ALSO BY FRAN GAGE

Bread and Chocolate:
My Food Life In & Around San Francisco

A SWEET QUARTET

A SWEET QUARTET

SUGAR, ALMONDS, EGGS, AND BUTTER

FRAN GAGE

North Point Press
A division of Farrar, Straus and Giroux
New York

North Point Press
A division of Farrar, Straus and Giroux
19 Union Square West, New York 10003

Copyright © 2002 by Fran Gage
All rights reserved
Distributed in Canada by Douglas & McIntyre Ltd.
Printed in the United States of America
First edition, 2002

Library of Congress Cataloging-in-Publication Data
Gage, Fran.
 A sweet quartet : sugar, almonds, eggs, and butter / Fran Gage.— 1st ed.
  p. cm.
 Includes bibliographical references.
 ISBN 0-86547-609-8 (hc)
 1. Desserts. I. Title.

TX773.G32 2002
641.8'6—dc21

             2002025545

Illustrations by Cyclone Design
Designed by Karen Schober

www.fsgbooks.com

10 9 8 7 6 5 4 3 2 1

For Sidney

CONTENTS

A Sweet Quartet

INTRODUCTION

WHEN I HAD A BAKERY, sugar, almonds, eggs, and butter were the sweet quartet that defined our everyday rhythm. We scooped sugar—granulated, powdered, brown—from large round tubs on casters into bowls set on scales as we constructed desserts. Every one of them contained some form of sugar. We scooped nuts too, almonds most of all, into the bowlfuls of sugar on the scales, or processed them to a powder. We cracked flat after flat of eggs, using some whole and separating others into yolks and whites. We cut sixty-pound blocks of butter into manageable slabs for rolling, beating, and melting. Then we mixed these four staples in countless permutations, using different proportions and baking techniques to create a profusion of pastries. The absence of any one of them would have brought our work to an abrupt halt—no more croissants, tart dough, *dacquoise*, no more chocolate cake with almond paste, no more brown-sugar scones.

Yes, there are other ingredients in a baker's repertoire. Flour gives her creations structure, and chocolate imparts its unreplicatable flavor. But while flour plays an important role in pastry, it is in the bread kingdom, not the dessert realm, that it reigns supreme. And chocolate's deep complexity demands an arena of its own. While chocolate will dominate the taste of any dessert that includes it, any combination of sugar, almonds, eggs, and butter will blend more harmoniously. I can't visualize a dessert that doesn't contain at least two of this sweet quartet.

The factors that get these ingredients into the kitchen in the first place are infinite and ever-variable: weather conditions, human trial and error, symbiotic relationships between plants and animals, technological innovation, genetic manipulation, and government intervention. A flaw in just one of these can mean a less-than-perfect product. Then, no matter how much alchemy the pastry maker employs, the resulting dessert will not be gold. But when all goes well and the ingredients arrive in a pristine state, wonders can occur.

◎

Desserts are sweet—sometimes just a hint, sometimes a punch—but sweetness is a defining quality, especially in the Western world. Our fondness for sweet food seems to be part of our genetic makeup, just as our attraction to music distinguishes us from other animals. Early people relied on fruit to bring this special taste to their diets. Tens of millennia ago, early *Homo sapiens* raided wild bee hives, braving stings from the inhabitants, for the pleasure of eating the insects' food. Later, people chewed fibrous sugarcane because it tasted good. Eventually, the canes were crushed to extract their sweet juice, and the first primitive sugar processing began. Cane sugar became a highly prized commodity and a staple of world trade. It reigned supreme until the eighteenth century; then a chemist extracted sucrose from beets, which could be grown in a wider range of climates. Today, much of our food contains sweeteners, most often corn syrup, so familiar a taste it may be hardly perceptible to us. Fortunately, fine desserts still depend on sugar to impart the taste that most of us crave.

Although other nuts are liberally sprinkled into desserts and pastries, almonds hold an exalted place in the desserts of the great cuisines, especially French, Viennese, and Italian. Their versatility is vast. Finely ground, they add texture as well as flavor to meringues, macaroons, tart dough, and *financiers*. Left whole, then cooked with sugar, they harden into a confection, to be broken into bits and swirled into ice cream or butter cream, or mixed with chocolate to make candies. If this cooked mass is ground between heavy rollers, the result is almond paste. With the addition of sugar syrup, almond paste becomes more pliable and can be rolled into sheets to drape over cakes or hand-shaped into confections. The preparation of the almonds themselves is almost as diverse as the desserts they grace.

Just as ancient people stole honey from bees, the first eggs eaten were pilfered from wild birds. When fowl were domesticated, eggs were still precious, and no wonder, as they are almost the perfect food, containing all the essential amino acids and most of the necessary vitamins. It wasn't until the twentieth century that a shadow fell over the egg because of its saturated fat content. More recently, a worry about salmonella bacteria in eggs has made people cautious about how eggs are cooked. Now people eat them with less abandon, rationing their weekly allotment. And they have strong opinions about the eggs they do eat—brown versus white, fertilized or otherwise, from chickens that roam versus those in pens, from chickens given organic feed versus those given commercial. Duck eggs roll into American kitchens occasionally too. Their yolks are larger and fattier, astonishing in custards. I almost bought an emu egg at a farmers' market last year, a heavy gray football with iridescent green blotches, but since one of them scrambled would feed fifteen or twenty, it seemed excessive for just my husband and me.

So many desserts and pastries, from *crème brûlée* to virtually every cake in existence, depend on eggs. Weighing less than two ounces, an egg possesses the chemical properties for countless baking feats. It is a powerful player in a baker's repertoire. Beaten egg whites trap air that can make a cake rise, bake into crisp meringues, or make a silky meringue to fold into a mousse or mound on a lemon tart. Egg yolks add their richness to ice cream, pastry, and butter cream. Heated and beaten with wine and sugar, egg yolks foam into an almost instant dessert.

Butter's unctuousness vies with its taste in determining its importance to pastries and desserts. Its starring role in puff pastry, with support from flour, water, and salt, is a prime example. If the ingredients were simply mixed together in a bowl, a leaden paste would result. But assembled in a certain way—fashioned into a soft dough made with the flour, water, salt, and part of the butter, then wrapped around a larger piece of butter, rolled and folded numerous times, resting between each "turn"—they make a delicate construction of hundreds of layers of dough interspersed with sheets of butter that, in a hot oven, will release steam, pushing the dough to triple its height and giving an incomparable tender crispness.

◎

How can I best convey my appreciation and spread my enthusiasm for these essential ingredients? With recipes, certainly, but each offers so much more. Each has a rich past, beginning before recorded history. And each has a complicated story to tell, right up to the present. I want to make the ingredients come alive, to celebrate their essences. However sterilely it is packaged, each begins on a farm. I realized I had to start there too. So I made phone calls and sent E-mails, looking for sources and information. Rather than merely talking to people who processed sugarcane, grew almonds, kept chickens, or milked cows, I knew I needed to visit the cane fields, then the mill and refinery. I needed to walk through an orchard with a farmer, not merely open a bag of almonds in my kitchen. I needed to peer inside a chicken coop; to visit dairy cows. My research took me far from home—to Louisiana, a major sugarcane producer in this country, and to France, home of the butter some think is the best in the world. Visits alone weren't sufficient; I needed to read to fill in the gaps, and to give the tales a sense of history. And I needed to taste. All the visiting and reading and time in my kitchen stirred memories, so I wove them into the stories too.

Although many desserts showcase one or another of these ingredients, like a true string quartet, their qualities are so intertwined that some of the recipes featured in a given section of the book would be comfortable in more than one chapter—meringue triangles with almonds, for example, could appear with equal ease after a discussion of sugar, almonds, or eggs. Sometimes one ingredient is the undisputed essence of the delicacy. Shortbread without butter? Each ingredient has its glories, and any two of them can unite to make a sterling dessert. But beware if someone offers you a delicacy that contains all four: It may be the pleasure experience of your life.

SUGAR

FROM THE HEIGHT OF A MAJESTIC BRIDGE over the Mississippi River, west of the New Orleans airport, I spotted an unwelcome bank of low, dark clouds in the late October sky. As I descended onto solid ground and the sun set, a torrent of rain began—exactly what I had hoped wouldn't happen: It's hard enough to navigate unfamiliar territory in the dark. Soon, however, the rain let up, and I continued west. In daylight, I would have seen the slow-moving water of the bayous, the thick vegetation and moss-draped trees of the swamps, and the sugarcane fields that line the road from one parish (the name for counties here) to the next. Instead, I concentrated on the wet pavement ahead and the directions beside me. After a few minor wrong turns, I arrived in Thibodaux, a small city on the Bayou Lafourche, about seven o'clock.

I had come to Louisiana's sugarcane country to learn more about how sugarcane is harvested and processed. Dr. Ben Legendre, a sugarcane specialist at Louisiana State University, had graciously agreed to show me around. He had spent the previous thirty-one years doing research at the USDA Agricultural Research Station at Houma, in the heart of the cane fields. But his involvement with the dominant crop of this region goes back even further. In 1937, his father revamped Thibodaux's sugar mill, and the family lived in a company-owned house on the property until Ben was fifteen years old. The family connection continues—today, one brother is president of the mill, and another is chief engineer.

My host, a tall man with a sturdy frame who drives a red Jeep with a bumper sticker proclaiming I ♥ SUGAR, met me at my lodgings. After dinner at a nearby restaurant, he took me to the mill. The rain had begun again, and I first glimpsed the mill through light mist: a huge structure topped by steam pouring from tall stacks. As we got closer, a holding bay mounded high with cut sugarcane came into sight. A crane mounted on steel runners moved along its tracks above the mountain of chopped cane. The operator lowered a hinged scoop into the tangled cane, picked up an eight-ton load, swung it to the right, and deposited it onto a conveyor belt. A steady stream of water washed the cane as it moved through a battery of rotating knives that chopped it into smaller pieces as it entered the building. Lights mounted on the roof cast an eerie glow, as if the whole scene were a clandestine operation.

We stopped at the side of the building and walked carefully across dirt that was turning to mud in the drizzle. I noticed an aroma of decaying vegetation; the washing water gets recycled. In the office, Ben outfitted me with a hard hat. I was ready to be initiated into the complexities of sugarcane processing.

We walked through a steel door onto the ground floor of the sugar mill, where we were greeted by thunderous noise, blasts of heat, and the feeble attempts of fans to cool the air. The whole building seemed to shake with the vibrations of the massive machinery; I felt as if I were in the belly of an ocean freighter. We passed rotating gears wet with oil and climbed stairs to a catwalk that led to the first mill, one in a series of six.

Each mill is a trio of grooved rollers, one positioned on top of the other two. Chopped sugarcane is pushed through, while steam-run turbines rotate the rollers and exert up to four hundred tons of pressure on the top roller, squeezing the juice from the plant fiber. But pressure alone won't remove all the juice, so the fiber is moistened with water as the mass passes from mill to mill. In an example of instant recycling, the spent fiber at the end, called bagasse, feeds the walk-in-size furnaces that fuel the machinery. I could feel their heat from fifty feet away.

We were standing at the second mill when a jarring *clank* resonated through the air. The man stationed at the shredder, just before the first mill, jumped to his feet and signaled to another farther along the catwalk, who hurried to a whistle and sent an ear-splitting blast through the plant. Then he shut down the conveyors that feed the mills. Ben ushered me out of the way as workers appeared out of nowhere. Something foreign was in the cane and had to be removed before it went into the first mill and caused damage. Men dug through the pile with shovels and pitchforks. After fifteen minutes of digging produced nothing, the operation restarted. "It must be small enough to pass through," Ben explained. "Last week they found a shard of metal a yard long, and another time a big piece of tree trunk."

Crisis averted, we walked to the next step in the process. The brown juice is clarified by heat and the addition of lime and polymers, which precipitate the impurities. The lime also increases the pH, protecting the sucrose in the heated juice from inverting, or making an irreversible change, into its two components, glucose and fructose.

Next we walked to large tanks spaced only a few feet apart, where the juice is separated from the solid gray-brown slush, aptly known as mud. "But there's still sugar in this, and we want to get as much as possible," said Ben. We moved to a large rotating drum caked with mud, which wets the mass, then extracts the sugar solution by vacuum. Ben scraped some off the drum and handed me the warm, dry matter. "This is used in health bars," he joked.

We walked to four towering tanks. These are evaporators; they remove some of the water and concentrate the juice to syrup, the penultimate step. Pressure in the tanks allows the juice to be heated to a higher temperature without boiling, losing moisture as it passes in sequence from tank to tank. I tasted the sticky brown syrup. It was intensely sweet, with a Brix of 60—60 percent of its weight was sucrose.

We navigated another set of open metal stairs that lead to the pans, a name left over from earlier times, when sugar syrup was crystallized in shallow pans placed over an open fire. Sugar boiling has always had a certain mystique, an art that was handed down from a master to his successors. Old-time sugar boilers relied on the appearance and feel of the syrup to determine its concentration—when a sample pulled between thumb and forefinger formed a string of a certain length, it was ready to start the crystallization process. Today, sophisticated instruments aid the process, but there's still artistry to it.

Instead of shallow pans, we stood in front of immense enclosed tanks, where the boiling syrup is seeded with sugar crystals, which grow to a desired size although they still remain in solution. I reached into the trough below the tanks and took some in my hand. It was dark brown with visible solids and the plasticity of Play-Doh. This massecuite, as it is called, drops to a centrifugal separator, whose spinning force removes the last of the liquid, leaving only the crystals. The revolutions slowed, then stopped. The color change was dramatic; I didn't expect the raw sugar to be so white. Ben scooped some from the side of the drum. Its warm sweetness melted quickly in my mouth.

Our journey finished, we wound our way back to the office, passing a truck being loaded with spent mud to be returned to the fields as fertilizer. The grinding would continue, one hundred people working one hundred days, splitting twelve-hour shifts, to process almost nine thousand tons of cane a day, until the last stock makes its way through the sugarhouse and is carried in crystal form to an adjacent warehouse. Its journey, however, isn't over. It needs another complicated step, the refining process, before it fills sugar bowls in thousands of kitchens.

The ability to discern sweetness, along with bitter, salt, and sour, is innate in human beings. Specific receptors on our tongues recognize these taste elements. But the foods available to early people produced more bitter, salty, and sour tastes than sweet ones; delicious sweet foods, at first limited to wild fruits and berries, were not an everyday experience. So people sought them out.

A cave painting found in Valencia, Spain, depicts two people pilfering honey from a hive. Wild bees provided honey, an intensely sweet liquid of several sugars that total three-quarters of its mass. It supplied more carbohydrates per mouthful, and thus more energy, than any other food. Honey was so revered that it was ritually offered to the gods. And sometimes it was the only food that tribal people took with them as they moved from place to place.

From a relief in a temple dating to about 2560 B.C., then later inscriptions and papyri, we know that the Egyptians developed a style of beekeeping that used cylindrical pipes for hives. The precious substance was extracted from the pipes and stored in jars. Later, the Hittites probably brought bees into Mesopotamia, for they were avid beekeepers. Their code of law, compiled between 1500 and 1460 B.C., showed a decrease in the fine for stealing a swarm of bees—bees must have become more plentiful and thus not so precious. As time progressed, beekeeping became more prevalent. Aristotle, Virgil, Varro, Pliny, and Columella all wrote at length about the practice. Honey was the chief sweetener in Greek cookery; the Romans, who had a preference for thyme honey, used honey not just for cakes but to preserve meat and fruit.

Although honey was the dominant sweetener in early times, it was not the only one. The Assyrians, who probably did not keep bees, used dates and fig syrup for sweetness, and the early people of Mesopotamia favored date syrup over honey, perhaps because it was more abundant. Regions that cultivated grapes used their juice. Egypt had a vast viticulture practice, and records of early Roman cookery describe sweeteners made from grape juice. Egyptian papyrus produced a sweet liquid; some varieties of trees exuded a sweet sap that could also be used in food. Pliny mentions sweet oil from palms—boiling palm flowers to make sugar remains a cottage industry in Southeast Asia today—and people in Australia and America may have used sap from eucalyptus and pine trees, respectively. Sugar-maple sap was well known to the Native Americans; along with dried berries, it was their only source of intense sweetness. North America did not have native bees; European settlers introduced honeybees about 1625.

⊚

Today, the sugarcane that grows in the highland valleys of New Guinea is the country's leading crop. A wild ancestor of the present-day plant also grew in these fertile valleys nine thousand years ago. Archaeological digs in the region have unearthed complicated drainage systems and terracing that are evidence of the first domestication of indigenous plants, including sugarcane.

From its homeland in New Guinea, the reed with the sweet juice traveled to the Philippines and India two thousand years after it was first cultivated. By the eighth century B.C., it had arrived in China, via India. Later, the cane itself was used as payment, indicating that the technique of sugar crystallization was not yet known. Authorities disagree on the origin of "the reed in India that brings forth honey without the help of bees" described by Nearchus, a general to Alexander the Great. It may have been sugarcane. A description by Dioscorides, a physician of the first century A.D., of a solid reed, like concrete honey with the texture of salt, good for the stomach, sounds like partially crystallized sugar. Pliny describes it as a honey that collected in reeds and was produced in small quantities and used as medicine. During this time, the kings of India drank grape wine imported from Rome, but common folk had to settle for drinks made from sugarcane juice, jaggery (a crudely refined sugar), molasses, and juice of rose-apple. Solid sugar, although not the pristine white crystals we know today, was looted from a palace in Persia in A.D. 627. Between the fourth and eighth centuries A.D., the major sugar-producing areas seem to have been the coast to the west of the Indian delta and the Tigris-Euphrates delta.

Sugar got a big boost during the Arab expansion. After capturing

Persia, establishing the caliphate at Baghdad, marching through Cyprus and Sicily, and controlling North Africa, the Arabs invaded Spain, carrying sugar as they went. They also brought sugarcane cultivation and sugar making to the conquered lands. As the Arabs moved forward, sugar became known in Europe. The Arabs brought sugar candy, sweet fruit syrups, candied capers, and probably marzipan, a sweet made from ground almonds and sugar. They made the first version of taffy by cooking sugar and water, adding pistachios, kneading it until it hardened, then cutting it into pieces.

Cultivation was not easy in some of these regions. Sugarcane is a tropical plant with a long growing season and a need for regular water if the sucrose content is to be optimal. To this end, the Arabs showed great inventiveness in developing irrigation systems. The growing and cutting of the cane, and the many steps required to extract the juice and crystallize the sucrose, is very labor-intensive, and slaves were used as the workforce, just as they would be during the years of burgeoning sugarcane cultivation in the New World.

That the Arabs went to such lengths to produce sugar attests to its important place in their medicine. Medicine of the early Middle Ages was a far cry from today's practice. Bacteria, viruses, antibiotics, hormones, anesthesia, and radiology were unknown. Disruptions in bodily function were diagnosed according to the theories of the second-century Greek physician Galen, who based his system on elements of the natural world—air, fire, water, and earth. Each had a unique characteristic: Air was cold, fire was hot, water was moist, and earth was dry. Coupling two of these characteristics produced a "complexion," and each complexion had a corresponding "humor." Four complexions were recognized—hot and moist, cold and moist, hot and dry, cold and dry. For example, hot and moist corresponded to the complexion sanguine, and the humor blood. In a healthy person, these elements were balanced; a tip in the scales resulted in disease. Treatment, then, attempted to rebalance the elements. Foods were categorized into the same elements, and the suitability of food was linked to the temperament of the person, although the formulations were complicated by subtleties and qualifications. Bitter almonds, for example, were considered heating to the first degree and drying to the second. Both sugar and honey were considered hot, and were used for coughs, difficult breathing, and sore throat.

The medicines themselves fell into nineteen categories, including syrups, lozenges, powders, poultices, and gargles. Sugar was included in every category, either in suspension to deliver the solid medicaments, or to heighten their effectiveness. As it is today, water was prescribed for those with fevers, but sometimes sugar was added to increase its "moistness," in accordance with Galenic principles. Sugar was also mixed with vinegar, with various combinations of ground vegetable seeds and roots, and with the juice of fruits and berries. Then as now, it undoubtedly helped the bitter ingredients go down.

Galen's theories were disseminated not only by the Arabs but thanks to Constantine the African, who settled in Salerno in the eleventh century and set about translating the works of Galen into Latin. Crusaders treated at Salerno took these ideas back to their homelands, and in Europe sugar was sold in apothecaries from the Middle Ages until the nineteenth century.

For a long time, the scarcity of sugar restricted its use largely to medicine. Even in households wealthy enough to use it in cooking, it was treated more as a spice than as a sweetener, mixed with ginger, saffron, cinnamon, cardamom, and especially black pepper. But gradually, sugar became more widely available. As Europe's honey supply declined during the Reformation—monasteries kept bees not only for their honey, but to make candles from their wax—sugar came to the fore, replacing honey in a number of sweet dishes. It was also used to counter bitter and sour tastes, and to give flavor to dull food.

From the sixteenth century onward, sugar had three principal uses: as a sweetener, as a medium to preserve fruit, and for decoration. Confectioners used *pastillage*, a mixture of sugar, water, and gum, to create fanciful decorations for food or the table. (French confectioners still use this substance, replacing the gum with gelatin.) They also cooked sugar syrup to various stages of concentration, so it could be pulled into decorations. The tables of the seventeenth and eighteenth centuries were laid with a strong sense of verticality (an aesthetic that seems to wax and wane even today, as "architectural" presentations go in and out of vogue). Elaborate figures and scenes, many not intended for consumption, adorned the tables of those wealthy enough to employ pastry makers.

Although Neolithic people knew that drying fruit allowed them to keep it longer, the preserving power of first honey, then sugar, was not recognized until Roman times. Dioscorides advised packing quinces in a vessel and covering them with honey; after a year's time, he noted, they became soft. Pliny improved upon the method by cooking the quinces and excluding air. Although he didn't know it, both steps discouraged the growth of bacteria, thus fostering preservation. But despite his having tasted the sugar coming to Rome from India, evidently he didn't realize that it could be used in place of honey in this method.

Arabic medical texts and cookbooks include directions for preparing fruit syrups and conserves, and these were taken up in the lands that the Arabs infiltrated. Candied fruits arrived in England in the fourteenth century from the Mediterranean, where they became an important offering at the feasts of the English kings. Candied sweets were called *dragées*, a word that today refers to sugar-coated nuts, silver confectionary balls used to decorate cakes, and sugar-coated pills.

Angelica, a plant noted for its curative powers, especially against the plague, was often preserved in sugar. Eventually, it passed from the realm of medicine into general use and was appreciated for its taste. Nuns in Niort, a small town in western France, made the preserving of angelica the work of their convent, and records from 1789 show that they exported ten tons of it that year, although the sugar blockade of the Napoleonic Wars cut production to two tons in 1810.

Production of fruit preserves swelled in the late nineteenth century as sugar became less expensive and more plentiful still and preserves became a staple of the English working class, replacing butter on the bread that accompanied sugar-laced tea and coffee. By 1900, sugar supplied almost one-fifth of the calories in the English diet.

On his second voyage to the New World, Columbus carried sugarcane shoots from the Canary Islands, along with men who were versed in cane farming. They planted the shoots in Spanish Santo Domingo, where conditions were ideal and the plants grew quickly. This made Spain the pioneer in sugarcane planting and processing in the New World. But the new industry had its bitter side. The Spanish also brought the practice of using African slave labor to the new colony. A trade triangle eventually emerged in the late seventeenth century: England sold goods to Africa; African slaves were sent to the Americas; and sugar replaced human cargo on the return trip. As the sugar-growing countries outlawed slavery one by one, domestic workers replaced the slaves. Although they were paid, the working conditions were severe—long hours of hard labor in the tropical heat. And the sugar itself remained a commodity that was largely out of the financial reach of the people who grew it.

Louisiana's role in sugarcane production started when Iberville, the founder of the colony, planted it in the late seventeenth century. But it wasn't until the Jesuits brought samples of the crop from Santo Domingo to their plantation on what is now Baronne Street in New Orleans that the region's production took root. By 1756, an entrepreneur named Dubreuil had built a sugar mill nearby, where he produced a liquid raw sugar that would be considered crude by today's standards. But the subtropical climate of Louisiana was not ideal for growing tropical sugarcane, and the sugar was of low quality. The new industry stumbled along until the end of the eighteenth century, when it got boosts from different directions. A more suitable cane variety was imported; sugar was granulated in a commercially successful way; the purchase of Louisiana from the French brought immigrants from the rest of the country to the sugar-producing regions; and steam power superseded animal power in milling cane. In quick succession, other inventions—evaporators, centrifuges, and condensers—increased production.

Sugarcane cultivation spread along the Mississippi from New Orleans north to Baton Rouge and west to the parishes of Lafourche and Terrebonne. As the industry grew, so did the need for labor, and once again slavery provided the workforce. By 1860, three hundred thousand slaves worked the sugarcane fields. The Civil War, which brought destruction to the land and liberty to the slaves, overturned plantation economics, but the industry slowly rebuilt itself. Then, in the first decades of the twentieth century, cane yields mysteriously declined. Finally, the most prominent perpetrator was identified—sugarcane mosaic virus—and between 1922 and 1924, the affected plants were replaced with varieties from Java known to be resistant to a similar virus. These hybrids were known as POJ, shorthand for Proefstation Oost Java, although Ben Legendre has rechristened them "Please Oh Jesus"—aptly, since the researchers who planted them must have prayed for their survival. The prayers were answered. Although not completely resistant, the new plants tolerated the virus, and by 1928, POJ varieties constituted 85 percent of the Louisiana industry's acreage.

The sugar business once again showed its less-than-sweet side in California. In 1846, Claus Spreckels left his native Germany for America. Lured by tales of prosperity, he moved to San Francisco and bought his brother's grocery store. Because the store didn't occupy all his time,

Spreckels, in a move typical of his future *modus operandi*, cast about for something additional to do. He started a brewery, then sold both it and the grocery. Although he knew little about sugar, he saw it as a profit opportunity and started a refinery with a brother-in-law in 1863. This step would eventually make him the sugar king of California; later, when he began refining sugar beets as well as cane, he dubbed himself the "Emperor" of the sugar industry.

Spreckels's refinery in San Francisco relied heavily on milled sugarcane from Hawaii. Following the Reciprocity Treaty between Hawaii and the United States in 1876, he moved swiftly to broaden his business opportunities. He booked passage on the steamer that sailed to Hawaii to announce the news, then promptly bought more than half the cane crop for the next year. In short order, he became friends with the Hawaiian king, Kalakaua, and the king's right-hand man, Walter Gibson—a gaunt man with sharp features and a shock of white hair, as depicted in a photograph of the time. These three men ran the country for the next eight years, often in eyebrow-raising circumstances. At one point, Gibson, the "Minister of Everything," held seven government offices. Spreckels, whose cash infusions bolstered the government, was awarded water rights for his burgeoning sugarcane plantation on the island of Maui, a title he had gained under dubious circumstances as well. At its height, the Spreckelsville plantation was the largest sugar estate in the world, and Spreckels instituted many innovations—a more efficient mill, electric lights, railroad hauling instead of mules and oxen, controlled irrigation, steam plows, and fertilization. Because he owned a shipping line and a refinery in San Francisco, Spreckels was the first planter to gain almost complete control of his sugar, from field to grocery shelf.

The blatant mishandlings were exposed by the Honolulu business community in 1886, and the triumvirate fell apart. Spreckels returned to San Francisco, and over the next seven years, Gibson and Kalakaua died. In addition, the McKinley Tariff removed duty on sugar brought to the United States and gave domestic growers two cents a pound.

There was talk of annexing Hawaii, which would mean the end of cheap labor supplied by the Chinese immigrants.

Although the annexation became reality in 1898, Spreckels didn't fare badly. He was still tied to Hawaii, both by his sugar kingdom and by holding half the public debt. And the beet-sugar refineries he'd established south of San Francisco ten years before were thriving. He knew there was more than one way to get sugar.

◎

For millennia, beets hid their potential to rival sugarcane, even though they were cultivated by Babylonian kings as early as 800 B.C. The Greeks grew them—Aristophanes mentioned them in two plays that were performed in Athens about 420 B.C.—as did the Romans after them, not for sugar or even for their roots, but primarily for their green leaves. The plants resembled our Swiss chard, which remains a member of the beet, or Beta, family.

By the Middle Ages, beet varieties had both edible leaves and large roots, which were also eaten. As the years passed, the red roots became prized for their sweetness. Olivier de Serres, a Frenchman writing about agriculture in 1600, extolled their virtues, promoting the roots as food and equating their cooked juice with sugar syrup. Imported sugarcane was still expensive, and a food with even a hint of its taste was prized.

Cultivation of beets was widespread by the seventeenth century, with some varieties used as animal feed, others favored by humans. But no one unraveled the mystery of their sweetness until the German chemist Andreas Marggraf, working in 1747, discovered that the sweet crystals in beets were the same substance as cane sugar. The discovery was groundbreaking, but he was only able to extract a tiny percentage of the plant's sugar. It took Franz Achard, a student of Marggraf who was cultivating a variety of vegetables that held promise as sources of sugar, to discover that white beets were richest in sugar. These prized beets became known as White Silesian, after the area where they were propagated. Unfortunately, the sugar content varied widely from plant to plant, but Achard was able to persuade King Frederick William III to fund a processing plant. Although Achard's first attempts were uneven, he demonstrated that large amounts of sugar could be obtained from beets. This meant that there was a possibility of producing domestic sugar instead of relying on expensive imported sugar from cane. During the Napoleonic Wars, when Napoleon wouldn't allow the importation of British goods into Europe and in retaliation England tried to cut off France from her colonies, beets provided Europe's only source of sugar. By 1806, West Indian sugar had vanished from Europe, and by 1811, more than forty small beet-sugar factories were established, most of them in northern France but some in other parts of Northern Europe where the plants could thrive as well. But the fledgling industry faltered. Two years later, the blockade was removed and cane sugar once again dominated the market.

The French didn't completely abandon sugar-beet production. Louis de Vilmorin expanded the work of Achard, improving breeding methods to increase sugar content and extraction methods to obtain as much sugar as possible. By 1830, the Germans were again building sugar-beet factories. By the late 1840s, Austria and Hungary produced substantial quantities of beet sugar, and by 1862, Austria had ceased importation of cane sugar altogether. Tax wars ensued, first on imported cane sugar, then, when imports dropped, on domestic beet sugar as well. These restrictions made the beet producers work harder, increasing their sugar yields and streamlining manufacturing processes. By the early 1900s, the majority of the world's sugar was produced from beets. This held until an international tax break for cane producers leveled the playing field again. By 1914, cane and beet sugar each claimed 50 percent of the sugar market.

Northampton, Massachusetts, sported the first American beet-sugar factory in 1838, but production was meager, and it closed in 1841. Other attempts at factories failed until, in 1870, E. H. Dyer, considered the founder of the beet-sugar industry in America, built a factory in California. Not many years later, Claus Spreckels built his factory, also in California. Later, Utah and Nebraska joined California as major centers of cultivation and production.

Unlike sugarcane, which must be milled and then refined, beets are processed in a single step, and can be made into sugar near the fields where they grow. First the large roots, which contain 16 to 18 percent sucrose, are washed and sliced into strips. A large tank, called a diffuser, removes the sugar by boiling the strips in many changes of water. The juice, now rich in sugar, is separated from the pulp, which goes for animal feed. Then this juice is treated somewhat like sugarcane in a refinery—clarified, filtered, boiled until crystals form, centrifuged, and dried—but there are two big differences. The process can produce only white sugar fit for human consumption, not the brown syrups and molasses that are part of the cane-refining process. And the whole operation gives off a disagreeable odor that can be detected for miles.

There's another difference, one that is controversial. Some say the sugars don't act the same in the kitchen. Chemists pronounce the white sugar from both sources equal, both 99.95 percent sucrose and 0.03 percent moisture. But what about the remaining 0.02 percent of other substances, minerals and proteins?

In 1999, food writers at the *San Francisco Chronicle* tackled the cane-versus-beet controversy. They made *crème brûlée* and sprinkled one ramekin with granulated white cane sugar and the other with sugar from beets. The accompanying color photograph needed no caption. The beet sugar burned, with black splotches on top of the custard, whereas the cane sugar produced an even golden-brown surface. Next the testers turned to brown sugar. Brown cane sugar is a combination of sugar and molasses produced during the refining process; brown beet sugar is really completely refined sugar that has been coated, or "painted," with cane molasses. Cookies baked with cane sugar were superior in taste and texture to those made with beet sugar, as was a cane-sugar *crème anglaise*. Experienced jelly- and marmalade-makers prefer cane sugar too. Betaine, a nitrogen-containing compound found in beet sugar, interferes with gel formation, so jellies made with beet sugar may not set. And when I studied at heralded pastry chef Gaston Lenôtre's school in France years ago, the teachers insisted on cane sugar for certain applications, especially those involving caramelization. Beet sugar produces excess foam when heated and sometimes crystallizes instead of coloring.

"Would you like to ride a harvester?" asked Ben Legendre, the second day he was my host in Louisiana sugarcane country. We headed for a field about an hour's drive from Thibodaux that belongs to an old friend of Ben's. (Ben's family has lived in Thibodaux for so long that he knows everyone and is related to half the town; last year, the head count at the Christmas dinner he and his wife host was eighty-two.) The bumpy ride, down a dirt path with sugarcane towering close to twelve feet high on either side, reminded me of a tour through the vineyards of Beaujolais many years ago, when the driver had raised our Citroën's suspension to clear the ground.

Ben's friend drove up in a dust-covered pickup. A tall, lanky man with blue eyes one shade lighter than his shirt got out and shook my hand. He didn't blink an eye at Ben's request, so we got into his truck and bumped along, the two men exchanged sugarcane shorthand as we went.

"I only got twenty-three [tons to the acre] this year on that old field. Should have pulled it out. But you don't know. It might have produced more."

"Are you harvesting from can to can't-see?" (That is, from dawn to dark.)

"No, we quit around four."

"This is the first time I've burned this harvest. Had to, the cane is so lodged [fallen over and tangled from recent winds] that we can't get the harvester through."

This last comment was made as we drove up to cane that had just been ignited. Black smoke rose from the crackling vegetation as the red flames swept through the tall patch. The burn was fast, leaving shreds of blackened leaves floating through the air. Just adjacent to the burned stand, debris from harvested cane smoldered on the ground.

We drove to where a yellow Cameco harvester/cutter traversed the field. Close to its side, a tractor pulled a large wagon. The harvester severed the stalks, then chopped them into shorter pieces called billets before dropping them into the wagon. It blew the lighter leaves back down to the ground. My companions signaled the driver to stop, and though he looked nonplussed at their request for me to join him, he lowered the machine so that the first step was a mere three feet off the ground. I grabbed the handrails and hoisted myself into the cab. The driver indicated that I should sit on a small cooler, first covering it carefully with a paper towel. Then I closed the door and we were off.

The machine turned on a dime, and we headed down the next row. We plowed through stalks as tall as fifteen feet, an impenetrable wall of green through the windshield. A video camera mounted just above eye level was trained on the ground behind us. It told the driver how efficient the cutting was—if the cane was sheared too far above the ground, he could lower the whirling blades.

The ride was much more comfortable than I had anticipated, with only an occasional bump—and I wasn't even in the padded seat with the suspension. It took me a minute to realize that the cab was air-conditioned too. But for the price tag—$220,000—it should be. A joystick in front of the driver controlled most of the operations; I was amazed at the constant small adjustments they required.

"How did you learn?" I asked the driver.

"You go to school for two days," he said nonchalantly, as if I too could learn.

After ten minutes or so, I got out. My short ride was great fun, but day after day of crunching through the fields would be monotonous—although I would choose the harvester over an open tractor exposed to the hot sun. And I know that I wouldn't even attempt to harvest sugarcane with a machete, the method still employed in many of the sixty-two countries where the crop is grown.

That afternoon, at the Cameco factory, which produced the harvester I rode, I saw a formidable display of these tools, thick-bladed and thin, scythelike and straight. There were wedge-shaped blades with hooks on the end, and one that resembled a hatchet. Most looked handmade and had wooden handles. The crudest one of all, from the Sudan, had a jagged, curved blade made by heating the metal springs from a car or truck and pounding them into shape. It would be slow going, felling the fibrous stalks with such an implement.

As I left the factory, I saw a cloud of smoke not far away. A neighboring farmer was burning his fields. Sizable pieces of burned vegetation, bigger than ordinary soot, floated through the air. "In Florida, you need a permit to burn," my tour guide said. "It's going to come to that here. My wife complains about the debris on our patio. I tell her I'll clean it up. This is how we make our living."

Ben and I were going to a public meeting of the Environmental Protection Agency regarding burning that evening.

Sugarcane farming has its share of environmental woes. Initially, the water used to wash the cane was dumped into the local bayous and streams. It took some time for people to realize that this sugar-rich water was harmful to the native ecosystems. Diverting spent water into local waterways is no longer allowed. The mill in Thibodaux spent one million dollars to develop a series of sizable ponds on a piece of land adjacent to the sugarhouse, where the water is pH-adjusted and aerated until it is safe to release into the bayou.

But today another issue is at the forefront, sparking animosity between the growers and their neighbors: burning. Fire has always been an important tool for farmers—to reduce unwanted vegetation that interferes with harvest or bed preparation, to control pests and weeds, and, under certain conditions, to stimulate new growth. Sugarcane debris, or trash, as the farmers call it, is a large portion of the plant. The jagged green leaves that grow along the stalk and jut from the top support the photosynthesis of the plant, but it's only the woody canes that hold the sucrose. The farmer doesn't want to shoulder the cost for transporting useless greenery.

To make hand-harvesting easier, cane fields are often burned first, which removes the unwanted vegetation without harming the stalks. Current-model harvesters can generally work a field without prior burning (the field I had seen burning the day before was an exception), but the unwanted leaves don't disappear. The debris left on the ground—eight tons of it per acre—doesn't deteriorate easily, because of its high fiber content. If it stays on the ground, it will impede the growth of next year's crop. So the farmers burn it. But as the acres planted with sugarcane increase (463,000 in Louisiana in 1999) and the towns near the fields expand outward, the two come increasingly into conflict. Burned debris on the ground causes smoke and dust, and if the wind conditions are wrong, both can engulf nearby houses; the effect is more dramatic if standing fields are burned.

A federal task force was created in 1996 to examine agricultural air-quality dangers. In November 1999, the group recommended a smoke-management program that included two tiers, one voluntary, the other more structured. The voluntary program focused on teaching farmers to evaluate weather conditions, area, and time of day, to keep disruption to a minimum. Now the Environmental Protection Agency was holding a public hearing on this matter before drafting an official policy. Ben and I drove to New Iberia to attend.

Holding the meeting during "grinding"—the harvest and milling operations—heightened the tension. The farmers were strained from the harvest, when they make all of their annual income. And the citizenry was correspondingly irate about the fouled air. Perhaps in order to keep flaring tempers cool, the meeting was held in a chilly, over-air-conditioned room.

The farmers gathered in the back, most of them casually dressed, except those who planned to speak. And their message was clear. "Without burning in Louisiana, we would have no sugarcane industry," stated a local farmer. Those opposed were just as firm, linking respiratory problems and medical bills to the practice. One woman gave the officials a bag of debris she had collected from her yard. Another said that the farmers were not following the voluntary guidelines and called for a ban on burning. The director of Louisiana State University's agricultural center emphasized more funds for research to develop alternatives to burning—varieties that shed their leaves, harvesting machinery that decreases trash, methods to speed up decomposition of the debris, perhaps the use of defoliating agents. The EPA representatives listened attentively, taking notes. A decision was months away.

As the meeting broke up, the two factions gathered and continued to talk among themselves, each reaffirming its position.

On the drive back to Thibodaux, Ben talked about experiments in other cane-growing countries to eliminate the debris. One notion had been to bale it, then use it as fuel—a promising idea, but the debris hadn't contained enough BTUs to make the practice economical. Another solution is needed, and soon.

On the last morning of my Louisiana sojourn, Ben Legendre took me to the USDA's research center at Houma. Over the years, its focus had shifted from diseases to breeding and selecting cane varieties that will produce more sugar, offer disease- and insect resistance, adapt to the climate, and lend themselves to mechanical harvesting. The laboratory work goes on at the original site; field trials are nearby at a three-hundred-acre farm.

Manicured lawns separated large greenhouses as we drove along the gravel road to the main building, which was a residence when the site was a plantation. It still looks stately, painted white, its four columns facing an expanse of grass. I imagined the scene as it must have been once—people sitting in chairs on the porch, enjoying a summer breeze, sugarcane fields as far as the eye could see. An old pecan tree, gravid with nuts, spread to the sidewalk where we parked.

We walked through the greenhouses, hot and humid at this time of year, and almost empty. In a few months, their tables would be covered with soil-filled containers incubating seeds. A few straggly plants in another greenhouse had light striations on their leaves, the telltale sign of the mosaic virus. In another room, a different sort of breeding was going on. In clear plastic containers the scientists were raising sugarcane borers, which have ferocious appetites for the plants until they pupate, eventually turning into very ordinary-looking moths. The scientists hope new cane varieties can fend them off.

We went outside to a modest stand of plants, the basis for the breeding program. Species of wild sugarcane were confined to containers to prevent them from invading the lawn. Other plants, hybrids from previous work, grew in pots lined up on carts with wheels. As we approached, I saw tall tassels on some of the plants. Sugarcane can produce flowers, a fact not known in modern times until the end of the nineteenth century, when a slave in Guyana discovered a plant whose top had fallen to the ground and was regenerating. Scientists want the plants to flower so they can control the cross-fertilization and develop new cultivars, but they must coax the plants to do so by alternating periods of darkness with equal periods of light. They do so by wheeling the carts holding the plants into a dark shed with retractable doors. Then they select plants whose traits they want to duplicate and play matchmaker.

"This is the bedroom," announced Ben as we went into a tall, warm greenhouse. "Harem" is a better word for it. One plant heavy with pollen is grouped with as many as six plants sporting receptive female flowers, then all are ushered into a private partitioned cubicle. Several such compartments run along one side of the building. The pollenizer plant is positioned above those to be fertilized, so gravity can help. Just to be sure, each day a technician taps the bar that holds the plants, so pollen will be dislodged. Even with extra help, the pollen won't disperse if it's too cold, so temperatures are regulated. The plants are left in their cozy quarters for two weeks; after all this pampering, the scientists want a good supply of viable seed.

When the deed is done, the tops of the plants with the now-fertilized seeds are bagged and moved across the aisle for drying. The seeds themselves are further dried in a small oven, then frozen for future planting. They are minute and plentiful. Between 1972 and 1994, almost forty-six hundred crosses yielded 7.3 million seeds. Imagine the possibilities, the permutations, the characteristics of the offspring! Each year, the researchers select batches of seed to plant. They start them in the greenhouses, then plant them in the ground at the nearby three-hundred-acre experimental farm. Once they are mature, the process continues; some are singled out and cross-bred again. Developing a variety with a specific set of characteristics is a painstakingly slow process. It can take thirteen years from the initial cross to the development of hybrid plants ready to release to farmers.

Our last stop was the farm. Experimental plots, each with cane grown for a specific set of traits, stood in rows. Even to my inexperienced eye, there was a difference among them—some taller, others bushier, a group with thicker stalks. As Ben got out of the car and disappeared between two rows, I realized why he had chosen a long-sleeved shirt on such a warm day. The stalks are sharp and brittle, and they dwarfed his tall frame. He emerged with a piece of cane, stripped off the outer, fibrous part with a penknife, cut off a piece a few inches long, and offered it to me. I put it in my mouth and chewed. It was pure sweetness, unmarred by any other flavor. I spit out the fiber and took another piece. The people who first discovered, long ago, that certain tall grasses growing wild possessed such a taste sensation must have been ecstatic. We bumped along to an adjacent row, where Ben cut another stalk. "This one is chewing cane," he said. He cut it into two pieces and handed them to me. They were surprisingly heavy. We drove back to the farm building.

My visit to the sugarcane country was drawing to a close. I thanked my host one last time, slipped my sweet gift under the strap of my suitcase, climbed into my car, and headed back to New Orleans, the taste of the sugarcane lingering in my mouth.

Molasses, a by-product of sugar making, became an important commodity in its own right. Initially the cane plantations distilled it to make rum. Early colonists on Barbados preferred to make spirits out of cane juice rather than crystallizing it for sugar. They shipped this "Barbados Water" to New England as early as 1647, before it was sent to the mother country. Other islands made rum from molasses, which also found its way to the thirsty in the Northern colonies. Along the way, someone realized that concentrated molasses would make the trip to New England without fermenting. So, in addition to the finished rum, New Englanders began importing molasses to make their own, and rum distillation was on its way to becoming the largest manufacturing industry in prerevolutionary America. By 1750, the city of Boston boasted sixty-three distilleries.

The British were irked, because some of the islands shipping molasses to New England were owned by other countries. The Molasses Act, drawn up in 1733, levied stiff duties on rum, molasses, and sugar if purchased from non-British sources. The new law wasn't applied until the 1770s, but when it was, it gave the American colonies an additional reason for declaring independence.

In time, American tastes changed; Scotch whisky and American blends superseded the drink from the cane. The number of New England rum distillers dwindled. Eventually, only one remained, Felton & Son. Heublein purchased it in 1981, then sold it the next year, closing the operation.

◉

Back in New Orleans, I had one last sugar mission—a visit to an artisanal rum distillery. I couldn't find the street on my map, but that didn't concern me until the morning of my visit.

The first taxi driver didn't know the way. "Frenchmen Street? Never heard of it. Is it in the Quarter?" I got out of the cab. The driver of another cab knew the way. "Maybe he just didn't want to go out there," he said when I mentioned the first cabbie's response. I knew my destination was in a slightly seedy part of town; now I began to wonder how safe it was.

"Smells like rum," said the driver as he pulled to a stop in front of an old warehouse. He was right. I was at Celebration Distillation, a young company that makes the only rum now distilled in the continental United States. I found the company through coincidences that Paul Auster would appreciate. And there would be more before the end of my visit.

In California's Anderson Valley, more than two thousand miles from New Orleans, and weeks before I planned my trip, I had stood in the tasting room of a friend's winery, admiring her new wine labels. She owns the paintings on which they were based—she and her husband had discovered the artist in his beginning years, when he sold paintings on New Orleans's Bourbon Street—and the artist had granted permission to reproduce his work on her labels. Later, while researching rum on the Web, I came across a paragraph describing how a now-prosperous New Orleans artist had gotten the notion to make rum from the local molasses. One of his French Quarter street scenes adorns the bottle. Something clicked. This was the same man whose paintings were on the wine bottles. I called my winemaker friend, who connected me to the company.

Meanwhile, I had sought out the rum without success at several liquor stores in my area. No one knew it. I called my contact with the company, who directed me to a tiny shop that sells wine and spirits and a few groceries, only a mile from my house—I drive by it almost every day. After some delay (the rum was out of stock the first time I went), I bought a bottle. The color was the first thing I noticed about it—dark with red undertones, like a rich, highly polished piece of furniture. My husband and I tasted some from a snifter. It was smooth, with a hint of caramel and vanilla, unlike any other rum I've tasted. Making it into daiquiris would be an insult. It deserves to be swirled and sipped from a brandy glass, or maybe served as an apéritif over a single ice cube with a squeeze of lime juice.

Back on Frenchmen Street, I walked up a ramp past rows of fifty-gallon oak barrels. The rum aroma intensified. Someone called to me from an enclosed mezzanine. It was Mark Stewart, the president and distiller. He ambled over, dressed in shorts and a faded blue T-shirt. There was no distilling that day, but he and Jonathan Kline, the other distiller, who was similarly attired, explained the process. The marketing director, Jed McSpadden, joined us as well.

Blue metal drums of cane syrup and edible molasses (in contrast to the final run of molasses from a sugar mill) sat in a small room. In another coincidental twist, I had sat across a levee of the Mississippi in the office of their supplier five days before with Ben Legendre. It had taken the distillers a lengthy search to find Caire and Graugnard, a producer of sugarcane specialties that had been willing to supply the small quantities of high-quality molasses they wanted.

To make the rum, a mixture of cane syrup and molasses is poured into white plastic barrels, water and brewer's yeast are added, then the mix is left to ferment for four days. At that point, it's into the still, a contraption that bears little resemblance to the small alembic stills used for cognacs, or the taller continuous stills I have seen used in Normandy to make Calvados. Steam heats the mix, vaporizing the alcohol, which travels up a curlicue of tubing, then condenses into a clear,

150-proof liquid. The "heads," the first alcohol that vaporizes, is discarded because it contains unwanted substances. The last part of the distillate, also discarded, is similarly tainted.

Next the liquid goes into once-used charred bourbon barrels, where it ages for up to three years, taking on color and developing flavor nuances. Before it is bottled, the rum is cut with water to 86 proof. As the company grows, Mark wants to age rum even longer. The distillers admire a fifteen-year-old rum from Haiti and see great potential for their rum if it can rest as long.

The bottling room was the final stop. "This is our blast-proof room," said Jonathan. The floor and three walls are heavy concrete; in the event of an explosion, only the unreinforced outside wall would collapse, leaving the rest of the building standing. It was the most economical way to satisfy the fire code, far cheaper than installing a sprinkler system in the entire warehouse, explained Jonathan. We said hello to the cellar manager (just back from touring with his rock band), who was painstakingly hand-attaching labels to special seven-hundred-milliliter bottles for export to France.

The tour finished, we visited the "research" room. Bottles of rum from what looked like every rum-producing country crowded one table. "Taste whatever you like," offered Mark. But 11 a.m. seemed too early for such a *dégustation*. Another table held bottles of experiments, a rum bitters and a rum flavored with plum and tangerine among them. Jars of dried orange peel, angelica root, gentian root, and other aromatics lined a shelf above the table. It looked as if the men had fun on the days when they weren't distilling.

Back in the office, I spied an old bottle with a peeling label on a shelf. It was a bottle of Herbsaint, the anise-flavored liquor produced in New Orleans. Mark guessed it dated from the sixties. Jonathan's mother-in-law had found it in her garage and, to the men's dismay, had emptied it. I took it in my hand to get a better look, and couldn't believe my eyes when I read the name of the producer: Legendre.

One more connection closed the circle of coincidences. As Mark drove me back to the French Quarter, he asked me where I grew up. "Pittsburgh," I said. The artist who started the company shares my hometown.

◎

Back home, I realized that there was one missing link to the sugar story. I wanted to see a sugar refinery, the last step in the process. Although the raw sugar that exits from the mill contains only a few impurities, they must be removed if the sugar is to be edible and not to spoil in storage. And the refining is as involved as the milling process. All told, it is an extraordinary amount of work to go to merely to extract what the sugarcane plant has created.

A week later, I stood on the roof of the C&H (California and Hawaiian) Sugar Refinery, a seventeen-acre complex that hugs the water in the tiny town of Crockett, thirty miles north of San Francisco. The sun was shining and a light breeze blowing. Below, a sailboat glided past, framed by the brown hills of late summer, following the Carquinez Strait to the top of San Francisco Bay. That day, the boat had the water to itself. There were no freighters transferring raw sugar to the phalanx of sky-blue silos, each with a capacity of eleven thousand tons, that stand near the water's edge. But freighters would be at the dock again, their holds full of processed sugarcane from Hawaii, Guatemala, Colombia, and other sugarcane-growing regions, including Louisiana.

The refinery started life as a flour mill; as a baker, I liked that progression. Joyce Greene, a chemist who works at the refinery, acted as tour guide. She led the way to the roof for a view of the silos, the place where the process begins. Sugars from different countries are stored separately, because the quality can vary. Then they are blended, so the refinery has a consistent starting base.

We left the roof deck and trooped down a flight of stairs to the room housing the large washing-machine-like drums that tumble the raw sugar with a sugar syrup to remove the film of molasses and then drain the syrup, leaving the cleaner crystals.

Next the crystals are melted and mixed with phosphoric acid and lime, which clings to impurities and brings them to the surface. Then the clear liquid trickles through bone-char filters, where most of the remaining color and minerals are removed. Finally, presses remove any bits of char. Now, almost completely purified, and with only a slight hint of color remaining, the liquid is ready to return to the crystal state.

We went from one area to the next, up and down the stairs, following the sugar trail. Handy open elevators, with foot stands and handholds, run continuously between floors, but we didn't take them. "They save a lot of climbing when you work here every day," Joyce admitted.

Most of the machines viewed so far didn't have much personality—their work was hidden under steel housings—but then we got to the pans, which looked like the pans at the sugar mill—tall cylinders where the liquid is transformed back into crystals. The sugar solution is seeded with very finely ground sugar to start the crystallization process, then boiled under vacuum so the cooking takes place at a lower temperature, which minimizes the risk of coloring the crystals. The pans had little windows running up the side, so I could see the sugar bubbling away, monitored by large dials registering temperature and pressure. One of the workers removed a sample and put it under a magnifying glass. I squinted through what looked like a small pile of slush to the naked eye, but was transformed into shimmering, irregularly shaped pieces piled on each other, like the three-dimensional view of a kaleidoscope. The length of time the syrup remains in the pans determines the size of the crystals. Fine sugar needs two hours; coarser granules, three and a half.

We walked back down the stairs to the centrifuges, a long row of round tubs about three feet tall, which eliminate the syrup and give the crystals a final wash. They were an imposing sight, hissing and belching, some dripping water, spinning and stopping at what seemed like random intervals, although an operator controlled them from a small partition at the end of the room. The clattering of the machines made conversation impossible. As I watched, sugar solution was poured into one, and the tub started to spin, whirling faster and faster. Within seconds, the color of the sugar changed from light brown to sparkling white.

Up two more flights. I could cancel my exercise walks if I worked here, I thought. Here, large drums tumble the sugar while hot air blows through them, dropping the moisture from 2 percent to .02 percent. Just across from the drums were my favorite machines, the screens, which separate the different-size crystals. I'd heard them *chug-chugging* like trains as we climbed the stairs. They are big rectangles, driven by a circular arm at one end and fed from above by cloth tubes that tremble as the sugar falls through them. The machines move like two-ton hula dancers, rectangular hips swaying, raised arms shaking. The screens rattle as the crystals fall through.

Now the refining process is finished, but the work is not done. Packing the sugar demands as much space as refining it. The bagging lines were our next stop.

One operation handles five-pound bags, which includes making the bags, filling and closing them, then rolling them along a conveyor belt to waiting boxes. This line fills 120 bags a minute; with three lines that run twenty-four hours a day for ten or twelve days straight, the factory can barely keep up with demand.

Brown sugar, in two-pound plastic sacks with zip-lock closures, is automatically packaged, flattened, then transferred to boxes by two flexible suction hoses that resemble legs doing a perpetual step-exercise. All the packages are weighed twice and passed through a metal detector. The same practice prevails on each packing line. "There are lots of moving parts in this building, and we don't want any of them to end up in the sugar," Joyce explained.

But it wasn't the look-how-fast-I-can-do-this bagging lines that most impressed me. It was the machines that make and box the sugar cubes. Perfect squares, perfectly equidistant from each other, move slowly along a narrow metal belt that runs the length of a large room. Although hundreds of thousands of cubes must travel along the belt each day, I saw only a handful on the floor. At the end of the belt, metal arms push groups of cubes together, enough to fit into one of the boxes waiting to be folded around it. The refinery is buying a new cubing machine, at a cost of more than a million dollars. The present machine may be outmoded, but it is a far cry from the original process. A photograph of the cubing room taken in the early 1900s shows two women cutting cubes from blocks secured in wooden frames. Their work uniforms are heeled boots, knickers with extensions that reach the ankles, short-sleeved smocks, and floppy caps. I wonder how many cubes they made in one day.

Joyce picked up a box without a lid and offered me a sugar cube. It was still warm and quickly melted on my tongue.

All this sugar needs a place to rest before it leaves the plant. Packaged sugar is palletized, bar-coded, and shrink-wrapped by a menacing machine that looks like something from a horror movie. Then the sugar is rolled into a cavernous warehouse where robots run by computers store and track pallets stacked thirteen high and fifty long. Each year, hundreds of thousands of metric tons of refined sugar leave the plant, to sweeten cups of coffee, get baked into wonderful desserts, lend to thousands of things the sweetness that only sugar can provide.

When I was growing up, my entire family went grocery shopping on Friday evenings. While my parents frugally mapped out dinners for the coming week, my brother and I raided the aisles for snacks; most, but not all, of our selections were rejected by the two with the purchasing power. If I pleaded hard, I was usually allowed a bag of my favorite candy—orange bulbous forms shaped like peanuts. I don't know why they were peanut-shaped; they certainly didn't taste like peanuts, or nuts of any kind. Nor do I know, especially today, what attracted me to them.

At home, while my parents unpacked cans, boxes of frozen vegetables, quarts of milk, and plastic-wrapped packages of meat, I sat on a stool next to the built-in cupboard and methodically ate one piece of candy after another, sometimes coming close to finishing the entire bag. I remember the texture of those ersatz nuts—thick and rubbery, but breaking down quickly after a few chews, like dense marshmallows. Just as distinct in my memory was the flavor, a chemically perfumed sweetness. And if I'm not mistaken, the orange color permeated my tongue, remaining long after I had swallowed the last bite. I haven't eaten one in decades. I thought they were gone from the market, but recently I saw bags of them in a grocery store. How the power of sugar endures!

My mother's favorite candy was more sophisticated. She loved Almond Joy candy bars. Peter Paul Candy Company introduced them—their first bar to contain almonds—in 1948, with the snappy slogan, "Oh Boy! Almond Joy!" For ten cents, my mother bought not one but two bars wrapped in the same package, two for the price of one being a sound marketing ploy in the inflated postwar market. Under a milk-chocolate coating, two roasted almonds sat on top of a coconut filling. I often pestered my mother for a bite and was rewarded with a mouthful of creamy coconut, a crunchy almond, and a whisper of chocolate. It was an education for my orange-tinged taste buds.

Until the mid-nineteenth century, candy making in the United States was a laborious process. Candy was either made at home or an expensive luxury, because it was so time-consuming to produce commercially. Then, in 1847, Oliver Chase, a Boston candy maker overwhelmed by orders for his handmade lozenges—rounds of sugar and peppermint oil, held together with gum arabic—rigged up a contraption that resembled a small clothes-wringer with holes cut in the rollers. Instead of stamping out rounds from a sheet of candy, he could roll the sheet through his invention, dramatically increasing his production capacity. A few years later, he patented a mill for powdering sugar, which increased the quality of his confections. These innovations were the nascence of what would become the New England Confectionary Company, which still makes Necco wafers today.

Another pair of clever candy makers invented a revolving steam pan, thus eliminating the constant stirring that had been required to make boiled confections. Another decided to use a native sweetener, maple syrup, rather than expensive imported West Indian sugar, to glue together the popcorn balls he sold from a cart. He also stumbled upon a confection made by immigrants from Syria called Turkish delight. It was delicious, but he couldn't decipher the source of its haunting taste until a missionary who had been to Syria provided him with a detailed recipe for the candy including the elusive ingredient, oil of roses. He added Turkish delight to his list of confections.

Confectioners searched out other new flavors, crushing herbs and other plants for their oil, stripping sassafras bark from the tree, gathering wild gingerroot. Other flavors came from abroad—vanilla from Mexico, cloves from the Spice Islands, licorice root from Europe. Gum arabic, from acacia trees growing on Mediterranean islands, held many of these confections together. But the unit of sale was still the individual piece of candy, attractively wrapped in cellophane.

All that changed when Milton Hershey made the first milk-chocolate bar in 1900, kicking off a candy-bar revolution. The next year, he added almonds, and combination bars featuring mixtures of nuts and nougat covered with chocolate weren't far behind. Initially, people didn't flock to the stores to buy these new bars, though; loose candy was more economical. World War I changed the picture. The U.S. government commissioned Hershey's to supply soldiers with candy during the war, and, given the conditions at the front, the rations couldn't be dainty bonbons. Hershey's chemists concocted a bar containing six hundred dense calories, which could withstand temperatures of up to 120 degrees Fahrenheit without melting, and packaged it in a waterproof box.

After the war, the market for wrapped bars took off, and over the ensuing decades, candy bars with every imaginable combination of ingredients appeared—coconut, caramel, toffee, crisped rice, fudge, nuts, and especially all-American peanuts. Most were covered with chocolate, either milk or bittersweet. And what fanciful names! Charleston Chew, Butterfinger, Powerhouse, Black Cow, Slo Poke, Milky Way, Munch, Oh! Henry, Mary Jane, and Baby Ruth. In 1923, the owner of the Curtiss Candy Company chartered a plane and dropped Baby Ruth bars by parachute over Pittsburgh, Pennsylvania. Too bad he didn't wait thirty more years, when I could have profited from his largesse.

Many of the candy-bar companies started small, then grew. But the competition was fierce. Bigger players bought out the small enterprises; some companies changed hands many times. Now Hershey owns Peter Paul, and they still make Almond Joy. Today, two giants, Mars and Hershey, control 75 percent of the candy sales in the United States, a market that totals a staggering fourteen billion dollars per year. The two are arch-rivals, with a history of sparring that spans the last century.

More recently, a unique marketing scheme that pairs snack foods with education has been developing. In 1982, a Massachusetts nursery-school teacher composed a poem about M & M's to teach her charges to count. She developed the concept into a book, but it took twelve more years to convince a publisher that this would sell. Now, with more than a million copies of *The M & M Brand Counting Book* sold, other publishers have joined the frenzy with brand-name books aimed at children, and many more are on the way. Not everyone is happy with this trend. Some pediatricians, parents, and publishers dismiss these books as pure advertisement and are aghast at their proliferation, even if some promote "healthy" snacks.

Still, a Web site that encourages children to do their own science experiments gives a cut candy bar as an example of a cross-section and challenges the viewer to identify a whole page of candy-bar cross-sections by brand name. I was glad to see that the first example was an Almond Joy.

Although Hershey and Mars are the giants of today's candy industry, small companies with a hands-on philosophy survive, even thrive. One is Charlotte's Confections, housed in a nondescript building on a suburban street not far from the San Francisco airport. I went there one morning to witness the making of old-fashioned peppermint twist-end chews, and to pay homage to the machine that works its magic to produce them.

The chief confectioner is José Chávez, and he is a man who loves his work. He never sits down; he regularly lifts heavy loads; he repeats the same task many times. Ah, but he's a candy maker. The heavy loads are bubbling cauldrons of sugar. Or fat cylinders of white nougat, some striped like a barber's pole, others containing a tiny green Christmas tree, also made from nougat, hidden in the center. Or blocks of chocolate wrapped in foil that he breaks up with a hammer, then deposits in a heated tub to melt.

José has worked for almost twenty years at Charlotte's Confections. "Charlotte" no longer owns the company, but the operation is little different from when it started sixty-five years ago; it continues to make candy the old-fashioned way. The most new-fangled addition is an expensive wrapping machine, and it's temperamental.

The ingredients José uses are those every candy maker knows well—sugar, corn syrup, egg whites, fat, and flavoring. But the proportions of the components and how long they are cooked, then mixed together, are crucial details.

"Of course, every candy maker has his secrets," I hinted

"The secret is in the heart," he responded. "If you don't love what you do, it shows in the candy."

When José was only eight years old, his father, a candy maker in Mexico, introduced him to the craft. José embraced it with enthusiasm and made it his life's work. His face glowed when I told him I had seen the Louisiana sugarcane harvest. Here is a man with a soul connection to sugar.

José and his apprentice, Javier, white bib aprons over their clothes, started another batch of peppermint chews. Reconstituted powdered egg whites whipped in the bowl of a 120-quart mixer. A propane-fired ring stood on the floor, cradling a copper kettle bigger than a baby bath. Sugar, corn syrup, and water bubbled inside. Nearby, a wooden pallet supported brown paper sacks, each filled with fifty pounds of granulated sugar. A white tank that looked like a small silo stood ready to dispense corn syrup. Although nuts weren't used that day, a roaster that looked like a pot-bellied stove sat next to the silo. It hasn't broken down during José's tenure.

When the temperature of the syrup reached the desired level, José and his helper picked up the kettle, moved it a few steps, then slowly poured the contents into the mixer bowl. The egg whites thickened and turned glossy. The candy makers mixed up another batch of syrup in the copper kettle and set it to heat. Just before it was hot enough, José added fat and a shot of peppermint oil to the beating mass in the mixer. The aroma of mint instantly wafted through the air. Then they added more sugar syrup, until the bowl was almost overflowing, and after a few more revolutions stopped the mixer.

A long table with a metal top waited, rigged with a special cooling system that sends cold water under the surface. The candy makers removed the bowl from the mixer, attached it to the chains of a hoist, and ratcheted it higher than the table. They rolled the apparatus to the end of the table, then tilted the bowl and slowly dragged the hoist down the length of it, as most of the warm white candy ribboned from the bowl. They pushed the candy to the upright extensions that boxed in the table's edge and smoothed the surface.

As the candy cooled, they mixed the small amount they'd reserved in the bowl with red coloring made from beet concentrate. Javier held a ball of the red candy in one hand and pulled with the other to make nine stripes at one end of the rectangle of cooling white candy. While it was still pliable, the men flipped it over, all one hundred pounds. They folded the end opposite the stripes onto itself, then folded again. Then they rolled the rectangle onto itself, so that the red stripes were on the outside. Next they cradled it in their arms as they moved it to a special machine, the "former," where it was massaged like a sore muscle. The machine turned it and pushed it toward three rollers, one on top of the other two—the same configuration as the rollers in the sugar mill. The nougat was slowly pushed through, its diameter shrinking dramatically. One more set of rollers thinned it even more. As it reached the end of the line, a cutter chopped off bite-size pieces—*ka-chunk, ka-chunk*—then two whirligig arms twisted cellophane around each one. Dressed up in their shiny coverings, the candies rolled down a chute and showered into a waiting bin. José gave me a handful of the soft pieces, which I slipped into my pocket.

The two candy makers can make eight batches of chews in one day. The flavor and look vary with the season and the holiday. In October, the nougat is orange, with chocolate Halloween faces in the middle of the rounds. For springtime, a lemon with a leaf announces the flavor. It takes an artist to make these fanciful images. Forms are available, but José uses only a V-shaped trough and works free-hand.

At another table, a worker was trimming rocky-road Easter eggs, a fusion of bittersweet chocolate and marshmallows. They were utterly unlike my memories of the bouncy rounds I roasted over fires as a kid, and certainly unlike the rubbery orange "peanuts" of my childhood. These were soft, sweet pillows just barely held together with gelatin and suspended in chocolate. José and his crew make them here—beating the ingredients in the mixers, pouring the mass on the cooling tables, cutting it with special rollers, then dusting the pieces with finely powdered sugar.

I collected more samples from the different production rooms—chews of different flavors, a new candy called Tidbits that combined squares of nougat with nuts. My pockets filled. I felt like a squirrel just before winter. I'm glad I chose the right jacket.

Sugar held its position as the supreme sweetener for centuries. But another sweetener, first developed in 1967, has significantly displaced it in the commercial food industry. High-fructose corn syrup begins as starch mixed with water. Acids and enzymes convert the starch to a dextrose solution, which is further concentrated. Another enzyme changes the dextrose into fructose. The development of this enzyme is the key to the process. The Clinton Corn Processing Company, the first to produce commercial high-fructose corn syrup, patented its special enzyme, calling it Isomerose. Their first syrup contained only 14 percent fructose. More sophisticated techniques led to syrups with higher concentrations. Eventually, the percentage reached 42, making this new product equivalent to sugar. Further advances helped the manufacturers make a super-sweet syrup, one that was 90 percent fructose. As sugar prices rose, commercial food and beverage producers realized they could save money by switching from sugar to high-fructose corn syrup, or HFCS. The syrup became industry-specific: 42 percent HFCS for canned fruits and condiments; 45 percent for soft drinks, ice cream, and frozen desserts; and the sweetest of all in foods marketed as low-calorie, where only a small amount was needed.

The Coca-Cola Company, one of the world's largest users of sugar in 1980, dealt the sugar industry a blow when it replaced half the sugar in Coke with high-fructose corn syrup. By 1984, all the sugar was gone. Pepsi followed suit. By the mid-nineties, per capita consumption of HFCS in the United States was fifty-five pounds, although probably few people realized that they consumed so much. Industrial food manufacturers use it as an inexpensive way to make processed foods more palatable, including those that we don't consider sweet. Even ketchup and sweet pickles get a dose of HFCS.

Even though this syrup is food-based, there was cause for alarm in some circles. The altered fructose isn't quite the same as the fructose found in ordinary sugar, and it may interfere with the body's use of essential trace minerals. Lab rats fed a low-copper, high-fructose diet died long before their life expectancy—five weeks instead of two years.

Another set of contenders—and sources of health concerns—are the artificial sweeteners. In 1879, a researcher at Johns Hopkins discovered a preservative that was sweet. Not only was it sweet, it had no calories. He called it saccharin, after the Greek word for sugar. It was embraced by dieters as well as diabetics, and during the war years of rationing, the population at large depended on it as a sugar substitute. Theodore Roosevelt, a diabetic, sang its praises and dismissed those who questioned its safety, although there was another undeniable, if harmless problem—saccharin had a bitter aftertaste. This was solved by the addition of cyclamate, another sweetener.

Cyclamate was soon used as a sweetener in its own right, mainly in soft drinks—No-Cal, Diet Rite Cola, and Tab among them. But in the 1960s, laboratory tests tainted cyclamate's reputation; it caused cancer in rats. By 1969, the FDA removed cyclamate from its "generally recognized as safe" list, then banned it altogether. Saccharin became the noncaloric sweetener of choice, but its ascendence was only temporary. Further tests implicated it as a carcinogen. Although still available, it has been required to carry "hazardous to your health" warnings since 1977.

In the 1980s, two more artificial sweeteners gained FDA approval. Aspartame, made from two amino acids, was approved in 1981. It is sold under the brand names of Equal and NutraSweet and has a mere four calories per packet. More important, it doesn't have saccharin's bitter aftertaste. This sweetener is used in many packaged foods and soft drinks, including Diet Coke and Dannon Light yogurt. Acesulfame K (Sweet One and Sunette), two hundred times sweeter than sugar, was approved in 1988. The FDA classifies it in the "generally recognized as safe" category, but some studies show an increase of tumors in rats and an elevated cholesterol level in diabetic rats to whom it is given.

The newest sweetener to hit the market is Splenda, with the full-mouth name of trichlorogalactosucrose, made by a patented process. Because it isn't absorbed by the body, there are no calories to worry about. And it has the endorsement of the star soccer player Mia Hamm. To me, the most interesting claim Splenda promoters make is that it is good for baking. (None of the others make this claim.) Because it is so sweet (six hundred times as sweet as sugar), a little goes a long way. So that a baker can measure it more realistically, it is mixed with dextrose and maltodextrin, much larger molecules which do provide two calories per teaspoon. Instead of a pinch, a recipe may specify one cup of Splenda, the same proportion of sugar one might expect in a recipe for cookies.

After all my reading about sugar substitutes, I decided it was time to put one to the test and chose Splenda, because it was touted for baking. A peanut-butter cookie recipe from the company's Web site seemed a good choice. I further stacked the odds in its favor by substituting butter for margarine and a real egg for the egg substitute called for in the recipe. The first thing I noticed in the directions was the order in which the ingredients were added. Rather than beating the butter-and-peanut-butter mixture with the Splenda, the normal course of events if one were using sugar, the egg, honey, and vanilla were added before the sweetener. I followed the directions. In my naïveté, I thought the Splenda would act as sugar would, creaming into the butter to make a light, homogenized base. Instead, the mixture separated into balls. I switched to a whisk attachment. No help. I added the rest of the ingredients without improvement. As I shaped the grainy dough into balls to be baked, I realized that I had never encountered dough with such a texture.

Cookies usually rise and spread in the oven. These did neither. Their taste was of peanut butter, but their sweetness didn't ring true.

These unusual cookies did have one saving grace: My husband's ailing diabetic aunt enjoyed them.

Sugar itself—the real thing—does not only come as sparkling white crystals. Regular granulated sugar, the backbone of the sugar world, probably sits in most American kitchens as a few ounces in a sugar bowl, a one-pound box pushed to the back of the cupboard, or a five-pound sack waiting to be baked into holiday cookies and cakes. In a bakery, a three-foot-high plastic tub may hold one hundred pounds, which will disappear quickly.

The same home kitchens might also have a small box of superfine sugar, which disperses more evenly and quickly in a batter (perfect for angel-food cakes) and dissolves faster, a boon for lemonade and iced-tea drinkers.

Powdered or confectioner's sugar is processed to a fine dust; the individual crystals aren't discernible. A baker might use this sugar to shower cooled cookies with a thin coating, or mix a little with milk or lemon juice to glaze a cake, or dust rounds of meringue just before they go into the oven.

Brown cane sugars are darker and moister than white sugar, because they still contain some of the dark cane syrup. As we have seen, brown sugar from sugar beets mimics this quality but is in fact completely refined, its dark color only surface-deep. Brown sugars have a more robust taste that lends a special character to some cookies and cakes. There are some very dark sugars, Demerara and Muscovado, less refined and with a stronger taste, that have been designer-packaged and given high price tags. They are used when an even more intense flavor is wanted, or to give a hint of their dark crunch when sprinkled on cookies and cakes.

Recently, "raw" or "natural" sugar has appeared on store shelves. This sugar isn't actually raw, but it is not as completely refined as white sugar. Some people think this makes it healthier. The ascendency of this sugar is reminiscent of the rehabilitation of dark bread and brown rice—shunned for a while and relegated to the peasants, then rediscovered and revered for its health benefits.

When I was in Louisiana, I visited a small family-owned operation that processes a dark, slow-flowing cane syrup and a turbinado sugar called Cajun Crystals, its crystals lighter and smaller than other free-flowing brown sugars. I used some to sweeten *palmiers*, leaf-shaped cookies made from puff-pastry scraps. In the oven, they caramelized like granulated sugar but stayed slightly crunchy, giving my *palmiers* a new personality.

Corn syrup can also be found on grocery shelves. Ordinary corn syrup is glucose, one of the sugars in sucrose. At least one major brand sold today contains high-fructose corn syrup, the specially treated syrup with added sweetness. Because corn syrup doesn't crystallize as easily as sucrose, candy makers add a little of it to sugar solutions. As the syrup boils down, the dissolved sucrose isn't tempted to revert to its crystal state, ruining the outcome.

Molasses is a liquid (just barely) sugar product prized for the flavor it brings to gingerbread and some candy. As we have seen, in the technical world of sugar milling and refining it has a specific meaning, and it isn't the sweet brown syrup in bottles on grocery shelves.

At the sugar mill, after the sucrose is crystallized, the sugar crystals are still suspended in thick syrup. The rotating force of a centrifuge separates the two, resulting in "A" sugar crystals and "A" molasses. This molasses is returned to a pan where it is crystallized and then centrifuged, separating the "B" sugar crystals from the "B" molasses. The resulting molasses is crystallized and centrifuged again, leaving

"C" sugar and the final or blackstrap molasses. But this is not the blackstrap molasses sold in stores. Instead, it is sold to companies that make cattle feed or produce alcohol.

When A and B sugar crystals are sold to refineries, they still have molasses clinging to them. The molasses is washed off, resulting in a syrup that is concentrated, then crystallized. The recovered syrup, called refinery molasses, must be further treated by pasteurization and filtration before it is fit for human consumption. Beet molasses isn't edible at all. Food-grade molasses is also made directly from cane juice, which can be clarified, evaporated, then filtered and pasteurized to produce a dark but sweet molasses called cane-juice molasses. Cane-juice molasses can be blended with refinery molasses. Manufacturers give these various food-grade forms of molasses different names—light, dark, blackstrap. Sulfured or unsulfured is now a moot point; sulfur isn't used in cane-sugar processing anymore.

In the kitchen, sugar in all its guises plays more roles than any other ingredient. In addition to adding sweetness, sugar crystals help trap air bubbles in a cake batter. The perfect example is a simple pound cake. Originally, these cakes contained a pound each of butter, sugar, eggs, and flour. The proportions in today's cakes are modified, and a chemical leavening and sometimes a liquid are added to provide a lighter texture. But the first step in making the cake is still the defining one: The baker beats soft butter, then gradually adds sugar, continuing to beat. The sharp edges of the sugar crystals help to trap tiny air pockets in the mix. As the beating continues, the two substances change their identity, becoming paler and visibly gaining volume. The trapped air contributes to the final texture of the cake.

In the oven, the higher heat on the exposed top of the cake and along the sides and bottom that are pressed against the pan browns the sugar on these surfaces, adding flavor and an appetizing appearance.

And because it draws humidity from the air, sugar keeps the cooled cake moist and fresh.

The cooking of sugar is the basis of the entire field of confectionery. A simple mix of water and sugar crystals in a pot undergoes a series of magical transformations when heated. It becomes a thin syrup to beat into meringues, then a molten mass that gives a brittle its crunch, and finally a thick brown syrup with a caramelized taste, just before the sugar burns and loses its sweetness altogether in a billow of smoke. Each stage gives a confection a different consistency—fudge, caramels, toffee, marshmallows, nougat, brittles, coatings for popcorn. Cream, butter, flavorings, and nuts change the taste, but the cooked sugar syrup provides the texture.

These stages are well defined, both by the appearance of the syrup and by its temperature. Thread, soft-ball, firm-ball, hard-ball, light-crack, hard-crack, caramel—as the temperature mounts, the syrup becomes more concentrated and behaves differently. Brave souls with quick reflexes test these stages by dipping an index finger into a glass of cold water, then quickly dipping the finger into the boiling syrup and back to the cold water. (I prefer the safer method of relying on a candy thermometer.) Syrup at the thread stage extends between thumb and index finger. The ball stages range from a flattened, soft ball to one that is firm and holds its shape when dropped into cold water. Syrup cooled to a light crack will break when removed from the water but stick to the teeth. Cooked to a hard crack, it snaps cleanly. The caramel stage is easier to identify; the syrup changes color, first to a light brown, then to a deeper amber.

Another use of cooked sugar removes it from the realm of food and elevates it to an art form. Sugar, water, and glucose syrup are heated; then this molten mass is poured onto a marble slab and folded upon itself with a spatula. When it cools enough for human hands, it is pulled like taffy until it stretches and is pliable. Then, quickly, before it hardens and shatters, the pastry chef shapes small pieces into petal flowers, attaches them to stems, and adds leaves. I spent a week at a school in France trying my hand at this artistry. There is a tension to the work—only very hot sugar can be pulled; when it cools, it loses its plasticity. The underlying fear of pain is augmented by creative anxiety. Some of the students had a natural flair for the work. The young man beside me deftly assembled multi-petaled roses and graceful tulips. Assuming that he made these creations every day at the restaurant where he worked, I asked him how he had gotten so proficient. "This is the first time I've done it," was his reply. Sugar pulling and I parted company when I returned to San Francisco.

Sugar lets us make ice cream and sorbets. The point in history when these concoctions metamorphosed from merely being chilled by the addition of ice to actually being frozen is hazy. The notion that confectioners of Catherine de Médicis made the first ices in 1533 has been refuted by many scholars. At least one (Elizabeth David) thinks it more likely that a Monsieur Audiger made the first ices in France about 1660. These early frozen confections would probably not pass muster today. They were stirred only occasionally—just enough to prevent the mix from freezing solid—resulting in an uneven texture containing chunks of ice, more like a granita than a smooth sorbet. Now we know that continuous stirring rapidly cools the sorbet and inhibits the formation of large ice crystals. The dissolved sugar also contributes to the final texture by lowering the freezing point; too little sugar makes a sorbet that is too hard.

Most home ice-cream/sorbet machines cool an inner rotating canister with a surrounding solution of water, ice, and salt. (Others employ an antifreeze-filled jacket.) The salt plays the external role that the sugar does inside the sorbet or ice cream: It lowers the freezing temperature so that the ice turns into liquid without a rise in temperature. This cools the sorbet faster, making it smooth on the tongue, devoid of crunchy crystals. Monsieur Audiger added salt to the cooling solution in his ice-cream makers too, but I bet he didn't know why.

Sugar is a powerful preserving agent. Fruits poached in sugar solutions of increasing densities become preserved. Sugar replaces the water in the fruit and renders it translucent and sweet. Although whole fruits and peels have been preserved this way for centuries, the birth of factory-produced preserved chestnuts, called *marrons glacés*, deserves special mention.

Chestnut trees are prolific in the Ardèche region of France, where they were called *l'arbre à pain*, or "tree of bread," because the dried, ground nuts were used as flour, especially among the poor. The local silk industry employed most of the population in the area until the latter half of the nineteenth century, when a disease killed the silkworms. With so many people out of work, an engineer named Clément Faugier saw an opportunity. He could put the manual dexterity of the silk weavers to good use by getting them to preserve the fruit of the ancient trees. Lack of a candy-making background didn't stop him. In 1882, he teamed up with confectioners and opened a factory. Former silk weavers peeled the nuts—only large nuts with few convolutions would do—then wrapped them in gauze, preparing them for poaching in increasingly dense sugar solutions. It was, and still is, an arduous task. Sugar slowly replaces the moisture in the nuts and transforms them into earthy candies to be eaten out of hand or crumbled into desserts. Today, the Faugier enterprise still produces many of the market's *marrons glacés*, although the chestnuts are apt to be Italian in origin rather than French. And in small confectioneries throughout France and Italy, preserved chestnuts are painstakingly made and proudly displayed at Christmas.

Sugar also preserves fruit in jellies and jams, a task better suited to home cooks than preserving whole fruits. In addition to sweetening the spread, sugar helps the fruit mixture gel. It attracts water molecules and binds with them, leaving the pectin molecules to twine around each other, creating the matrix that traps the fruit-and-sugar solution. Acid, either in the fruit or added, promotes gel formation too. None of this chemistry was known to early makers of marmalades and preserves; they learned by trial and error which fruits and how much sugar to use.

TWO MODERN POUND CAKES

These two cakes would be equally at home in the butter or egg chapters: Sugar, butter, and eggs are their backbones. Here the formula of the classic pound cake has been modified for a lighter texture.

1. POPPY SEED CAKE WITH CHOCOLATE SWIRL

Chocolate-enriched batter swirled into the cake just before it goes into the oven adds visual flair in addition to taste. Its Bundt shape makes it equally welcome at breakfast or after dinner.

Use a good-quality chocolate so the flavor comes through.

1 CAKE, 10 SERVINGS

Soft butter for the pan
4 ounces bittersweet chocolate, finely chopped
2 cups (10 ounces) unbleached all-purpose flour*
1½ teaspoons baking powder
¼ teaspoon fine sea salt
2 tablespoons poppy seeds
15 tablespoons (7 ounces) unsalted butter, at room temperature
1½ cups (10½ ounces) granulated sugar
3 large eggs, at room temperature
1 teaspoon pure vanilla extract, preferably Madagascar Bourbon
½ cup buttermilk, at room temperature

Preheat the oven to 350°F.

Generously butter a 2-quart Bundt pan.

Put the chocolate in a medium metal bowl, then place it over a pan of simmering water. When the chocolate has melted, remove it from the heat and whisk it a few times. Let it cool to room temperature.

Sift the flour, baking powder, and salt together. Add the poppy seeds.

Put the 15 tablespoons of butter in the bowl of a heavy-duty mixer. Beat it with the paddle attachment at medium speed until it is creamy and smooth. With the mixer on low, add the sugar in a steady stream. Beat the butter and sugar on medium speed until the mixture is lighter in color and fluffy.

In a separate bowl, beat the eggs together with a fork. With the mixer running, dribble the eggs into the butter and sugar.

Add the vanilla to the buttermilk.

Alternately add the dry ingredients and the buttermilk to the mixer bowl, starting and ending with the dry ingredients. Stop and scrape down the sides of the bowl when necessary.

Add about ½ cup of the batter to the melted chocolate and fold the two together. Now fold the chocolate mixture into the rest of the batter. Fold only 2 or 3 times, leaving swirls of chocolate in the batter.

Pour the batter into the pan and smooth the top with a spatula. Place it on the middle shelf of the oven, and bake until the top is brown and a skewer inserted into the center comes out clean, about 45 to 50 minutes.

Cool the cake. Unmold it, and place it, right side up, on a serving plate.

*In each of the recipes in this book, I give measurements for dry ingredients in volume first, followed by the equivalent in weight. Although either can be used, weight is generally considered a more accurate measure. Bakers themselves do not agree on the equivalencies, but here are those I use:

all-purpose flour: 1 cup, unsifted = 5 ounces
cake flour: 1 cup, unsifted = 4½ ounces
granulated sugar: 1 cup = 7 ounces
brown sugar: 1 cup, firmly packed = 6 ounces
powdered sugar: 1 cup, unsifted = 3½ ounces
almonds: 1 cup, whole blanched = 5⅓ ounces

2. Pumpkin Swirl Cake

Pumpkins speak of fall, and the autumn months are the best time to make this cake. Sage pairs with pumpkin in savory dishes. The *soupçon* of sage in this cake gives it a different twist.

The pumpkin can be cooked a few days ahead.

1 CAKE, 10 SERVINGS

> *1 small pumpkin, either sugar pumpkin or* rouge vif d'étampes
> *Soft butter for the pan*
> *2 cups (10 ounces) unbleached all-purpose flour*
> *1½ teaspoons baking powder*
> *¼ teaspoon fine sea salt*
> *1 teaspoon ground cinnamon*
> *½ teaspoon grated nutmeg*
> *¼ teaspoon ground cloves*
> *15 tablespoons (7 ounces) unsalted butter, at room temperature*
> *1½ cups (10½ ounces) granulated sugar*
> *3 large eggs, at room temperature*
> *1 teaspoon pure vanilla extract, preferably Madagascar Bourbon*
> *½ cup buttermilk, at room temperature*
> *1 teaspoon finely chopped fresh sage, about 5 leaves (don't use dry sage)*

Cook the pumpkin:

Preheat the oven to 375°F.

Line a large baking pan with parchment paper.

Cut the pumpkin into halves. Place the pieces on the baking pan, cut side down. Bake in the oven until a skewer pierces them easily, about 30 minutes.

Cool the pumpkin halves. Scrape out the seeds and discard them. Scrape the flesh out of the rinds. Purée the flesh in a food processor. You will need ¾ cup of purée for this recipe. Save the rest for another use. (It makes great soup.)

Make the cake:

Preheat the oven to 350°F.

Generously butter a 2-quart Bundt pan.

Sift the flour, baking powder, salt, cinnamon, nutmeg, and cloves together.

Put the 15 tablespoons of butter in the bowl of a heavy-duty mixer. Beat it with the paddle attachment at medium speed until it is creamy and smooth. With the mixer on low, add the sugar in a steady stream. Beat the butter and sugar on medium speed until the mixture is lighter in color and fluffy.

In a separate bowl, beat the eggs together with a fork. With the mixer running, dribble the eggs into the butter and sugar.

Add the vanilla to the buttermilk.

Alternately add the dry ingredients and the buttermilk to the mixer bowl, starting and ending with the dry ingredients. Stop and scrape down the sides of the bowl when necessary.

Stir the sage into the pumpkin purée. Add about 1 cup of the batter to the pumpkin purée and fold the two together. Now fold the pumpkin mixture into the rest of the batter. Fold only 2 or 3 times, leaving swirls of pumpkin in the batter.

Pour the batter into the pan and smooth the top with a spatula. Place it on the middle shelf of the oven, and bake until the top is brown and a skewer inserted into the center comes out clean, about 45 to 50 minutes.

Cool the cake. Unmold it, and place it, right side up, on a serving plate.

Ginger Scones

These breakfast treats shun pearly-white sugar; they prefer brown sugar and molasses for a more robust taste that doesn't wilt when faced with the bits of ginger in the dough. A sprinkling of raw sugar crystals on the top adds a final gutsy touch.

If you want hot scones for breakfast, a few minutes of organizing the night before helps you get these in the oven quickly. Combine the dry ingredients with the gingers, cut the butter into pieces and refrigerate it, and mix the buttermilk with the molasses. In the morning, the scones will be ready to bake as soon as the oven is hot.

6 SCONES

1¾ cup (scant 9 ounces) unbleached all-purpose flour
¼ cup (1½ ounces) firmly packed dark-brown sugar
1½ teaspoons baking powder
½ teaspoon baking soda
¼ teaspoon salt
2 teaspoons ground ginger
1 tablespoon chopped candied ginger
1 tablespoon chopped fresh peeled ginger
8 tablespoons (4 ounces) unsalted butter, refrigerator-temperature,
    cut into ½-inch cubes
½ cup (4 ounces) buttermilk, plus some for topping
1 tablespoon light molasses
Raw sugar crystals for topping

Preheat the oven to 375°F.

Line a baking pan with parchment paper.

Mix the flour, sugar, baking powder, baking soda, salt, and gingers in a medium bowl. Add the butter and, using your fingertips or a pastry cutter, mix it into the dry ingredients until it looks like a coarse meal. The butter pieces will not be uniform in size.

Stir the buttermilk and molasses together. Pouring with one hand and mixing with the other, add the liquid to the coarse meal to make a rough dough. Turn it out onto a lightly floured work surface, and knead it a few turns, until it just comes together. Pat the dough into a 7-inch disk, and cut it into 6 wedges.

Put the wedges on the baking pan. Brush the tops with buttermilk, and sprinkle them with raw sugar crystals.

Bake the scones in the middle of the oven until they are brown on top, about 20 minutes.

Serve them while they are still warm.

MOLASSES SPICE CAKE

Molasses lends its earthy taste to many American dishes, from Louisiana's *gâteau de sirop* to Boston brown bread. This recipe is cross-cultural—a combination of spices long used in parts of Europe, particularly Belgium and Germany, and molasses, the product made popular by the New World sugar industry.

This cake can stand alone, or become a very adult dessert with a dab of the rum sauce from the Pineapple with Rum Sauce recipe on page 64.

ONE 9-INCH CAKE, 8 SERVINGS

> 1⅓ cups (6⅔ ounces) unbleached all-purpose flour
> ¼ cup (1 ounce) rye flour
> 1½ teaspoons baking soda
> ½ teaspoon ground cinnamon
> ¼ teaspoon ground cloves
> ¼ teaspoon grated nutmeg
> ¼ teaspoon salt
> 1 teaspoon anise seeds
> 6 tablespoons (3 ounces) unsalted butter, at room temperature
> ⅓ cup (2 ounces) firmly packed dark-brown sugar
> 1 large egg, at room temperature
> ½ cup light molasses
> ¾ cup (6 ounces) buttermilk, at room temperature
> ¼ cup (1 ounce) raisins

Preheat the oven to 350°F.

Put a disk of parchment paper in the bottom of a 9-by-3-inch cake pan.

Sift the all-purpose and rye flours, baking soda, cinnamon, cloves, nutmeg, and salt together. Add the anise seeds.

Beat the butter in the bowl of a heavy-duty mixer with a paddle attachment until it is creamy and smooth. Add the brown sugar, and beat until the mixture lightens in color. Crack the egg into a small bowl and break it up with a fork. With the mixer running, dribble the egg into the butter and sugar. Beat in the molasses.

Alternately add the dry ingredients and the buttermilk to the mixer bowl, starting and ending with the dry ingredients. Stop and scrape down the sides of the bowl when necessary. Mix in the raisins.

Pour the batter into the pan and smooth the top with a spatula.

Bake the cake on the middle shelf of the oven until it is puffed and a skewer inserted into the center comes out clean, about 30 minutes.

Cool the cake, still in the pan, on a rack. Invert the cake onto a plate, peel off the parchment paper, then put it on a serving plate, right side up. Serve it at room temperature.

BEAUJOLAIS AND PEACH SORBET

The fruitiness of wine and peaches adds up to more than the sum of the two parts. The alcohol in the wine allows you to use less sugar to lower the freezing point of the liquid, so the sorbet isn't overly sweet. The beautiful color seems to enhance the taste.

Use the sweetest peaches you can find, at the peak of the season.

1 QUART

> *1 pound ripe, flavorful peaches*
> *1½ cups (12 ounces) Beaujolais, preferably a* cru, *not* nouveau
> *½ cup (3½ ounces) granulated sugar*

Blanch the peaches: Bring a large pot of water to a boil. Have a bowl of cold water handy. Put the peaches in the boiling water, bring back to a simmer, and cook the peaches about 30 seconds to loosen the skin. Remove them from the simmering water, and plunge them into the cold water. The skin should come off easily. Cut the peaches into halves, and remove the pits. Cut each half into ¼-inch slices.

Bring the wine and sugar to a simmer, stirring occasionally until the sugar melts. Add the peach slices to the simmering wine. Bring the wine back to a simmer, and cook the peaches for 1 minute.

Use a food processor to blend the fruit and wine into a purée.

Refrigerate the purée for 4 hours or overnight.

Churn the purée in an ice-cream maker according to the manufacturer's instructions.

Serve the sorbet in goblets or dessert bowls.

Green Tea Granita

The proportion of sugar to liquid is low in this recipe. Although the sugar slows the freezing process, it is not enough to stop it completely. If left in the freezer too long, the granita becomes a block of ice.

Once the mixture is cool, it will freeze to the proper texture in about 3 hours. If you forget to stir it and large chunks become frozen, take it out of the freezer, break up the frozen parts, and leave it in the refrigerator for about 15 minutes before returning it to the freezer.

Piled high in a parfait glass, this makes a refreshing dessert.

1 QUART

> *4¼ cups (18 ounces) water*
> *4 green-tea bags*
> *¾ cup (5¼ ounces) granulated sugar*

Bring the water to a boil. Put the tea bags and sugar in a large bowl that will conduct heat easily, such as stainless steel. Pour the water into the bowl, and give it a few stirs to dissolve the sugar. Let the tea cool to room temperature. Remove the tea bags, pressing down on them to extract as much flavor as possible.

Put the bowl in the freezer.

After 1 hour, the granita should begin to freeze. Remove the bowl from the freezer, and break up the frozen bits with a fork. Return the bowl to the freezer. Mix the granita, breaking up any large frozen chunks, every 30 minutes, until it resembles crushed ice. This should take about 3 hours.

Spoon the granita into tall glasses and serve.

PINEAPPLE WITH RUM SAUCE

Pineapple and sugarcane both grow in tropical countries. Maybe that's why this dessert works so well. The sweet-tart crunchiness of the fruit is smoothed by the rum-flavored sauce. Use a dark rum for the best flavor.

From the outside, ripe pineapples should be yellow to golden in color. A leaf pulled from the center of the top should come out easily.

4 SERVINGS

> *1 large ripe pineapple*
> *6 tablespoons (3 ounces) unsalted butter, at room temperature, cut into chunks*
> *½ cup (3½ ounces) granulated sugar*
> *¼ cup (2 ounces) dark rum*
> *2 large egg yolks*

Cut the green top and the bottom from the pineapple. Stand it on a work surface and peel it with a knife by cutting from top to bottom, removing the outside husk and the "eyes." Slice it into 8 rounds, ½ inch thick. Remove the cores. (An apple corer works best.)

Cover the slices and refrigerate them if you're not proceeding immediately, but bring the fruit back to room temperature before you do proceed.

Divide the pineapple slices among 4 serving plates.

Put the butter, sugar, rum, and egg yolks in a heavy-bottomed saucepan over low heat. Whisk them together until the butter is melted. Continue to cook the sauce, stirring constantly, until it thickens and coats a spoon. An instant-read thermometer will read 160°F. Don't let it boil, or the yolks will scramble.

Nap—lightly coat—the pineapple with the sauce. If you have Cardamom Coins (page 217), put a few on the edge of each plate.

POPCORN BALLS WITH CASHEWS

These are fun treats for both children and adults. Take them on a picnic.

Cooking the sugar syrup until it just begins to caramelize gives the popcorn more flavor, but handle it carefully to avoid getting burned. The ground coriander mixed with the nuts adds a subtle spice tone.

ABOUT TEN 3-INCH BALLS

½ cup (3 ounces) salted cashews
¾ teaspoon ground coriander
½ cup popping corn
Flavorless vegetable oil for popping corn (optional)
Salt to taste
2 cups (14 ounces) granulated sugar
½ cup (4 ounces) water
2 tablespoons light corn syrup
1 tablespoon unsalted butter
1 teaspoon pure vanilla extract, preferably Madagascar Bourbon

Preheat the oven to 375°F.

Lightly toast the cashews on a baking sheet until they are lightly browned, about 5 minutes. Let them cool, then roughly chop them with a knife. Mix them with the coriander.

Pop the corn, either in a corn popper, in batches in a microwave, or on top of the stove. If you're using the stovetop, choose a large pot; ½ cup of corn will pop into about 8 cups. Cover the bottom of the pot with a light film of flavorless oil. Heat it over high heat. When a drop of water dropped into the pot sputters, add the corn. It should cover the bottom of the pot in one layer. Cover the pot. The corn should start to pop in 1 to 2 minutes. When it starts, shake the pan occasionally until the popping noises cease. Remove the lid. (If you've used a corn popper or a microwave to pop the corn, transfer the popcorn to a large pot with a lid.) Season the corn with salt to taste. Sprinkle the nuts on top, and cover the pot to keep the corn warm.

Mix the sugar, water, and corn syrup in a medium heavy-bottomed saucepan. Use an unlined copper sugar-pot if you have one. Cook the syrup mixture over medium heat, stirring once or twice, until the sugar dissolves. Wash any sugar crystals from the sides of the pan with a brush dipped in cold water. Continue to cook, without stirring, until the syrup shows just a hint of golden color. This may take 10 to 15 minutes. Check the color by putting a drop on a white plate. When the syrup is ready, turn off the heat. Stir in the butter and vanilla. The syrup will be very hot.

Pour the syrup over the corn, and mix everything together with a wooden spoon. The syrup will start to form threads as it cools, and the corn will start to clump together. When this happens, mix it for 2 more minutes, then gingerly touch the palm of your hand to the corn to test the temperature. If it's too hot, wait a few more minutes. When you can handle the corn, press it between your palms into balls 3 inches in diameter. If the mixture stops sticking together before you finish, heat the pot over low heat to remelt the sugar.

Let the balls cool on a tray covered with parchment paper. When they are completely cool, store them in plastic bags.

Variation:

To make these for a dessert buffet, shape the corn into smaller balls, 1½ inches in diameter.

PEPPERMINT LOLLIPOPS

Lollipops have long been considered children's fare, but now grown-up restaurants are bringing them to the table as fanciful after-dinner bites. These have a clean and refreshing taste. If you like sweetened coffee, stir a cup with one of these instead of a spoon.

Order the lollipop sticks from a candy supplier.

10 LOLLIPOPS

Flavorless vegetable oil for the pan
1 cup (7 ounces) granulated sugar
½ cup (4 ounces) water
⅓ cup (2½ fluid ounces) light corn syrup
½ teaspoon pure peppermint extract

Lightly coat a rimless unwarped baking pan with the vegetable oil.

Place 10 lollipop sticks, evenly spaced, around the perimeter of the pan, with the sticks extending perpendicularly beyond the edges of the pan.

Mix the sugar, water, and corn syrup in a medium heavy-bottomed saucepan. Use an unlined copper sugar-pot if you have one. Cook the syrup mixture over medium heat, stirring once or twice, until the sugar dissolves. Put a candy thermometer in the pan. Wash any sugar crystals from the sides of the pan with a brush dipped in cold water. Continue to cook, without stirring, to 300°F, almost 10 minutes.

Remove the thermometer from the pan. Add the peppermint extract, and stir the syrup 3 or 4 times, just enough to distribute the flavoring. Wait until the bubbles subside and the syrup cools slightly, 1 or 2 minutes.

Holding the protruding ends of the sticks to keep them in position, pour a small puddle of syrup, 2½ inches in diameter, around the end of each stick that lies inside the pan. Work quickly, so the syrup doesn't cool too much and become too thick to pour.

Release the lollipops from the pan when they are just cool, about 5 minutes. If they become very hard, they may break upon removal.

When they are completely hard, wrap each pop in cellophane.

ALMONDS

IN 1914, FRANK MEYER, a botanist employed by the United States Department of Agriculture, found late-flowering bush almonds in the mountains near Taochow, China. During the same expedition, he found samples of the genuine wild peach. They were important discoveries, which overturned the long-held belief that almonds and wild peaches, which are in the same genus, had evolved from the same stock, then migrated in different directions, peaches moving east into China while their cousins the almonds traveled west. Darwin himself had concluded that the peach was a modification of the almond, because no wild peach trees had been found when he was writing. But Meyer determined that they evolved from separate stock; both trees are natives of a dry region of China. Small almond trees that produce hard, bitter nuts still grow in the Tian Shan mountains, which separate China from Kazakhstan; there the dry summers and mild wet winters are not unlike the climate of the almond-growing region in California. Stray seedlings probably grew along the early trade routes, where people picked the nuts and helped the trees' dissemination.

The assumption of a common origin for the two kinds of tree was natural. The pits of both peaches and almonds contain amygdalin, as do those of other fruits in the rose family—plums, cherries, apricots. Amygdalin, a substance capable of being synthesized into cyanide, exists not only in the pits, but in the bark and leaves as well. Since we don't eat the leaves or bark of any of these trees, this presents no problem. Nor do we eat the pits of almonds' relatives. But we approach almonds in a different way—we throw away the leathery hull and eat the pit. We eat almonds inside out.

Only one gene makes the difference between a bitter-almond tree and a tree whose nuts are sweet. Sweet-almond trees have a gene that has mutated so that the tree either doesn't contain or cannot synthesize amygdalin. This mutation may have occurred very early in the life of almond trees; bitter and sweet probably existed side by side. Early people probably rejoiced at finding the kernels from some trees to be sweet instead of bitter. But, faced with trees that produced only bitter fruit, they learned to use heat and water to make the bitterness go away, as they did with other crops, like cassava, that are toxic unless treated in some way. At first thought, it seems odd that people would gather dangerous food and even cultivate it. But such foods survive in the wild and become dependable crops; herbivores keep their distance, leaving the harvest for the humans who know how to tame the foods into palatability.

Settled village life, based on wild nuts as food, may have preceded the beginning of agriculture. The ability to store food was essential to a settled life, and nuts have this capacity, as do cereal grains. There is new evidence that sedentary village societies, dependent on almonds and pistachios, existed ten thousand years ago in the highlands of eastern Turkey. This significantly predates cereal agriculture in the region. So the staple food of very early societies may have been almonds. They grew readily in today's Iran and Iraq and along the Mediterranean. Hebrew writings of 2000 B.C. place them in what is present-day Israel. Almonds were tucked into the tomb of Tutankhamen when he died, about 1352 B.C., to provide food in his next life.

By 2000 B.C., maybe earlier, people began cultivating trees instead of merely gathering wild nuts. Some experts argue that early plant cultivation was vegetative propagation—planting branches of a plant in the ground, or even grafting one plant to another—because this would have been easier than planting seeds. Others suggest that the cutting up and burying of plant parts began as a religious rite, representing the sacrifice and burying of a god.

Whatever the origins of these practices, they were discovered and used thousands of years before the science of plant genetics was developed. Grafting techniques may predate history and may have been initiated in different places: The Chinese have grafted trees since remote times; the Greeks knew grafting; the Bible describes better olive trees resulting from grafts; Pliny the Elder described the technique.

In the case of almonds, vegetative propagation had a particular advantage. Propagating almonds isn't the same as propagating heirloom tomatoes. The seeds of early tomatoes produced plants with duplicate fruits; a planted almond seed may not grow up to produce the same fruit as its parents. The diversity of the resulting trees was a genetic advantage, although perhaps not one that the early planters understood: The trees could pollinate each other. But some 25 percent of them went back to their ancestral roots and produced bitter almonds.

Cutting a piece of an almond tree with favorable fruit and planting it in the ground, or grafting it to another tree, is a better way to duplicate the preferred fruit. Most early grafts were a form called inarching, which occurs in nature and was copied by farmers. When parts of two different trees are wedged together—for example, when the branch of one tree gets stuck in the fork of another—a union can occur. This type of juncture differs from other grafting techniques in that both parts are rooted. In contrast, bud grafting, a present-day technique, inserts only the bud from one tree into the rootstock of another.

Almonds are mentioned in the Bible, and are the only nuts cited except pistachios. They were used in exchange for grain during a famine in Canaan; to indicate God's chosen one—"the rod of Aaron . . . had sprouted and put forth buds and produced blossoms, and it bore ripe almonds"—and as a foundation for the menorah. They were linked to spring and to fertility. Today, sugar-coated almonds are still given to guests, especially in Italy and France, at baptisms (pink for girls, blue for boys) and at weddings and anniversaries.

The Persians and Arabs mixed ground almonds with water to make "milk." People in early China gave infants almond milk, considered almost sacred, instead of animal milk. Almonds figured in the cuisines of the Mediterranean, often in savory dishes. The cookbook of Apicius, a collection of Greek and Roman recipes from the first century A.D., includes them in recipes as diverse as stuffings for chicken and sausages, as a thickener in sauces, and in one sweet instance as an ingredient in cakes drizzled with honey. Persians gave the Romans, as well as the Arabs, the idea of thickening sauces with ground almonds, a custom that carried forward into European kitchens and was widely practiced until it was surpassed by roux, a mixture of flour and butter, in seventeenth-century France.

Spain, an early cultivation site for almonds, provided most of the almonds used throughout Europe. The country is still a major almond-growing region today, ranking second to California. Spain's almond acreage actually exceeds that of California, but the yields are less, probably because controlled irrigation and the placement of hives in the orchards for pollination are not commonplace.

Another Arab concoction was a sort of primordial trail mix—balls of dried bread crumbs, dates, almonds, and pistachios, held together with a few drops of sesame oil, that travelers could easily carry. A recipe for this exists in the *Baghdad Cookery Book*, written in 1226. Other recipes include sweet mixtures of almonds, pistachios, dates, sugar, and rose water, ingredients that were to form the basis of confectionery. Indeed, there are recipes in the book for two confections that still exist, in somewhat altered form, today. One is for taffy with pistachios, pulled until white, then cut into pieces. The other is for marzipan—a mixture of honey, sugar, almonds, musk (a favorite flavoring of the time), rose water, and starch that was cooked, then made into a paste. A similar mixture of ingredients went into almond torrone, although it was closer to French nougat than to marzipan in texture; it arrived in Italy in 1260, brought by the conquering count of Valois, and it remains a favorite Christmas gift throughout the country. Almonds appeared in many Italian confections and pastries. In a display of utter excess, Count Fieschi, lord of Lavagna, ordered a gargantuan cake that stood thirty feet high for his wedding in 1230. For its frosting, he chose almond paste.

The nuns of Italy, many living in closed communities, became excellent pastry makers, and the tradition lives on. Maria Grammatico, a contemporary woman who spent her adolescence in a convent in Sicily, learned the craft so well that she opened a pastry shop that still exists in the small town of Erice. Almost all her pastries contain almonds, not just any almonds but the Sicilian nuts that may contain a small percentage of bitter almonds, giving them a more intense flavor.

As the confectioners' art grew, so did the use of marzipan. Eighteenth-century cookbooks contain as many as seventeen recipes for the confection, adding preserved fruit and egg whites to the basic mix of almonds and sugar. The English Queen Elizabeth was fond of marzipan (as of all sweet things) and received many molded creations of the paste from admirers, including a depiction of St. Paul's Cathedral.

The Germans have loved marzipan since it arrived in the sixteenth century from Venice. They sought out the best almonds for it, and trade guilds regulated its sale; only apothecaries were allowed to sell it, much to the chagrin of confectioners. The proportions of almonds to sugar varied endlessly, as did the amounts of bitter almonds and other flavorings, such as honey. Neideregger, a marzipan maker in Lübeck since 1805, still boasts two hundred varieties. Because the amount of sugar in marzipan makes it stiff, a confectioner can mold it into shapes, then color it. Molding lifelike fruits and fanciful animals from it has become an art form in itself. A pastry maker can roll it into sheets to drape over cakes.

❧

Almonds came to New England about 1840. Since they belong to the same genus as peaches, settlers thought they would thrive in the same climate, a miscalculation. Almonds bloom before peaches, which exposed them to the wild swings of early-spring weather on the Eastern Seaboard, when frosts can kill the blossoms. California offered a milder climate, and eventually its central valley, with its long, rainless summer, would become the only important almond-producing site in the country. Father Junipero Serra brought almond seeds with him from Spain when he came to California in the late eighteenth century to establish his missions, but it wasn't until the next century that an almond industry was established.

Some of the first commercial growers planted seeds. Then Félix Gillet, a nurseryman in California, brought almond trees from the Languedoc region of France in the middle of the nineteenth century. Within a few years, plantings were scattered around the state. In 1863, an orchard in Yolo County sold five thousand pounds of nuts for twenty to twenty-two cents a pound, a price good enough that another grower proclaimed that no other crop was as profitable. The same grower hoped that one day California would supply the entire country with almonds. Little did he know that his wish would be granted, and then some.

These early enterprises had varying success rates. Growers struggled to develop varieties best suited to their areas, but they failed to take into account a very important fact. Almond trees are not self-fertilizing; they need cross-pollination. For Augustus Hatch, a shortage of grafting buds led to a serendipitous discovery. In 1879, he planted two thousand seedlings for grafting but ran out of budwood. From the remaining two hundred graftless trees, he selected four that looked promising, christening them Nonpareil, IXL, Ne Plus Ultra, and La Prima. La Prima didn't live up to its name, but he subsequently discovered that plantings of the other three resulted in high-quality, consistent yields. This combination became the basis for the California almond industry, and the soft-shelled, sweet Nonpareil is the favorite variety today, constituting 50 percent of the crop.

As the industry grew, new problems developed. In addition to selecting varieties, honing growing conditions, and striving for good yields, other concerns included selling the harvested nuts, because individual growers had little leverage with the buyers. In 1897, seventy-one growers banded together to form the Davisville Almond Growers Association. Their joint efforts led to higher prices for their nuts. Other small associations formed, but their size became a handicap. Members had no way of predicting crop volumes or demand in world markets; they remained at the mercy of the buyers. A grower named J. P. Dartitz became convinced that only a larger, central organization would give the growers the leverage they needed. He gathered officers of all the smaller organizations in the state, ten men including himself, at a meeting in Sacramento on May 6, 1910, and proposed banding together all the almond growers. The mood was tense; he wasn't sure of the outcome. But when a vote was taken, all present agreed. A state organization of all the almond growers was born. They called their new corporation the California Almond Growers Exchange, and they chose Blue Diamond as their almond's brand name, equating the nuts with the most precious of gems. They built a processing plant in Sacramento that has expanded over the last ninety years to cover ninety acres. It is the world's largest almond factory.

Now four thousand members have annual sales of five hundred million dollars. California is the major supplier of almonds not only to the country but to the world. I once saw pallets of California almonds on the loading dock of a large chocolate producer near Paris.

Harvesting the nuts in those early years was extraordinarily laborious. When the hulls split in the fall, revealing the brown shells inside, it is time to collect the nuts. But the nuts don't fall; they prefer to stay on the tree. Growers hauled tarpaulins to the fields and covered the ground around the trees. Then workers smacked the trees with poles, dislodging the nuts. To reach the nuts on the top branches, they climbed into the trees. Workers stuffed the nuts into cloth sacks and moved them to a nearby shed in the field. Then two men grabbed the corners at one end of the tarpaulin and dragged it to another stand of nut-laden trees.

Women, dressed in ankle-length dresses, many with their hair piled in buns on top of their heads, were the hullers. Sitting on up-ended boxes at a table under the shade of a tree, they removed the hulls from mountains of almonds by hand. The hulled nuts dried on wooden flats in the sun, then were transported in horse-drawn wagons to warehouses. Eventually, mechanical hullers took over the tedious handwork, and trucks and rail replaced the horses.

After World War II, mechanization moved into the orchards as well. Tractor-mounted "knockers" began to replace hand-harvesting in 1943. Self-propelled sleds sacked the almonds. In 1946, a grower named Elmer Keaton rigged up a contraption fashioned on his wife's carpet cleaner; an old Buick motor powered a fan that sucked in almonds and debris, then separated the nuts from the leaves. Variations on this theme, using rotating brushes, came next. These innovations meant that fewer people could harvest more nuts in less time.

Wendy D'Elesoua of Big Tree Organic Farms manages a cooperative of twelve growers in the northern part of the San Joaquin Valley. She agreed to take me on a tour of the orchards and small processing plants at harvest time, so I headed east from San Francisco. It was late September, and the hills of the Altamont Pass were brown, some in shadow. Rows of three-point windmills, looking like a Christo installation, twirled furiously, generating electricity. The freeway dropped to the valley floor, and the light changed to a glare. As the road straightened out, the speed limit accelerated to seventy and the drivers did the same. I drove over the San Joaquin River, then turned south to Modesto.

Wendy met me in the lobby of the Doubletree Hotel, clearly the most important building in town. The California Almond Board is housed on the top floor and uses the hotel for its meetings throughout the year. I left my car in the parking lot and climbed into Wendy's car. We drove out to an orchard so I could see a tree shaker at work.

We were met by Ray Marino, the owner, a trim man dressed in jeans and cowboy boots and sporting a baseball cap that bore the inscription "Professional Rodeo Cowboy Association." When I asked him about it, he said he'd been a rodeo rider but had given up the sport.

A shaker machine driven by a farm worker lumbered down a row between the trees. It was low to the ground, like a yellow bug, with large arms resembling pincers jutting from the front. The operator dismounted, oiled the front grasping parts, then strapped heavy rubber pads to them to protect the trees. He climbed back on and, surrounded by a protective cage, started up the motor. The machine crept up to a tree. Then the pincers advanced and locked onto the trunk. The machine shook the tree violently for thirty seconds, sending almonds and leaves cascading to the ground. "That's the end of one almond tree," I thought, fully expecting it to topple over once the machine unleashed it. But when the machine released its grasp, the tree was still upright. The driver moved to the next tree in the row and gave it the same treatment.

These were Fitz almonds; we freed some from their hulls and shells, then tasted them. They were very moist and slightly bitter. After the nuts had sat on the ground for ten days or so to dry out—an important step if they are to be hulled and shelled properly—workers would rake them into windrows for the shelling company to pick up.

Next we drove to Wendy's brother's farm. The land between the rows was more bare here, and the earth drier. We tasted a nut from the ground. This one was a Carmel, with a deeper flavor than the Fitz, a taste I associate more with almonds. A concrete-lined canal runs along the back of the orchard. Although there are heavy rains in the winter, most of the San Joaquin Valley growing season is dry. With annual rainfall of only fourteen inches, the trees need irrigation. Large valves line the canal at intervals. But the farmers can't turn them on at will. They have to make appointments with the water district—day, hour, length of time. Before the valves open and the water gushes forth, the farmers make small earthen dams, enclosing four rows of trees at a time. Then they flood the ground.

Our next stop was a shelling company. We pulled into the lot next to a mammoth steel building. Behind it, an overhead auger was spinning a mountain of hulls that challenged the building's height. A heavy-duty truck pulled up in front of the office and drove onto a scale, where the weight of its load was recorded. Then the almonds dropped through a large grate in the ground to begin the journey that would free them of their outer layers. First they entered a noisy machine that removed sticks and rocks; then they moved into the building itself, where the noise rose to an eardrum-splitting level. Bob Skittone, the owner of the company, explained the process before we donned earmuff protectors and entered the building; the few words he shouted inside were practically inaudible.

The nuts are repeatedly rubbed over heavy metal plates studded with almond-size holes. When a nut is free of its hull and shell, it fits through one of the holes on the bottom screen. But it isn't an all-or-nothing proposition. Some nuts are more stubborn than others, which is why they pass through nine such screens, until eventually all are freed. As the nuts fall through the screens, belts carry them to a huge bin. Some of the nuts are chipped in the process. The owner tasted one and made a face. "Too green. Should have left them on the ground longer," he said. "The growers complain, but if they're not dry, this is what happens."

The detritus of almond shelling, comprising rocks, sticks, hulls, and shells, is a much greater volume than the nuts themselves, but none goes to waste. The rocks and sticks go back to the ground, the hulls are a component of cattle feed, and the shells become cattle bedding.

The shelling operation only runs during the harvest, two months of the year. "We spend the next ten months overhauling the equipment," explained Skittone.

Next the almonds journey to a packing plant. We stopped at a small market for water, since the heat of the day was building, then continued on to the California Independent Almond Growers. A family-owned business run by a middle-aged couple, the plant occupies a low, corrugated steel building with several unhitched trailers parked near the entrance. Before we went inside, Wendy showed me the fumigation chambers, large steel enclosures that hold stacked wooden boxes filled with incoming almonds. Once the nuts are inside, a steel door drops into place and a worker injects phytoxin, an insecticide that kills pests and their larvae, but not their eggs. A second application is needed after the eggs hatch. Because this plant processes both conventional and organic almonds, another method is used to rid those almonds of pests. Inside the building, boxes of organically grown almonds are covered with heavy plastic wrap, which is taped to the floor. A thin hose delivers nitrogen, which replaces the oxygen under the tent. The nitrogen environment doesn't harm the almonds, but insects, including larvae and eggs, cannot survive. Fourteen days in this oxygen-free atmosphere kill the bugs, which then drop through the wooden bins to the floor.

As we walked toward the room where the almonds are separated, Wendy said, "Hear that noise?" It sounded like rushing water. "It's the almonds," she said. We opened the door and saw a vibrating machine that moved not cascading water but almonds over a series of screens that separated them by size. The machine sorting was only the first step. Next the nuts traveled at a good clip along conveyor belts where women in hairnets manually removed those with chips or insect damage.

At California Independent Almond Growers, this is the end of the almond processing. The nuts go into boxes to await delivery. We tasted several as we walked through. They were Nonpareils. Although these are considered to be the king of almonds, I might prefer the Carmels.

Another nearby plant takes almonds through an additional step. The processing plant sat behind the modest house of the family that owns it. Toni Conway, a diminutive woman wearing a red-and-white polka-dotted dress with matching earrings, greeted us cordially as we stepped into the office. As soon as we entered, the aroma of roasting nuts enveloped us. "We're running your father's almonds today," Toni said to Wendy. In addition to separating almonds, the Conways also produce sliced almonds, roasted almonds, and almond butter. "I'm sorry to rush you through, but I have to go to the bank before they close," apologized Toni. She led us through the processing room, past a woman patiently removing damaged nuts from a conveyor belt. In the back, another woman was hosing water into an almond-filled box. "We wet them to prevent shattering when they go through the slicer. If the almonds are blanched, they're not as dry, so they don't need water," Toni explained.

The wet almonds passed through a heater before being dumped into the slicer—a small machine, considering the work it does. The slicer deposited the nuts into little containers on a moving belt. Another machine separated out imperfect nuts, which the Conways make into almond butter. Large bins of processed nuts stood almost to my shoulder.

In a corner of the room stood the roaster, a tired machine that roasts batch after batch of nuts, four hundred pounds at a time, for forty-five minutes. I was practically salivating from the aroma. "We need a new machine, one that's bigger. This one slows us down," said Toni before dashing to the bank.

Our appetites piqued by the roasting almonds, Wendy and I took our leave and headed to a nearby restaurant for a late lunch.

◎

After the busy work of the harvest, January is a quiet time in the California almond orchards. The trees that blanket the San Joaquin and Sacramento Valleys are pruned skeletons. They look lifeless, but flower buds that began the previous summer are starting to emerge from their dormant state. By the middle of February, the trees will wear white blossoms as if covered with snow, even though snow rarely falls in these fertile valleys, the only places in the United States that meet the climatic requirements that the trees demand. It must be cold in the winter but frost-free after February, and the summer months must be warm and dry.

Exacting climatic conditions aren't all the trees need to produce mature nuts. Unlike other nut trees, almonds produce flowers, like stone-fruit trees, instead of catkins, like other nut trees, and the pollen of one variety must be transferred to a tree of a different variety for pollination to occur. Orchard breezes can't move the heavy, sticky substance, but honeybees can.

Just when the trees are stirring to renew their annual cycle, honeybees, sequestered in hives during the winter, are also awakening, as if they know their services will soon be needed. The cold months are hard on the bees. Pollen and nectar sources are gone, but there are still mouths to feed, and the bees must generate enough heat to keep the inside temperature of the hive high enough so they can survive. In the best of times, the fall brood is small, pollen and honey stores are plentiful or supplemented by a careful beekeeper, and the colony of bees survives the winter.

In January, when the almond-tree buds are stirring, the queen bee of the hive starts laying eggs in the hexagonal wax cells that the worker bees build. A new mating session isn't necessary; her one-time fling provides enough sperm to last about two years. In top form, a queen can lay an egg a minute, and can determine whether each egg is fertilized or not. The fertilized eggs become worker bees, all female, but incapable of reproducing, thanks to pheromones the queen produces, assuring her supremacy. The unfertilized eggs develop into the loafing drones, whose sole purpose is mating.

In three days, the eggs hatch into wormlike larvae. They are the impetus that drives the worker bees out of the hive in search of food. The worker bees feed these grubs for six days, then cap their cells. In their dark, silent, hexagonal homes, the larvae metamorphose from worms to insects, and after twenty-one days, if they are worker bees, chew their way free. This worker bee can perform tasks of which neither of her parents was capable. She is a housekeeper first, then, after a few days, graduates to the role of nurse bee, feeding larvae. After a week, she takes on the duties of receiving and storing nectar and tending to the queen, feeding her the royal jelly that the worker bee secretes from special glands. Next she makes wax, the building material for the hive, and acts as a guard, patrolling the hive entrance on four legs, wings up and antennae straight out, alert for intruders. Only after three weeks of hive chores does the new worker become a field bee, foraging for food and water. Meanwhile, the coddled queen continues her life's work—laying eggs.

As the bee colonies build their numbers throughout January and into February, farmers, sometimes miles away from the beehives, watch their trees for impending bloom. When the blossoms are about to transform the trees into white statues, the farmers call the beekeepers and arrange delivery of rental hives. Because they want to pollinate every flower, the farmers need as many as three large hives per acre, more than local bee supplies can meet. Hive rental has become big business. The *American Bee Journal*'s "Help Wanted" column runs ads from farmers looking for bees, as well as ads from beekeepers looking for people to drive trailer trucks (good driving records required) the length of California, depositing and picking up hives.

The bees must be in the fields during the crucial three days when pollination takes place, but to ensure the best results, the farmers keep them about a month. They also plant some pollenizing varieties that bloom before the main crop, and others that bloom after. And they hope other, nearby flowers don't contain more nectar than the almonds, thereby luring the bees to them instead of to their trees. They also hope that the weather cooperates, producing temperatures above fifty-five degrees, preferably closer to sixty, with a minimum of clouds and wind, conditions under which the bees do their best work.

At the critical moment when the needs of the trees and bees dovetail—one needing pollen transfer, the other needing a plentiful food source—the beekeepers move into action. At the end of the day, when all the bees are home from their foraging efforts, the beekeepers tightly strap each hive. Then, depending on the size of the operation, the hives are loaded into a truck or a large tractor trailer. Large operators use forklifts.

The bees don't like to be disrupted and would prefer to be left alone when it's dark, but during this special time they are jostled all night as the trucks carry them to the waiting orchards, often crossing state lines. The drivers strive for a predawn arrival, to position the hives before the bees venture out. Then, dressed in space-suit garb to prevent stings from the irritated insects, they hurriedly unload their charges before heading bleary-eyed to bed. It's an edgy time for all—bees, beekeepers, and farmers.

Bob Burres, a California beekeeper, explained his routine during impending blossom. He has two trucks with booms. At dusk, he stacks the hives by twos, picks them up, loads them on the truck, and ties them down. Then he sleeps for four hours. By 2 a.m., he's on the road, traveling in the dark to get to the orchards by sunrise. After unloading the bees, he drives back home and sleeps for another three hours. This is his schedule for the next ten days. "The first load is the worst," he says. But he adds, "I still get excited after twenty-one years."

When the sun comes out, the foraging bees go to work. They fly
to the nearby trees, collecting nectar and pollen, moving from flower
to flower, returning to the hives only when the special pollen-carrying
sacks on their hind legs are full and their honey stomachs are en-
gorged. Back at the hive, they transfer the fruit of their gatherings to
house bees and then, in a highly skilled form of communication, tell
other worker bees how to locate the food source. They do the wagtail
dance; the direction of the wagging points the way. And it's just not a
vague shake of the abdomen: It indicates the correct direction in rela-
tion to the position of the sun, and the distance.

The trees shed pollen during the evening and early-morning
hours. By late afternoon, the bees have collected it all. The bees
gather pollen each day until the flowers stop producing it. Then the
bees' work is done, and the beekeeper picks them up. For Bob Burres,
picking up the bees isn't as exhausting as the delivery. He drives to the
orchards, loads the beehives, and drives home. The bees spend the rest
of the night on the truck while he sleeps. By sunrise, he's outside
again, stacking the hives on firm ground. The timing of the pickup is
just as important as the timing of the placement, not for the trees this
time, but for the bees. With the queen in full egg-laying mode, the
brood is expanding, and the acres of almond trees without nectar or
pollen no longer give sustenance. The beekeeper repeats his nocturnal
voyages to other flower sources, ending up as far away as Texas.

Because of increasing acreage planted in almonds, and farming
practices that plant more trees per acre, the demand for bees continues
to grow. In 1999, 950,000 beehives were placed in the almond orchards of California. With an average of twenty thousand bees per
hive, that means that nineteen billion bees flitted from flower to
flower that February. And that's just for the almond pollination.
Throughout the country, bees help pollinate thirteen major crops,
from apples to blueberries.

This dependence on the bees is dramatically different from 1909,
when the first colonies of honeybees were rented for apple pollination

in New Jersey. Then, wild bees helped pollinate crops. Later, insecticides that killed unwanted pests also drastically reduced the number of wild bees. Then a new scourge arrived—tracheal and varroa mites—and wild bees became even more scarce. These same mites attack honeybees, necessitating medication by the beekeepers. More trouble is in sight; the effectiveness of a widely used drug is waning, and there's nothing on the horizon to replace it.

☙

An amateur beekeeping friend introduced me to bees after a trip to our country house with him was slightly delayed when he took delivery of his first shipment of bees and needed time to get them settled. That weekend, his talk of the complexities of the hive stirred my curiosity, and I borrowed some of his books. Then I borrowed more from the library. There may be more written about bees than about any other animal. Karl von Frisch won a Nobel Prize for his discoveries about bee communication and sight. The information seemed never-ending. The bees lured me into their world; maybe I could install a hive in our country orchard, I mused. The apple trees would be more fruitful if we had bees.

I saw a flyer at a farmers' market announcing beekeeping classes and called the number. There was one final class for the year in Sacramento, an hour-and-a-half drive. I signed up. "Bring a hat and a veil," said the woman on the phone. Not owning a proper specimen of either, I hastily grabbed a straw hat and a long scarf as I left the house.

It was unseasonably cold in the state capital, and overcast, weather that bees don't like. A group of twenty or so would-be beekeepers assembled in a classroom at the agricultural-extension office, drinking instant coffee and eating locally made doughnuts. Some had driven farther than I. It was a mixed group that included both men and women, some children, people with experience and neophytes. Ten minutes before starting time, our teacher, a tall, lanky man with movie-star looks, loped into the room wearing jeans and a colorful shirt. "Any volunteers to help me carry in stuff?" he asked. Several people followed him and returned with books about bees, smokers, brood boxes, supers, frames, telescoping tops, hive tools, bee suits, and a box of hats and veils (to my relief). He announced that there was a lot of material to cover, so he would stick to a strict schedule: "Your heads will be swimming by the end of the day." In the afternoon, he promised to open hives on the lawn beside the building so we could experience the bees up close.

He launched into his presentation, adding many facts to my expanding knowledge of the insects. Humans have been allied with bees as far back as there are records. The earliest gatherers broke hives apart to collect honey, thus killing the bees. It wasn't until the nineteenth century, when Lorenzo Langstroth invented movable frames, that people could harvest honey without completely disrupting the hive. Langstroth discovered "bee space," the interval that bees naturally leave between their combs. This space, five-sixteenths of an inch, lets the bees pass each other as they move through the hive. Langstroth deduced that respecting this distance when building inside frames for combs would allow him to remove combs to harvest honey, then replace them. The era of modern beekeeping had arrived. "But the bees don't know they're living in something you built," our teacher reminded us. "As far as they're concerned, they live in a hollow tree. Bees are wild animals. The beekeeper is the servant of the bees, not the other way around." Our ebullient instructor paced the front of the room, turning at the wall to march in the opposite direction. By the third hour, I made a connection—his movements mimicked the dance of the bees.

After lunch, theory turned to practice. We donned the rather clumsy getups that looked like hard hats with mosquito netting dangling from the brims. These offer protection for two things that bees associate with the enemy—hair and eyes. (Bears are notorious hive robbers.) Also, bees see red as black, a warning color. After hearing that, I removed my red earrings and hid them in my pocket.

We filed out to the lawn, where hives awaited. Eschewing veil or gloves, our leader showed us how to light a smoker; then he lightly smoked the entrance to the hive. This tricks the bees into thinking that their home is on fire, so they hurry to the honey to gorge themselves in preparation for flight. Then he carefully pried the cover from one of the hives and lifted out a honeycombed frame covered with bees. They were in constant motion. Within seconds, many were flying around the group. Our teacher removed more frames, one at a time, showing us the brood and the cells filled with honey. He discovered that the workers were making queen cells; they weren't happy with their leader and secretly planned to replace her. Then he found the queen, a small one. Maybe she wasn't up to her queenly tasks.

We moved to an empty hive to watch as a package of bees were introduced to their new home. The bees were clustered around the queen, who was in a special cage. After brushing the bees from the cage with his bare hands, our teacher attached the queen-bearing cylinder to a frame of the open hive. Then he invited people to pick up a handful of bees and shake them gently (quick, jerky movements can cause stings) over the frames. "Who wants a handful of bees?" he asked. No one wore gloves. He gently scooped them from their traveling box and dumped them into outstretched palms. The kids, showing fearless curiosity, were first in line.

My vision was restricted by my too-big hat, which kept falling down over my eyes. And bees were flying everywhere. I wanted to hold the bees, but an inner caution made me hesitate to extend my hands; I found them in my pockets instead. I was reminded of my sugar-pulling class, when molten sugar of taffy consistency had to be handled to be worked into fancy shapes but would burn if held too long. Just as I was about to ask for a handful of bees, someone asked, "How do I get them off?" He was gently shaking his hands, but the bees clung to him instead of falling onto the hive's frames. "Be patient, just keep shaking them gently. Remember, no jerky movements," replied our teacher. That did it. My hands stayed jammed deep in my pockets. Maybe I wasn't quite ready for the bees.

A soft drizzle started to fall. It was time to wrap up the demonstration. Our teacher overturned the box holding the remaining bees in front of the hive. To a member, they marched in.

⊚

Not all bees exhibit such docile behavior. Some colonies are persistently aggressive, ready to attack when the beekeeper opens the hive. The queen dictates the ambience of the colony, and replacing her can entirely change the personality of the hive.

The Africanized strain of bees are always testy and easily provoked. Their productivity, not their nastiness, is what prompted the introduction of twenty-five queens into Brazil in 1956 for a special breeding program. Unfortunately, excessive swarming is a characteristic of these bees, and many escaped from the hives. At the slightest provocation, they will sting in large numbers, much more readily than their European cousins. And the bees will follow nest intruders, such as beekeepers, for a much longer distance, up to two miles.

These so-called "killer bees" have slowly been migrating north. They were discovered in Texas in 1990, and over the southeastern corner of California by 1997. Small swarms of Africanized bees get a toehold in a new region by taking over colonies of European bees, but the beekeepers are fighting back. Frequent hive inspections can detect takeovers when the population is small, and introducing a new queen each year keeps the European genes dominant.

Another South American import is causing consternation among beekeepers and sleepless nights for almond growers. Fire ants have invaded beehives in several states; they were discovered in southern California in 1998. Their ferociousness and nasty bites are a problem. If anything disturbs their nest, a large mound above the ground, they attack all at once. Agricultural inspectors have stationed themselves at California's borders to inspect beehives for the unwanted ants. If any are found, the drivers, some from as far away as Texas and Louisiana, are turned back. And since half the bee colonies needed for pollination come from out of the state, the tougher inspections have led to a shortage of bees. During a recent harvest, one farmer who needed four thousand hives had only fifteen hundred. As his trees blossomed, so did his anxiety.

Neither killer bees nor fire ants were on John Lagier's mind when I visited him during almond bloom. The weather was. Rain pelted my car, and my windshield wipers were running full-tilt from the time I left San Francisco until I pulled into his road. Not a good day to visit orchards, I thought. But the first sight of the delicately flowering trees, blushed only slightly pink as I crested the Altamont Pass, spurred me on. The almond trees really are the harbingers of spring here; every other plant in sight was dormant.

By the time I pulled into John's driveway, the rain had stopped. He met me at the door, dressed in a plaid shirt and jeans; his droopy mustache gave him a forlorn look that matched the dismal day. But his smile returned when he offered me a handful of caramelized almonds, still warm from the copper kettle in his commercial kitchen.

"Are you ready to walk in the orchards?" he asked, looking pointedly at my shoes. "Sure," I answered, and I changed into yellow boots. He added a parka and a brim hat to his own attire.

We left the building and walked past bare cherry trees. After a few minutes, John pointed out a lone blossoming tree. "It's a wild tree, probably from a seed," he said. "The nuts from it are very bitter." I had been trying to find bitter almonds, without much success. John spied a blackened hull near the top of the tree and jumped to retrieve it. But when he broke it open, the nut was gray with mold. Too bad. I would have to wait months for another opportunity.

Down a side road, John's almond trees were on our right, a neighbor's cherry trees on the left. We turned into a row between the trees and stopped at a stand of hives. They were silent, and a solitary bee hovered outside. John pried the top from a hive. The bees scurried on the frames and emitted an alarm scent at the intrusion. John closed the hive and peeked in another. There were plenty of bees inside, but none wanted to venture into the chilly air under cloudy skies.

This year, John ordered one hundred hives for his thirty-six acres of trees. The beekeeper, one he has used for a long time, dropped them off a few weeks ago, and they will stay for three more.

Each row of Nonpareil trees, the dominant variety, was flanked by a row of Carmel on one side and Butte on the other. These were the pollenizers. The Nonpareil trees were in full bloom, waiting for bee activity, which didn't look promising that day. I asked John if he was worried about the inactive bees. He admitted that he was, but the wet weather brought him other worries as well. The rain-soaked blossoms were prime targets for a fungus that causes brown-rot blossom blight, although the cold weather was actually an ally against the fungus. A few days ago, he'd sprayed with Nutrimix, an organic substance, to protect the trees against the fungus. "Sort of like homeopathic medicine," he said. Because he farms organically, it's the best weapon he has. Conventional farmers apply fungicides. A careful inspection of a few trees didn't reveal the culprit. John exhaled sharply, with relief. The other affliction that concerned him was shot-hole fungus, whose name defines it—it eats small round holes in the leaves. Cold weather doesn't deter it, and if unchecked, it can defoliate the trees. John found a leaf with signs of infection. His brow furrowed, and worry clouded his face. He will spray with a compost tea, hoping that the good organisms will overpower the bad. "I don't sleep well at this time of year," he admitted.

Before we headed back, John cut two souvenir branches for me—a Nonpareil covered with open blossoms, and a Butte not quite in full bloom. Back in his office, a phone call returned him to business. He handed me two pouches of nuts to go with my tree branches, and I thanked him and headed for my car.

◎

All of the almonds cultivated in California, regardless of their variety, are sweet almonds. But in Europe, bitter almonds are still prized—a few are often added to almond meal in France to heighten the flavor, and a portion of the almonds in German marzipan are bitter. American companies were not forthcoming about the ingredients in their almond pastes and marzipans, citing proprietary information. A company noted for its spices and extracts was no more informative about its formulas. Pure almond extract is a mixture of bitter almond oil and alcohol, and the source of the bitter almonds is probably China. There is also a relatively inexpensive product called "kernel paste," which derives an almond flavor from apricot kernels. And scientists can produce benzaldehyde, the substance responsible for almond flavor, in a laboratory without ever coming close to an almond or apricot; this is the flavor agent in imitation almond extract.

Dr. Sam Cunningham, director of research and development at Blue Diamond Growers, shed some light on this confusing issue. He gave me a diagram showing the sequence that changes the amygdalin found in apricot kernels and almonds into hydrogen cyanide and benzaldehyde. He reminded me of what the early eaters of the nuts deduced long ago—that hot water dissipates the poison, leaving the aldehyde, which accounts for the special taste.

Sam led the way to his lab and opened a refrigerator. He rummaged through plastic bags of nuts and containers holding possible new products and held out an open bag to me. "Here, try one of these." Inside were small, blanched bitter almonds that were split in two. Their bitterness had been removed. I popped one in my mouth. It had a strong extract taste, and produced a slight tingling of my tongue because of the acid in the aldehyde. He selected another; the taste was the same. Then he found a bag of nuts from South Africa, unblanched and still bitter. He offered me one. "You first," I said. He put one in his mouth and, after the initial chew, contorted his face. I put mine in my pocket to try at home, at a moment of invincibility.

For several days, the almond sat like a flattened, tan teardrop in a cup on the kitchen counter. After passing it several times, I decided to try it one afternoon. I cut off a very small piece (reducing the amount of toxin ingested, I figured), put it in my mouth, and chewed. It wasn't as bitter as I'd expected, and it had a strong almond-extract flavor. I rather liked it.

Green almonds are another curiosity. By the beginning of May, the blossoms on the trees have metamorphosed into infant nuts. Fuzzy green hulls hang from the trees. When the soft hulls are opened, they reveal a startling green hue, the color of kiwi fruit. Cradled in this thick, protective coating lies a virgin-white almond. The shell is paper-thin, and the inside, which has not yet hardened into the nut we know, is gelatinous. The taste only vaguely approaches that of an almond. Its soft fruitiness reminds me more of a lychee or logan fruit. It takes five more months for the soft jelly to harden into a mature nut.

In the south of France, a bowl of green almonds might appear with apéritifs. Friends would break into the soft hull and slip the fragile kernels into their mouths between sips of *vin cuit*.

I bought a few pounds of these immature nuts from John Lagier at the Ferry Plaza Farmers' Market in San Francisco and added them to panna cotta. Their alluring taste and very slight crunch made a distinctive dessert, sort of a fancy take on the "almond milk" made long ago.

Some special almond confections have attained premier status over the years. In each case, a story accompanies the delicacy's ascent.

Praslines de Montargis are almonds with a history. When I read the tale, I wanted to drive south from Paris to the town of Montargis, straight to the Church of the Madeleine, to see if the shop that made these confections so long ago still stood across the street.

In the seventeenth century, the duke of Plessis-Praslin had a cook named Clément Jaluzot. Watching an apprentice scrape caramel from a bowl with one hand while he popped almonds into his mouth with the other, Jaluzot speculated that the two ingredients would be delicious together. He cooked almonds in sugar until they were individually coated with a hard covering. They were an instant success. He later set up a shop in town, the Confiserie du Roy, to sell his special almonds. How they came to be called *praslines* isn't clear, but theories abound. Perhaps the inventor named them for his employer. Or perhaps one of the duke's many female friends, to whom he gave boxes of the candies, named them in his honor. In another story, King Louis XIII dispatched the duke to Bordeaux to negotiate a dispute with the local magistrates. When they refused him entrance to the city, he decided to invite them to a banquet, which dazzled them and allayed their concerns. At the end of the meal, they ate the sugared almonds and named them for the duke.

Later, the Confiserie du Roy became the Confiserie Mazet. The building was reconstructed in 1920, relying on documents from the seventeenth century, and the shop still makes *praslines* from the original recipe and ships them worldwide.

My husband and I had appointments to visit creameries west of Paris, not the right direction for stopping at Montargis, and our tight schedule precluded a detour. A few hours out of Paris, when we stopped at a snack bar on the autoroute, a sign at the entrance announced a boutique with regional specialties. I wandered in and saw yellow boxes with gold trim labeled "*Véritables Praslines—Mazet de Montargis.*" What a find! But back in the car, when I opened the box,

I thought I had misunderstood how the candy was made: The almonds were dark, as if they were covered with chocolate. I bit into one. It wasn't chocolate, just dark caramelized sugar, very crunchy. French pastry chefs bake everything very brown, and these candies were made according to the same philosophy.

Today, the general term for these candied nuts is "praline," but the nomenclature can be confusing, because it also refers to the sugar patties famous in New Orleans, made with pecans rather than almonds. To a French pastry chef, *praliné* is sugar cooked with almonds, poured onto a marble slab in a single mass, and allowed to cool. Then it is ground up and added to butter cream or whipped cream to give cakes a sweet, almond crunch or mixed into melted chocolate to make candies. The aroma when the sugar melts and cooks the almonds is almost intoxicating; when we made this in my bakery, as soon as it was cool enough we broke off pieces to sample.

Confections that have become synonymous with Provence are *calissons*. Although their origin is obscure, there is mention of a cake of almonds, flour, and dried fruit called *calisone* in a Latin text of 1170. Venetians made almond cakes called *marcipane*, "Mark's bread," in honor of their patron saint. By 1275, almond cakes made in Venice were called *calisone*. *Kalitsounia*, similar confections found in Crete, were made from almond paste, walnuts, sugar, honey, orange and lemon zests, cinnamon, and cloves. They were shaped into crescents and baked. As sugar became more plentiful, it was used to preserve fruit, which was added to the mix. Today's *calisson* is a lozenge-shaped paste made from almonds, sugar, and/or honey, preserved fruit—often melon—and orange-flower water. A white icing of egg whites and powdered sugar finishes the top.

These confections experienced a resurgence in the seventeenth century, when they acquired a role in a religious ceremony commemorating the end of the plague. In August 1629, the plague struck the population of Aix. Despite quarantines, the malady spread, and by January of the following year, twelve thousand people had perished. The survivors sought divine intervention to end the devastation. They promised to hold an annual procession to the Church of Notre Dame de la Seds on the anniversary of the plague if God would intervene. The plague subsided, then disappeared (whether because of divine intervention or because the disease ran its course, we can only speculate).

The following September, the plague over, the citizens walked solemnly through the streets to the church. Following a mass, *calissons* blessed by the archbishop were distributed on the plaza in front of the church. The people believed the confections protected them against illness and gave them strength. And, keeping their promise, they held this procession, replete with banners and ringing bells, not only every September, but also at Easter and at Christmas, until the Revolution. The *calisson* may have taken its distinctive shape during these years, the almond-shaped oval mirroring the shape of renderings of the Christ child and the Holy Father on the fronts of cathedrals. The bottom of the confection was made from host wafer, as it still is today.

The tradition of the procession was revived in 1996. Although the church has changed, the townspeople dress in costume and march to church on the first Sunday in September to distribute *calissons* from baskets.

Honey and nuts are an old pair. When the Greeks came to France about 600 B.C., settling in present-day Marseilles, they made a nougat with honey, pine nuts, and walnuts especially to celebrate feasts and in honor of the goddess Artemis, whom they associated with bees as a giver of life. As the Greeks spread out from Marseilles, they took nougat with them.

This early nougat was made with honey and without almonds. The Greeks were excellent beekeepers, and there was a profusion of blossoming plants in Provence to provide pollen and nectar for the bees. Although the Greeks knew almonds, it wasn't until the twelfth century A.D. that the trees arrived in Provence, imported from the east. Almond trees grew in Marseilles, but those that grew around Aix were more fruitful. During the Middle Ages, Aix was a major center of almond commerce, but small growers eventually switched from almonds to lavender, a more profitable crop. The candy makers, wanting high-quality almonds, augmented their supply with nuts from Greece and the eastern Mediterranean.

Almonds were considered a dessert for all seasons and held a place of honor, either alone or mixed into nougat, among the thirteen desserts symbolizing Christ and the twelve apostles that are the grand finale to the traditional Provençal meal eaten after midnight Mass on Christmas Eve. During the Middle Ages, large quantities of almonds were consumed, caramelized first in honey, then in sugar, and doused heavily with spices. The fourteenth-century book *Ménagier de Paris* specified that the best of these treats were from Provence.

Montélimar, a town to the north of Provence, became celebrated for its nougat, so much so that the name of the town became synonymous with the candy. Montélimar owes its status to Olivier de Serres, who planted almond trees near the town in the seventeenth century. The fruit of the trees provided the impetus for the revival of this ancient confection—the updated version is a cooked syrup of honey and sugar poured into beaten egg whites, which whiten and aerate the candy. Almonds and pistachios are added at the end.

A legend describes the naming of this confection: An elderly woman of Montélimar made a special treat of honey, sugar, nuts, fruits, and eggs that she frequently gave to her friends. Upon receiving her delicious offering, the friends exclaimed, "*Tu nous gâtes*" ("You spoil us"), which got shortened to *nougat*. However, this may be more legend than truth. When the word was added to the dictionary of the

French Academy in 1762, its origin was attributed to the Provençal *nougaioun*, which means the seed of a stone fruit. An earlier origin is from the Greek word *nôgalon*, a cake made from honey and nuts.

There are at least three major producers of nougat in Montélimar, and I have seen Montélimar nougat in specialty stores in northern California. But the owner of a confectionary store in Paris gasped when I asked for nougat from Montélimar, dismissing it with a quick shake of her head. She steered me to the "*véritable*" item—*nougat noir*, made with honey and almonds, and *nougat blanc*, the egg-white version, from deep in Provence. When I tasted them, I couldn't complain.

There is a circular connection among bees, honey, almonds, and humans. Bees, and therefore honey, evolved with flowering plants in Cretaceous times, probably in Africa. The two had a symbiotic relationship—the bees provided pollination for the plants, and the flowers' nectar sustained the bees. The insects gradually spread to other temperate regions. When humans arrived, they realized that bees produced a sweet substance, and they wedged themselves into the picture. As knowledge about bee behavior increased, people became better beekeepers. It wasn't so much a question of managing the bees; it had more to do with observing and learning their habits. The bees were in control.

A similar thing can be said about early almond farmers. People chose for propagation almond trees that had mutated from their forerunners, changing their bitter nuts to sweet. In a way, the trees paved their own destiny.

The bees helped the almond trees grow mature nuts. And the bees carried the nectar from the flowers of the trees back to the hive, where they transformed it into honey for food. But the humans intervened again. They collected some of the honey—not all, if they were careful beekeepers—for their own use. The bees were content, as long as their hives were not too disrupted and there was enough honey left for them. Then, unbeknownst to the hardworking insects, the humans paired the fruit of their labors with the nuts they had helped to produce, closing the circle.

The almonds that early people gathered, then later cultivated, contributed important components to their diets. They knew that the nuts tasted good; they didn't know that the amino acids, calories, fats, and vitamins that they ingested when they ate a handful of these seeds provided many aspects of a well-balanced diet. Indeed, the concept of a well-balanced diet did not yet exist. But the nuts curbed people's appetites and provided a source of energy.

As dietary habits became more sophisticated, almonds continued to be used in both savory and sweet preparations. But, while they are still an integral part of many savory dishes in the Mediterranean and Middle East, and are a staple in vegetarian cooking the world over, their main use in the United States has been in baked goods and confections. Milton Hershey led the way when he paired milk chocolate with almonds, a winning combination. But as California almond production and imports of almonds soared, growers needed another market outlet. The scientific community provided this. It touted almonds as a healthy food, rich in minerals, providing energy at a lower cost than most other foods, and containing highly nutritive protein that is easily digestible—in short, a remarkable vegetable food, one whose extended use "cannot fail to improve the American dietary," according to one nutritionist, writing in 1926.

By the 1980s, however, the fat scare had eclipsed almonds' healthy image. An ounce of almonds has 160 calories and fifteen grams of fat. Nut consumption declined, and the USDA's food pyramid, issued in

1992, placed nuts with meat, poultry, fish, dry beans, and eggs, recommending only two to three servings from this group daily.

About ten years ago, food scientists began to rethink nuts. Studies looked at nut consumption and its relationship to heart disease. Papers began to appear in scientific journals. One study concluded that eating nuts one to four times a week decreased the risk of coronary heart disease by 25 percent; when nut consumption rose to five or more times a week, the benefit rose to a 50-percent reduction in disease risk. Other studies showed that diets high in monounsaturated fats and low in saturated fats lowered both total cholesterol and LDL cholesterol. Even more surprising, the addition of almonds to a low-saturated-fat diet being followed by people with high cholesterol levels lowered those levels, even though their total fat intake was higher.

Nuts contain heart-healthy compounds that may be responsible. Almonds are particularly high in vitamin E and magnesium; the first prevents oxidation of LDL cholesterol, thus reducing cardiovascular risk, and the second helps maintain heart rhythm. Nuts also contain arginine, an amino acid that lowers cholesterol and relaxes blood vessels, and phytochemicals, whose health benefits are being studied. They are a good source of dietary fiber, which aids digestion and is believed to lower cholesterol. And their naturally occurring monounsaturated fats inhibit blood-clot formation and may help dissolve already-formed clots.

Another fatty acid, the polyunsaturated omega-3, is emerging as a protective substance against a wide-ranging number of maladies, including heart attacks, rheumatoid arthritis, Crohn's disease, and bipolar affective disorder. Oily fish, such as tuna and salmon, contain omega-3 fatty acids—and so do almonds.

Oldways Preservation & Exchange Trust, an organization whose mission is preserving traditions and fostering cultural exchange in the fields of food, cooking, and agriculture, rethought the food-guide pyramid in light of a traditional Mediterranean diet. The incidence of heart disease, cancer, and diabetes is lower in the countries surrounding the Mediterranean. Consumption of vegetables, fruit, and grains is high; intake of saturated fats is low. People living in these countries eat twice as many nuts as we do in the United States. Olive oil features prominently in the cuisine of the region, and although it is a fat, its components, low saturated fat and high monounsaturated, primarily oleic acid, give it a healthy profile. Nuts, particularly almonds, have a similar composition. Oldways moved nuts closer to the base of the pyramid, even with fruits and vegetables, and recommended significant daily doses of all three. A Latin American diet pyramid, also developed by Oldways, recommends that nuts be eaten at every meal!

The Almond Board of California took an innovative approach to encourage people to eat almonds. They mounted a national campaign to educate women about their risk of heart disease, encouraging them to make dietary changes—such as eating almonds, three ounces a day for thirty days. They dubbed the campaign the Almond Cholesterol Challenge. The Almond Board's Web site gave information about diet, cholesterol, heart disease, and research studies, and offered recipes. The Challenge message was aired on television. Two editors from *Better Homes and Gardens* took it on, and the magazine published the results: Both editors lowered their cholesterol levels.

The research into the benefits of this ancient food continues.

Almond processors make it easy to cook and bake with almonds. The nuts are available in every conceivable form—whole, slivered, diced, and sliced, in their natural state or blanched. The slight tannic edge to the skin gives a more pronounced flavor; a blanched nut tastes sweeter. The majority of the crop is the Nonpareil, a sweet variety with a papery shell that is easy to remove and a skin that slips off after a brief dunk in hot water. Other varieties have a bitter edge.

Since almonds are harvested just once a year, it's best to keep them tightly wrapped in the refrigerator or freezer to prevent rancidity. A light toasting before use will accentuate their flavor, but watch them closely: A burned nut is acrid.

Many cuisines use almonds ground to a fine powder in place of flour to make cakes; the meal adds a nutty taste and a denser texture. Mixed into tart or pie dough, it adds flavor. Larger pieces of nut, from thin slices to chunky batons, provide either the whisper of a crunch or a pleasing chewiness to cakes, cookies, and breads. They can also garnish cakes and cookies or be mixed into toppings for crisps. Whole nuts find their way into baked goods too, but really shine in confections—cooked in hot sugar syrup, then eaten out of hand or shattered, ground up, and mixed with chocolate; enveloped in a molten mass of syrup and beaten egg whites, cooled, and cut into pieces; folded into candy bars.

Almonds that are damaged or otherwise judged unworthy to be sold as first quality are pressed for their oil, which is distilled to make extract or used in cosmetics. A baker needs only a few drops of almond extract to ratchet up the intensity of a cake or shortbread. Or almonds can be roasted and ground into butter like their more common cousin, the peanut.

Almond paste and marzipan, the two pastes made from almonds, sugar, and glucose, differ with respect to their sugar content and texture. The typical formula for almond paste is 65 percent wet almonds and 35 percent sugar. Its stronger almond flavor can stand up to chocolate in a cake or be used as a base for candy. The almonds in marzipan are ground finer, and there are fewer of them in proportion to the sugar, so the paste is whiter and more malleable, a property that has long let confectioners mold it into shapes. Commercial producers formulate some marzipan so that it can be rolled into long, very thin sheets by mechanical rollers, then draped over cakes. How unfortunate that this refined paste wasn't available when Count Fieschi married in 1230!

ALMOND BUTTER COOKIES

Peanut-butter cookies, an American classic, are transformed with the substitution of almond butter. An extra dose of chopped almonds accentuates the taste.

Almond butter is available in health-food stores and many supermarkets. Mix it before using, because the oil tends to separate to the top. Buy the chunky style.

Because there is not an oven that truly heats uniformly, turn the pan around halfway through the baking.

ABOUT 30 COOKIES

> ½ cup (2⅔ ounces) whole blanched almonds
> 1¼ cups (6¼ ounces) unbleached all-purpose flour
> ½ teaspoon baking soda
> Pinch of fine sea salt
> ½ cup (4¾ ounces) almond butter
> 8 tablespoons (4 ounces) unsalted butter, at room temperature
> ½ cup (3 ounces) firmly packed light-brown sugar
> ⅓ cup (2½ ounces) granulated sugar
> 1 large egg, at room temperature

Preheat the oven to 375°F.

Toast the almonds on a baking sheet until they are lightly browned, about 5 minutes. Let them cool, then roughly chop them with a knife.

Line a large baking pan with parchment paper.

Sift the flour, baking soda, and salt together.

Put the almond butter and the unsalted butter in the bowl of a heavy-duty mixer, and beat with the paddle attachment until they are mixed together. Beat in the brown and granulated sugars, then the egg. Add the flour, baking soda, and salt, and beat until the dough is uniform. Beat in the nuts.

Take about a tablespoon of dough from the bowl and roll it in your palms, shaping it into a ball. Put it on the baking sheet and continue with the rest of the dough, placing the balls about 2 inches apart. Press the tops of the rounds with the tines of a fork, flattening the cookies to ½-inch thickness.

Put the baking sheet on the middle shelf of the oven, and bake until the edges of the cookies start to turn brown but the centers are still slightly soft when pressed with a finger, about 12 minutes.

Remove the pan to a rack to cool. Store the cookies in an airtight container at room temperature.

ALMOND CHOCOLATE DROPS

Finely ground almonds, rather than flour, give these cookies structure, and they also add a little crunch. Use a good bittersweet chocolate so the flavor shines through.

ABOUT 36 COOKIES

> *1½ cups (8 ounces) whole blanched almonds*
> *¼ cup (1 ounce) powdered sugar, sifted*
> *2 large egg whites, at room temperature*
> *¼ cup (1¾ ounces) granulated sugar*
> *1 ounce bittersweet chocolate, finely chopped*

Preheat the oven to 300°F.

Line a large baking pan with parchment paper.

Use a food processor to finely grind, but not pulverize, the almonds. Mix the almonds with the powdered sugar.

Put the egg whites in the bowl of a heavy-duty mixer. Beat the whites with the whisk attachment, starting on medium speed. When they start to froth, add about a third of the granulated sugar, and beat until they become opaque and increase in volume. Add another third of the sugar, and beat until they start to become firm; then turn up the mixer speed, add the remaining sugar, and beat until they are stiff but still glossy. The whites will hang in soft, droopy peaks from the whisk when it is lifted from the bowl. Using a spatula, fold the almonds and powdered sugar into the whites by hand, then fold in the chocolate.

If you are adept with a pastry bag, pipe the mixture into 1-inch rounds, 1 inch apart, onto the baking pan. Don't use a tip; the nuts and chocolate may clog it. Or drop the batter onto the pan from a teaspoon.

Put the pan on the middle shelf of the oven. Bake the cookies until they are lightly brown, firm on the surface, and able to be detached from the paper, about 20 minutes.

Remove the pan to a rack to cool. When the cookies are completely cool, store them in an airtight container at room temperature.

FINANCIERS

Although not immortalized in literature as Proust's *madeleines* are, these small almond cakes are quite popular in France. Their name is probably derived from their shape—a thin rectangle, like a gold bar. A hefty quantity of almonds gives them their distinctive taste and texture. Lightly browned butter is a key ingredient; it enhances the nutty flavor.

For these cakes I have a set of special molds that I bought in Paris. If you can't find them, use another low, small mold, such as a barquette, or a brioche mold 3 inches in diameter at the top.

Coat the molds well with very soft, but not melted, butter. (Melted butter tends to pool in the bottom of the molds.) A foolproof method is to brush the molds with the soft butter, then refrigerate them for a few minutes before brushing them again. This way, every speck of metal will be well coated.

SIXTEEN 3¾-BY-2-BY-½-INCH CAKES

> Soft butter for the molds
> 1 cup (5⅓ ounces) whole blanched almonds
> 14 tablespoons (7 ounces) unsalted butter
> 2½ cups (9 ounces) powdered sugar
> ½ cup (2½ ounces) unbleached all-purpose flour
> Pinch of fine sea salt
> 5 large egg whites, at room temperature

Preheat the oven to 450°F.

Carefully butter the molds so that no trace of metal is showing.

Use a food processor to finely grind, but not pulverize, the almonds.

Melt the 14 tablespoons of butter in a medium saucepan, and cook it until it stops sputtering and turns a light shade of brown, about 5 minutes. Remove the foam that rises to the top as the butter cooks. When the butter is the correct color, pour it through a fine sieve into a bowl, and let it cool to room temperature.

Sift the powdered sugar, flour, and salt together. Whisk in the almonds. Whisk the egg whites into the mixture. (Note that the whites are not beaten before they are added.) Add the butter, leaving any brown specks in the bottom of the bowl, and whisk until everything is uniformly combined.

Put the molds on a baking tray. Using a ladle, fill them three-quarters full.

Put the tray on the middle shelf of the oven, and bake for 5 minutes.

Turn the oven down to 400°F, and bake until the cakes are light brown, 10 more minutes.

Cool the cakes before unmolding.

Round Almond Cakes

Almond paste is the dominant feature of these dainty rounds, which contain only a wisp of flour and cornstarch. The very slow addition of the eggs beats plenty of air into the batter, giving these cakes a light, almost spongy texture. Use almond paste that is 50 percent almonds.

Bake the cakes in fluted tart pans with solid bottoms. Float them on a thin layer of fruit purée for dessert, or eat them for breakfast.

SIX 4-INCH CAKES

Soft butter for the pans
6 tablespoons (3 ounces) unsalted butter
10 ounces almond paste, at room temperature
4 large eggs, at room temperature
3 tablespoons cake flour
3 tablespoons cornstarch
2 tablespoons brandy
3 tablespoons sliced unblanched almonds

Preheat the oven to 375°F.

Butter six 4-inch, 1-inch-tall tart pans with solid bottoms.

Melt the 6 tablespoons of butter, and let it cool to room temperature.

Put the almond paste and one of the eggs in the bowl of a heavy-duty mixer, and beat with the whisk attachment on medium speed until the paste and egg are mixed together. This will make the almond paste a little less dense.

Beat the remaining 3 eggs in a small bowl with a fork. With the mixer on medium, drizzle about a tablespoon of egg into the bowl. The almond paste will still be quite thick, but it will start to become lighter around the whisk as it absorbs the egg. Continue adding small quantities of egg to the bowl, letting the paste fully incorporate each addition before adding more. Add the egg in 5 stages; it should take about 5 minutes. The paste is ready when it becomes pale and thick.

Hand-whisk the flour and cornstarch together in a medium bowl.

Whisk about ½ cup of the egg–almond-paste mixture into the flour and cornstarch, or just enough to absorb the starch and make a thick batter. Whisk in the brandy.

Using a spatula, fold the rest of the egg–almond-paste mixture into the batter in 2 additions. Fold in the melted butter in 3 additions.

Pour the batter into the molds, and sprinkle sliced almonds over each one. Bake the cakes on the middle shelf of the oven until the tops are golden, about 20 minutes.

Cool the cakes, then remove them from the pans.

Marzipan Ruffle Cake

Marzipan is almond paste's cousin, slightly firmer in texture and more pliable, because it contains more sugar. Because of its flexibility, it can be molded into different shapes—animals, fruit, and flowers are common—or rolled into sheets and draped over cakes.

ONE 9-INCH CAKE, 8 TO 10 SERVINGS

The cake:
⅔ cup (3 ounces) cake flour
4 large eggs
½ cup (3½ ounces) granulated sugar
3 tablespoons (1½ ounces) unsalted butter
½ teaspoon pure almond extract

The finish:
1 teaspoon kirsch
*Sugar syrup—¼ cup (2 ounces) granulated sugar heated and
    dissolved with ¼ cup (2 ounces) water*
2 cups (16 ounces) heavy whipping cream
1 tablespoon granulated sugar
½ pint raspberries or other ripe berries
Powdered sugar for rolling the marzipan
7 ounces marzipan, at room temperature

Bake the cake:

Preheat the oven to 375°F.

Line the bottom of a 9-by-3-inch round cake pan with parchment paper.

Sift the cake flour into a small bowl.

Put the eggs and ½ cup sugar in the bowl of a heavy-duty mixer, then place this bowl over a pan of simmering water. Whisk by hand until it reaches 140°F, about 3 minutes. Return the bowl to the mixer. Put the butter in a medium bowl, and set it over the simmering water to melt while you proceed.

Beat the eggs with the whisk attachment at high speed until they become pale, thick, and almost triple in volume, 8 to 10 minutes. Remove the bowl from the mixer. Sift half of the flour over the beaten eggs, and fold it in by hand with a rubber spatula. (This will be the second time the flour is sifted.) Sift and fold in the rest of the flour.

Remove the bowl containing the butter from the water. Stir the almond extract into the butter. Fold about one-fifth of the egg mixture into the butter, then pour the butter-enriched batter into the mixer bowl and fold it in.

Pour the batter into the pan, and bake it on the middle shelf of the oven until the top is lightly browned and the cake starts to pull away from the sides of the pan, about 20 minutes.

Cool the cake in the pan on a rack.

Finish the cake:

Run a table knife around the edge of the cake pan, and turn out the cake onto a work surface. Leave the parchment paper in place. Turn the cake right side up. Using a serrated knife, cut the cake in half lengthwise, through its equator. Overturn the top half onto a 9-inch cardboard round or a serving plate. You will work on this half of the cake first.

Add the kirsch to the sugar syrup. Brush some of the syrup onto the cake on the serving plate.

Whip the cream until it forms soft peaks, adding the tablespoon of sugar halfway through. Put one-quarter of the cream in another bowl, and fold in the berries. Spread this on the cake on the plate.

Overturn the other half of the cake onto the first, and peel off the parchment paper. Brush this half with the remaining sugar syrup. Put the cake in the freezer for 20 minutes so the filling becomes firmer.

Remove the cake from the freezer, and apply a thin layer of the remaining whipped cream to the top and sides, making it as smooth as possible.

Lightly sift some powdered sugar on a work surface. Shape the marzipan into a ball, then roll it into a disk about 12 inches in diameter.

Pick it up and turn it as you work, adding more powdered sugar if needed to keep it from sticking.

Trim the edges for smoothness. Put the marzipan disk on a rimless cookie sheet dusted with powdered sugar. Lift and softly pleat the rim of the marzipan disk, standing the pleats on the cookie sheet (practice with a napkin), until you have a cap of the same diameter as the top of the cake. Tilt the cookie sheet over the cake, and slide the marzipan on top. Dust it with powdered sugar.

Refrigerate the cake until serving.

GREEN ALMOND PANNA COTTA

If you live near an almond-growing region, or know someone with almond trees, collect a few immature almonds in the early spring to make this dessert. The infant nuts, with their fragile white shells and soft insides, offer a faint crunch and a whisper of almond taste to this comforting combination of milk and cream. A little almond extract heightens the flavor, but be careful. Extracts differ in intensity; add half the amount, mix, and taste. If it needs a little more, add the remainder of the amount.

FOUR 6-OUNCE SERVINGS

> 8 ounces green almonds in their shells
> 1½ teaspoons unflavored gelatin
> 2 tablespoons cold water
> 1½ cups (12 ounces) heavy whipping cream
> ¼ cup (1¾ ounces) granulated sugar
> 1 cup (8 ounces) whole milk
> ½ teaspoon pure almond extract
> 20 fresh Bing cherries (optional garnish)

Crack the fuzzy hulls of the almonds, being careful not to smash the fragile nuts inside. Free the nuts, and set them aside.

Sprinkle the gelatin over the water in a small bowl, and let it soften, about 3 minutes.

Heat the whipping cream and the sugar, stirring to dissolve the sugar. Add the almonds, and bring the liquid to a simmer. Turn off the heat, add the softened gelatin, and stir the liquid until the gelatin is dissolved.

Stir in the milk and half of the almond extract. Taste the mixture. If it needs more almond flavor, add the rest of the extract.

Pour the mixture into ramekins. Refrigerate them until the creams are firm, at least 4 hours and up to 2 days before serving.

Serve the panna cotta in the ramekins, or, for a fancier presentation, unmold them by dipping the ramekins in hot water for a few seconds and turning them out onto serving plates. Garnish the plates with a few pitted Bing cherries; the first of the cherries should be in season when the almonds are green.

A Trio of After-Dinner Almonds

Almond-accented treats that can be made ahead provide a dessert-after-dessert to go with coffee. All three praise the almond: a modern version of an early "trail mix"; a simple combination of dates and almonds, dressed up with chocolate; and a sophisticated French confection.

The caramelized almonds in the third confection can be eaten as is—an almond brittle beyond belief.

1. Almond Rounds with Figs, Pistachios, and Orange

ABOUT 24

8 ounces almond paste
2 (about 1 ounce) dried figs, finely chopped
2 tablespoons (1 ounce) pistachios, finely chopped
Zest of 1 orange, grated
6 drops orange-flower water
Powdered sugar for finishing

Line a large baking pan with parchment paper.

Knead the almond paste, figs, pistachios, and orange zest on a work surface by hand. Sprinkle the surface lightly with powdered sugar if the paste sticks. Flatten the paste, and drop the orange-flower water in different places on the surface. Knead again.

Roll small pieces of paste between your palms to make balls about 1 inch in diameter. Put them on the baking sheet. Cover the pan with plastic wrap, and refrigerate it.

Bring the candies to room temperature. Just before serving, roll each ball in sifted powdered sugar.

2. Dates Filled with Chocolate Cream and Almonds

ABOUT 48

48 (10 ounces) pitted dates
¼ cup (2 ounces) heavy whipping cream
4 ounces bittersweet chocolate, finely chopped
48 (2 ounces) whole blanched almonds

Cut one side of the dates from top to bottom to expose the space that housed the pit.

Bring the whipping cream to a boil in a small pan. Remove it from the heat. Add the chopped chocolate, and let it sit for 5 minutes. Whisk the chocolate into the cream until it is smooth. Let it sit at room temperature until it thickens slightly, about 10 minutes.

If you are adept at piping with a paper cone, use one to fill the pit spaces in the dates with chocolate cream, or fill them with a teaspoon. Nestle an almond, flat side down, on top of the chocolate.

Refrigerate the dates, but bring them to room temperature before serving to heighten the taste of the chocolate.

3. Chocolate Balls with Caramelized Almonds

Flavorless oil for the baking sheet
1¼ cups (9 ounces) granulated sugar
¼ cup (2 ounces) water
1⅔ cups (9 ounces) whole blanched almonds, at room temperature
8 ounces bittersweet chocolate, finely chopped

Lightly oil a baking sheet with a flavorless oil.

Mix the sugar and water in a medium heavy-bottomed saucepan. Use an unlined copper sugar-pot if you have one. Cook the syrup over medium heat, stirring once or twice, until the sugar dissolves. Put a candy thermometer in the pan. Wash any sugar crystals from the sides of the pan with a brush dipped in cold water. Continue to cook, without stirring, until the thermometer reaches 248°F.

Remove the thermometer, and turn off the heat. Add the almonds. Stir until the sugar syrup clumps and turns opaque. Over low heat, continue stirring until the sugar remelts and coats the nuts with a caramel-colored syrup. This will take about 20 minutes. If the nuts start to smoke, remove the pan from the heat for a minute, turn down the heat, and continue to cook.

When the sugar has melted again, carefully pour the almonds in the syrup onto the oiled baking sheet. Be careful—the almonds will be very hot.

When the candy is cool, break it apart. Store it in an airtight container (not in the refrigerator) until you are ready to make the chocolate balls.

Melt the chocolate in a bowl over simmering water.

Use a food processor to grind the candy into a powder.

Mix the candy powder and the warm chocolate together.

Drop the mixture by teaspoonfuls onto a baking sheet covered with plastic wrap.

Refrigerate the candies until firm, but bring to room temperature before serving.

EGGS

IN TODAY'S WORLD, the cycle of egg-chicken-egg is discontinuous. What once flowed in a natural sequence has been compartmentalized. Even small farms with roosters and hens producing fertile eggs don't hatch the chicks; the eggs go to the fertile-egg market to be consumed by humans. Other humans, often hundreds of miles away, keep carefully selected breeding stock that produce eggs that will become new chickens. But these eggs don't go directly to the farmers. They are shipped in a dormant state to a hatchery and leave as peeping balls of fluff after twenty-one days in a temperature-and-humidity-controlled gestation. Computers have replaced mother hens, because broodiness, the ability to sit on eggs and turn them many times a day until they hatch, has been bred out of many chickens.

Nature's way takes too long when there is an arms-folded, foot-tapping population demanding fresh eggs every day. Who wants to wait for a hen to take more than fifteen days to lay a clutch of eggs, perhaps as many as fifteen, settle down on them for three weeks until they hatch, then spend several more weeks raising the chicks, and not lay any eggs in the meantime? To an old-fashioned hen, this is the natural way to proceed, but people want an uninterrupted supply of eggs.

Taking eggs from under hens, eating some, and hatching others is not a new concept. Chinese literature from the third century B.C. describes mud incubation ovens. The Egyptians also devised elaborate chambers for hatching eggs. Thick walls of mud brick held the heat, which was provided by smoldering dried camel dung and straw. Rows of ovens lined the outside walls, with pens for the hatchlings in the middle. The hatchery manager lived in one corner of the building. He filled the chambers with eggs, examined them after five days to see if they were fertile by holding them in a ray of light from the chimney, and carefully manipulated the fire to regulate the temperature. Touching the eggs to his eyelids helped him discern the amount of heat needed. This ancient method was employed in Egypt up to the twentieth century.

A modern hatchery is a far cry from the smoke-filled Egyptian chambers, as I discovered on a visit to the Petaluma Poultry Hatchery, north of San Francisco. A moderate-size building with a loading dock at the back sat at the end of a paved road in an industrial part of town. The only signage was the street address. I pulled the door, only to find it locked. A man appeared and let me in. After climbing into a protective jumpsuit, plastic foot-coverings, and a paper hat, I was ushered through another door. The coverings protect the chicks from disease-carrying bacteria and viruses from the outside. I followed my escort to an office and was introduced to the manager, Armando Chavira. The view from a window looking into an adjoining room so distracted me that I could hardly shake his hand. Hundreds of baby chicks bobbed in two steel tubs as if they were riding a merry-go-round. But for now this special chick room remained a mystery. We left the office, walked to the end of the hall, and turned into the receiving room. Towers of cartons holding light-brown eggs stood along one wall. They had arrived after a three- or four-day journey from Arkansas. By nine days, they must be in the incubators. After that time, hatchability decreases.

A worker unpacked the eggs, discarding any with cracks, unusual shapes, or excessive dirt, then loaded them into plastic containers on metal buggies. Each buggy holds 4,950 eggs. When twelve buggies were full, a worker wheeled them across the hall into the incubation room, which was our next stop. Four stainless-steel doors, sporting the name "Chick Master," lined the walls. Armando opened one, and I peeked inside. The racks were tilted at a forty-five-degree angle, a position that is changed every hour by computer control, keeping the developing embryos from sticking to one side of the shells.

Thermostats maintain the incubation temperature at 99.4 degrees

Fahrenheit and the humidity at 55 percent. Although the fertilized ovum starts dividing even before it leaves the hen's body, its march from ovum to bird is halted by the sudden drop in temperature when it is laid. The controlled environment of the incubator, the mechanical mother, nudges the blastodisc, two layers of primordial cells, into completing its journey. By the second day, close to sixty thousand hearts are beating. By the fifth day, reproductive organs differentiate, and roughly half of the embryos are female. By day thirteen, most organs are present, the skeleton begins to calcify, and the developing chicks are covered with down.

After eighteen days of incubation, workers transfer the eggs to trays where they rest in single layers in preparation for hatching. Next they are wheeled into a hatcher room and placed in machines that look like the incubators but have a higher humidity and a slightly lower temperature. The increased humidity softens the shells so the chicks can peck their way out.

We walked from the incubator room to the hatching space. Armando opened one of the steel doors. I heard a chorus of peeps above the whirring fans. Some of the chicks had already emerged. Others were still inside the shells, peeping. By the next day, they too would have pecked their way free.

A few trolleys in the middle of the room could barely contain their vocal charges. Armando reached into a tray and scooped up a few chicks to show me how they were feather-sexable, a trait that has been bred into the birds. He fanned out a wing, exposing two sets of feathers. On this chick, they were the same length, the telltale sign of a rooster-to-be. The next two were the same. "Where are all my girls today?" he asked. His fourth examination revealed one set of feathers to be longer than the other. A girl. The difference was easy to spot.

Across the hall, the trays full of shell, puffs of down, and chicks were emptied onto a conveyor belt, and the trays were run through a giant washing machine. The chicks rode the conveyor belt into the room I had first spotted from Armando's office. The "merry-go-rounds" turned out to be circular tubs with conveyor belts on the bottom. Women wearing surgical masks sat on stools at the edge of the tubs, fanning the chicks' wings to determine sex and removing any sickly chicks. Males went down one chute to another moving belt, females to a second. At the ends of these belts, more women waited. They vaccinated each chick, then packed them all into color-coded boxes (blue for boys, and, in a change from stereotype, yellow for girls). These were meat chickens; the males would go to farms to be raised as free-range chickens, and the females would be raised organically.

The last stop in the chicks hatchery sojourn was the adjacent temperature-controlled room. Early the next morning, they would be loaded onto trucks and moved to the farms. Having absorbed what remained of the yolk in their eggs before hatching, they would need neither food nor water until they reached their new homes.

Before the days of chicken sexing, telling a baby pullet from a cockerel was difficult, so difficult that people didn't even try. Hatcheries sold "straight-run" chicks just as they came from the eggs, females and males together. The farmer who was interested in laying hens bought at least twice the number needed, since roughly 50 percent of the chicks would turn out to be males.

Then he fed the hungry birds for weeks, waiting patiently until the cockerels started to show their maleness by developing combs. If the chickens were White Leghorns, the dominant breed for laying, the cocks not only didn't produce eggs, they weren't very good for meat either.

About 1918, James K. Hirst, a Petaluma poultry man visiting Japan, heard rumors that people could determine the sex of day-old chicks. He investigated, asked questions, took notes. Then he returned to Petaluma and quietly started three new businesses, the

Welty, the Truby, and the Eureka Hatcheries. The first two sold White Leghorn chicks, and the Eureka Hatchery sold day-old chicks guaranteed to be pullets (presumably at a higher price). Not surprisingly, customers buying from Welty and Truby began complaining about the unusually high number of cockerels in their shipments, sometimes as many as 85 percent.

The claim of the Eureka Hatchery chilled the heart of every other hatchery owner in town. Hirst knew something none of the others could fathom: He could differentiate between a pullet and a cockerel the day chickens hatched. Rivals tried to discredit him in the press; they tried lawsuits; they banded together and insisted on inspection of hatcheries, including approval of all advertising. Hirst offered his knowledge to the USDA for the price of 1.25 million dollars, but Uncle Sam wasn't buying. Boycotted and ostracized, he closed his businesses and left town. Years passed before chicken sexing was reintroduced.

The Japanese who showed Hirst how to sex chickens had learned the technique from the Chinese. Kiyoshi Masui, a professor of veterinary anatomy in Tokyo, presented a paper on chicken sexing at the Third World's Poultry Congress at Ottawa in 1927. Six years later, he published a book entitled *Sexing Baby Chicks.* The knowledge disseminated, first to England, then to Canada and the United States.

The Japanese method is vent sexing. The vent of a chicken is the opening where the digestive, urinary, and reproductive systems merge. A chicken sexer, with the aid of a strong light and a magnifying glass, upends the chick and looks for an organ called the genital eminence, which is half the size of a pinhead. If it's present, the chick is a male.

This skill was soon in high demand. Chicken-sexing schools opened. For the final exam, candidates were expected to sex one hundred chicks with 92-percent accuracy, and they had to be speedy. During the spring hatching season, tens of thousands of chicks hatched daily; it took marathon sessions to check them all, separating the prized females from the disposable males. Top chicken sexers boasted of their records—Heimer Carlson of Petaluma sexed fifty-six million chicks in his career of fifty-five years, including one span of seven days and nights when he slept only twenty-one hours. Hugh Grove, another legendary sexer, traveled from state to state following the business. Chickens were his specialty, although he also sexed turkeys, both wild and domestic, geese, ducks, even canaries. The only animal he declined to examine was an emu. "Too big," he said.

Knowledge of chicken genetics broadened about the same time that vent sexing began. Breeders determined that the speed with which chicks grow feathers is sex-linked. A gene on the sex chromosome makes the difference. A fast-feathering male bred with a slow-feathering female will result in chicks with the reverse characteristics. As I had seen at the hatchery, the difference is easy to note by examining the chick's wing. However, this predictability only holds for the first generation, because the resultant males won't have the requisite gene combination.

Vent sexers are still important in those instances when feather growth or color doesn't play a part in the breeding, but there aren't many left. The skill is difficult to learn, and the next generation of would-be sexers isn't interested. As a Texas poultry breeder drawled to me, "Who'd wanna look at chickens' rears all their lives?"

Fossils of birds that existed 150 million years ago reveal that modern birds have lost some distinguishing characteristics—lizardlike tails and teeth—of their early ancestors. But one trait continues: feathers. Birds are divided into many subsets, and the wildfowl are in a subfamily of the pheasants, so placed because of the similarity of the molt of the tail feathers. But the wildfowls' comb earns them their own genus—*Gallus*, meaning "comb." These birds roamed from India and China, through Southeast Asia, to the Pacific Islands, a belt where they may first have been domesticated. Darwin, after careful study, determined that all domesticated varieties came from the Red Jungle Fowl, although others think that as many as four species of wildfowl may have contributed to today's chicken.

Although early people benefited from wild birds—removing eggs from their nests, slaughtering them for meat, using their plumage for decoration—the compelling impetus for the domestication of chickens might not have been food. Chickens have long been esteemed as birds of sacrifice, and both the animals and eggs have been invested with magical powers; this position of religious and occult importance may have provided a more important reason for keeping them. Roosters, with their irascible tendency to fight, were also raised to provide entertainment, and cockfighting is still practiced in many cultures, legally or not.

But certainly the Chinese valued both chickens and eggs as an important source of protein. They even devised a method of preserving eggs by burying them in a mixture that included tea leaves and clay and turned the eggs black, with a strong sulfury taste. Even today, these "thousand-year-old" eggs are a challenge to the Western palate. Like the Egyptians, the Chinese were also skilled egg brooders, and they had a taste for partially brooded eggs, perhaps a holdover from a time when people gathered wild eggs. The half-formed chickens inside are still considered a delicacy in some Asian cultures, particularly the Philippines, where eating them is thought to contribute to a man's virility. Some hatcheries in California still produce half-brooded duck eggs, called baluts, and sell them to Asian markets. A friend of mine had a shocking introduction to these special eggs. Seeing a woman carefully examining a selection of eggs in a market, he decided to buy a few from the same batch. His fellow shopper seemed surprised and asked if he liked them. "Oh, yes," he answered. The next morning, he brought a pan of water to a simmer and toasted slices of bread, looking forward to poached eggs for breakfast. With the crack of one eggshell, this usually very adventurous eater lost his appetite. "There's obviously something we don't know about how to prepare these," said his wife. He might have consulted Pliny the Elder, the prolific Roman naturalist, who suggested unborn chicks cooked in the shell and mixed with sour wine, flour, and oil as a remedy for dysentery.

When the Persians conquered India, they adopted the Indians' interest in raising chickens for cockfighting, eggs, and meat. These tastes spread, first to Greece, then to Rome. The Greeks began to differentiate birds for laying and birds for meat and produced both varieties, in addition to keeping the mandatory cocks for fighting. Pliny the Elder discoursed on many birds, both wild and domestic. His observations on chickens were elaborate, if somewhat askew. (He thought that thunder would kill the embryos in incubating eggs.) Aristotle was the first to record his findings upon opening eggs as each day of incubation passed, and later, the Roman philosophers Varro and Columella made their own contributions to the chicken commentary. In Roman kitchens, eggs were cooked with milk and honey to make early custards, or fried in oil, or used as a binder in sausages and casseroles. The Romans introduced these recipes to the Celts during the time they occupied their land.

Following their heralded place in Roman writings, eggs and chickens descended into their own dark ages as the years passed. Chickens still laid eggs and graced dinner tables, but chroniclers were silent about them. During the fourth and fifth centuries, the Catholic Church's ideas about fasting, which had been promoted earlier by St. Anthony and St. Augustine, became more rigid. The fasts dictated abstinence from animal products on specific calendar days—the thirty days of Advent preceding Christmas, the forty days of Lent preceding Easter, Wednesdays, Fridays, the evenings before holidays, and sometimes a third day of the week. This added up to a good portion of the year. For the wealthy, the restrictions afforded an opportunity to experiment with meatless, nondairy dishes, such as using almond milk in place of cream, but the poor had fewer choices. And transgressors were obliged to donate alms to the church—such a significant number in Rouen that the money collected built a steeple known as the Butter Tower, for the cathedral.

The Tuesday before Ash Wednesday, Mardi Gras, became an occasion to deplete the cupboards of all meat and eggs. It also became a day of wanton excess—overindulging in food and drink before the somber abstinence of Lent. People also preserved eggs—not only chicken eggs but peacock, turkey, duck, goose, and guinea-fowl eggs—by dipping them in fat or wax and sometimes decorating them until the fast was over, on Easter Sunday. Although Jews don't observe Lent, they observed a prohibition against eggs laid on the Sabbath.

Special pastries, rich in eggs, also graced the Easter table; some are still made today. In the south of France and in Albania, colored eggs adorn traditionally shaped loaves of bread. Pastries with eggs mark Easter in Italy: in Tuscany, an egg-enriched bread perfumed with Vin Santo and anise seeds; in Naples, a bread with eggs baked into the top; in Sicily, *la pupazza con l'uovo*, the doll with an egg, the shape of the pastry changing in each village. Eventually, the egg shape was mimicked—instead of eggs themselves, people exchanged egg-shaped chocolates, some simple solid confections, others large and hollow, hiding more edibles or even jewels.

Chickens from Asian strains accompanied Columbus to the New World, but they weren't the first poultry there. Chicken bones dating from A.D. 1000 have been found in Central and South America. Araucana hens may be a cross between an American grouse and an Asian chicken brought by pre-Columbian explorers. These chickens, prized for their pale-blue and green eggs, are still raised today.

It wasn't until the sixteenth century that chickens regained their former glory, thanks to a Renaissance man named Ulisse Aldrovandi. A professor at the University of Bologna who served at royal courts, traveled extensively, and corresponded with the Pope, he believed that an understanding of plants and animals was essential to understanding philosophy. Throughout his life, he worked on a exhaustive tome, nine volumes total, on animals. One volume focused on chickens. He repeated Aristotle's experiment of cracking open incubating eggs day by day to record the development of the embryos; he observed that one could place newborn chicks under another hen to be raised if the transfer was made at night; he advised disposing of hens when they were three years old and keeping cocks as long as they could perform their impregnation duties. Other notations were more philosophical. He waxed eloquent on the contribution of chickens to the human race: "They furnish food for both humans who are well and those who are ill and rally those who are almost dead. Which condition of the body, internal or external, does not obtain its remedies from the chicken?" And he sided with church dogma, and the majority of believers, when commenting on the inevitable question: "It is stated in the sacred books that the hen existed first."

French cookbooks began appearing in the fourteenth and fifteenth centuries, documenting a variety of uses for eggs. One of the earliest, *Ménagier de Paris*, written in 1392 by an unknown author, included many recipes for egg batters that were sprinkled with sugar after cooking. Later editions of the *Viandier*, first printed in Paris in about 1490, contain a recipe that sounds like zabaglione, although the liberal use of cinnamon and rose water dates from the Middle Ages. A recipe in a 1555 book entitled *Liure Fort Excellent de Cuysine* includes a recipe for "imitation snow" that uses stiffly beaten egg whites, a treatment that would become a staple of later pastry making in the form of meringues. By the end of the sixteenth century, nascent layered pastries, and pâte à choux for baking, frying, and poaching, were in evidence. *Le Pâtissier François*, which appeared in 1654 and is usually attributed to Pierre François de la Varenne, used batters lightened by foams of sugar and eggs to make sweet cakes. Baked meringues and macaroons appeared in a 1691 book written by François Massialot, and a 1790 edition of Menon's *Cuisinère Bourgeoise* lists, in addition to a wide range of sweet baked goods, other creative uses for eggs—a bedtime drink of yolks and hot water, beaten whites applied to sore eyes, powdered membranes from inside the shell for relief of fever blisters, even the shells themselves as toothpaste.

Settlers in the New World brought cooking methods from their homelands, although the soil and climate conditions affected what they cooked. *The Compleat Housewife*, written by E. Smith in 1742, had recipes for sweet cakes that depended on eggs for leavening rather than yeast. Two New England cookbooks, *American Cookery* (1796) and *The American Frugal Housewife* (1832), give recipes for soft gingerbreads and puddings, of which eggs were a component. And a recipe called "Hasty Pudding" from *The Virginia Housewife* (1824), was a liaison of milk, eggs, and the ubiquitous cornmeal, sweetened with molasses.

With the opening of the port of Canton in 1834, Chinese chickens were exported to England for the first time, and the results of Chinese breeding caused quite a stir. The first flock, three "Chochin" birds, didn't look like any chickens in England, and the queen contributed to their popularity by taking a liking to them. They were also far superior to the English chickens in both weight gain and laying ability. The birds were put on display. Thousands came to see them. Their exotic looks convinced people who had never thought of keeping chickens that they needed a few of their own. A poultry show in Boston began a similar chicken craze across the Atlantic. Ordinary citizens kept a few chickens; farmers bred the Chochin and other imported breeds. A race to develop better breeds ensued, and eventually three laying hens came to the fore: the White Leghorn, the Rhode Island Red (which produced brown eggs, still a favorite in New England), and the Barred Plymouth Rock, a dual-purpose bird, good for both eggs and meat.

Before these breeds of chickens appeared in California, either overland by wagon or by ship around the Horn, the early Spanish settlers brought and bred their own Castilian stock. Their motivation wasn't much different from that of the people who first domesticated chickens: They wanted them foremost for the sport of cockfighting, then for eggs, and finally for meat.

Settlers moving west included chickens in their wagons. Supplies along the route were scarce, and those few shopkeepers who had eggs demanded high prices for them. Isabella Bird, who traveled to the Rocky Mountains in 1873, wrote that she collected eggs in the days before Thanksgiving so she could make her traditional pudding. Sometimes it was so cold that the eggs were almost frozen; she had to thaw them out before cooking them.

Once called the "Egg Basket of the World," Petaluma, California, has only one remaining commercial chicken farm. Steve Mahrt's business, Petaluma Farms, is seventeen years old, but his father was also a chicken rancher, so he's been around chickens all his life. And his wife, Judy, grew up in the hatchery business not far away.

It wasn't easy to see the chickens. Concern about transmitting diseases to the birds keeps them out of the reach of visitors. But on a chilly day in June, I arranged to see the operation.

The ranch lies at the end of a lane. Low-slung chicken coops stand in the distance, and a series of interconnected buildings near the parking lot serve as offices. Steve, a cheery man with an easy smile, bounded into one of them. After a few introductory remarks about his business, he walked me down the road to a chicken coop. The birds seemed a little startled when we approached, so we stopped about ten feet away and watched through the chicken wire. Brown chickens—Rhode Island Reds—strutted around the floor and on a raised shelf, cackling and pecking the dirt. White roosters, one for every ten hens, walked among them, standing tall and looking important. A raised mezzanine in the middle held cubicles where the hens laid eggs.

Like human females, hens are born with all the eggs they will ever produce, albeit in microscopic form. Although they have two ovaries as embryos, their adult bodies will only be able to accommodate one of the mature organs, so only one develops, usually the left. The ovary contains several thousand germ cells. The young hens, called pullets, reach sexual maturity at about eighteen weeks of age and start laying eggs. The germ cells are surrounded by epithelial cells; the entire group is called a follicle. These epithelial cells play several crucial roles as the follicle grows: They collect molecules of yolk made by the liver and transported via the blood, and deposit them in the developing ovum. They help synthesize sex hormones, which are responsible for important behaviors of laying hens, including mating.

A laying hen will have follicles in different stages, some just beginning to grow, others about to release the ovum into the opening of the oviduct. Pituitary hormones, in turn influenced by the hen's perception of external events, such as the hours of daylight, also guide follicular development and pinpoint the moment of ovulation. In natural conditions, hens' laying cycles decrease in winter, not a good time to raise young.

When the ovum erupts from the ovary, it travels along the oviduct, a slow passage of twenty-four hours. If the hen has mated, like the Rhode Island Reds at Petaluma Farms, she will have sperm in the part of the oviduct that is close to the ovary. The sperm will fertilize the egg, and it will continue its travel, twisting its way along as it acquires concentric circles of white. Next the two shell membranes are formed, and finally the newly formed egg moves to the uterus, where it absorbs calcium and takes its final shape. Another pituitary hormone stimulates contractions that release the egg from the hen's body. After a brief rest, another follicle erupts, and the process begins anew. By two years of age, the hen's rate of egg-laying declines, and her days of commercial production are over.

Although there are some exceptions, wild birds generally lay eggs only once a year, in the spring. Since the early days of domestication, chickens have laid eggs on a more regular cycle, either because as their keepers removed the eggs the hapless birds continued laying—in hopes of accumulating a clutch large enough to sit on—or because the keepers selected hens that produced many eggs. Still, left to her own devices, a contemporary hen molts in the fall and does not lay eggs for several months, until the longer spring days trigger the laying cycle again. When she resumes egg production, her output is less than in her premolt days. Someone figured out that a hen could be forced to molt, which would bring her back into egg-laying mode faster and at a good production rate. Although books I consulted advocated decreasing or even withholding food and water for as long as four days to force a molt, both Steve Mahrt and a rancher with a much larger operation assured me that a lower-calorie diet does the trick.

Besides fertile brown eggs from Rhode Island Reds, Petaluma Farms produces unfertilized white eggs from Single Comb White Leghorns and organic eggs from a specially fed flock. At the moment, however, Steve's pet project is a flock that lays eggs containing docosahexaenoic acid (DHA), an omega-3 fatty acid. Through a special process patented by Gold Circle Farms in Boulder, Colorado, marine algae, the source of omega-3 fatty acids in cold-water fish, are harvested, dried, and added to chicken feed. The nutrient is passed on in the eggs, which contain eight times more DHA than other eggs.

These compounds are vital to a healthy cardiovascular system: They help maintain heart rhythm and a healthy lipid profile in the blood, and they help prevent narrowing of blood vessels. In addition, they appear to be necessary for normal visual and cognitive development in infants; one study found that infants fed a formula supplemented with these long-chain polyunsaturated fatty acids were better at problem solving than infants fed a nonsupplemented formula, and that this difference remained even after the supplemented formula was stopped. Adequate maternal levels of DHA also appear to be necessary to carry pregnancies to term.

Unfortunately, most American diets are sorely lacking in these long, gangly chains of beneficial nutrients. By adding them to eggs, researchers have devised a way to get people to eat them. Four of the eggs a week will supply all the DHA a person needs. But because they cost more, the people most in need may not buy them.

Still, such developments are a boon for the much-maligned egg. Steve gave me some of the special eggs when I left. They tasted fresh and good, especially spiked with a shot of righteousness.

☙

Before the Gold Rush, long before Petaluma became known as the "Egg Basket of the World," people in nearby San Francisco rekindled the ancient practice of gathering wild birds' eggs to supplement the meager local supply of chicken eggs. The source was a huge colony of murres, sharp-beaked and web-footed brown-and-white birds that inhabited the Farallon Islands, twenty-seven miles offshore from the Golden Gate. The season started in May, when the birds gathered on the islands to mate. Collectors labored under dangerous conditions—angry birds and steep, slippery rocks. Even though each female laid only one egg per season, the population was so large that thousands of dozens of eggs were collected. The eggs were bigger than chicken eggs, conical-shaped with almost red yolks. The ruthless gathering by the Pacific Egg Company, which monopolized the murre egg business, led to a decline in the bird population and thus in the number of available eggs. The growing band of chicken farmers in Petaluma realized that murre eggs wouldn't always dominate the market; they wanted to be the main egg-supplier.

The Petaluma River supplied a soft, swift journey to San Francisco, whose population burgeoned after gold was found in the hills to the northeast in 1849. People in communities near San Francisco were raising chickens too, but transporting eggs over bumpy roads resulted in many broken ones.

The weather in Petaluma—warm days, cool nights, and mild winters—was perfect for raising chickens. When the railroad was completed, more people moved west; many settled in this new chicken town, where starting a small poultry farm wasn't difficult. It was an international group that arrived—from Scandinavia, Europe, Russia, and Japan, as well as from other parts of the United States. The daily lives of these early chicken ranchers were arduous. Family members divided tasks. The men took care of the chickens in sickness (which was frequent) and in health. They were also jacks-of-all-trades—constructing chicken coops, repairing broken equipment, transporting chickens and eggs. The women of the household, with the help of the children, took charge of the baby chicks and the eggs. Eggs had to be collected every day, then cleaned, either with water or sandpaper, and packed, all by hand. In those days before chicken feed was fine-tuned, the family cooked a daily ration of feed, made up of potatoes, soybeans, horse meat, and whatever else was available. It always included vitamin-rich kale, which the ranchers grew themselves, and oyster shells, dredged from the bottom of the San Francisco Bay and carried by barge to Petaluma, to make the hens' eggshells strong. Besides the chickens, the family usually had a cow or two, for milk and butter. The family kept what they needed and sold the excess. Rabbits and pigs were raised for food. And everyone had a kitchen garden.

By the end of the nineteenth century, Petaluma supplied more than half the eggs in San Francisco. As the demand for eggs grew, the farmers decided that the hens' way of producing eggs was just too slow. Two immigrants, one from Canada, the other from Europe, invented a method of interrupting the cycle by incubating and hatching the eggs instead of leaving this task up to the whim of the hen.

Lyman Byce was an inventor from the days of his youth. He teamed up with Dr. Isaac Dias, a local dentist who was developing an artificial incubator. The two worked on their invention, an octagonal cabinet on turned wooden legs that looked more like a piece of furniture than farm equipment. A kerosene lamp provided heat, and the rancher turned the eggs by hand twice a day. In 1879, "Petaluma Incubators" went on the market. Three years later, Dias received a patent on the machines. The partnership came to an abrupt halt with the death of Dias in a hunting accident in 1884. Byce continued to run the company. Showing a unique flair for marketing, he caused quite a stir at the county fair in 1892 by hatching ostrich eggs as the expectant mother watched from a nearby enclosure. Next he hatched alligator eggs, and, in his most flamboyant effort, he displayed a human baby resting comfortably inside one of his inventions.

Detractors decried artificial incubation as unnatural, against God's wishes, and downright dangerous. But others recognized the promise the technology held for streamlining the poultry business, and the Petaluma Incubator Company continued to grow. In 1902, Byce took the company public. Then his incubator took the gold medal at the St. Louis Fair, bringing national notoriety to a small town in California. Buoyed by the prize, he built a new production site to fill the increasing orders.

Christopher Nisson is credited with starting Pioneer Hatchery, the first commercial hatchery on the West Coast. In 1880, he bought a Petaluma Incubator. Then he bought more. Soon his flock was two thousand strong. He started hatching eggs for neighbors, including eggs from their special flocks. He also developed brooders equipped with hovers (special canopies designed to keep the heat close to the ground) warmed by kerosene heaters to help the chicks survive the first few difficult weeks of life. His chicks were in demand. In 1892, he freighted live chicks, at eight cents each, to a town at the foot of the Sonoma Valley—one of the first such shipments.

He also introduced the "colony-house" method of raising chickens. The birds roamed outdoors during the day, then roosted at night in floorless houses built on runners. When the droppings piled up, he hitched the house to a horse and moved it to another location. Just like the beekeepers, he found it easier to move his stock at night, when they were sleeping. The methods that he pioneered are still used today, although the business that he founded closed its doors in 1958.

As the hatchery business took off, Petaluma entered its heyday. Chicken coops dotted the rolling hills; hatcheries and feed stores lined the streets; there was an annual Egg Day Celebration complete with a parade (still an annual event), even a chicken pharmacy. At its peak, the town boasted thirty-six full-time commercial hatcheries, shipping chicks all over the West and Midwest. Must Hatch was the largest hatchery in the world in 1929. It took up a city block and could hatch more than a million and a half chicks every three weeks.

The increase in hatcheries meant there were more hens, but there were other factors contributing to the increase in the overall number of eggs. After the flurry of imported strains from Asia, by the end of the nineteenth century, it was clear that the Leghorn, from Livorno, Italy, was the ace egg-layer. The invention of the trap nest, which held an individual hen in a compartment until her egg could be marked as belonging to her, helped the ranchers selectively breed the hens that laid the most eggs. In 1932, Pioneer Hatchery sold either "standard chicks" that would lay two hundred eggs a year or "specials," bred using trap nests, that might lay two hundred fifty.

The adoption of artificial lighting in chicken coops also increased the number of eggs, circumventing the hens' instinct to lay fewer eggs as the days grew shorter. However, it required a drastic change in chicken management—the hens had to be kept in windowless buildings so that the prolonged light could do its work. All this fine-tuning resulted in a dramatic increase in the hens' production. And other improvements—knowledge of nutrition, disease control, hygiene—pushed production still higher as the years passed.

The Depression took its toll on Petaluma chicken ranchers, however. Profits dropped to negative figures. Ranchers owed money to feed companies and hatcheries, who sometimes took the chickens in payment. Some ranchers tried to add more hens to cut losses, but the crowded conditions led to outbreaks of fowl plague, a contagious disease that could easily decimate a flock. World War II reinvigorated the industry. Feeding the fighting soldiers demanded innumerable eggs, not in the shell, but dried and powdered. In 1945, Petaluma hens produced fifty-one million dozen eggs. But after the war, the town's fortunes again declined.

Crowded conditions made the chickens more susceptible to disease, which the industry countered with vaccines and antibiotics. But the hens' confinement also meant that a mechanized system was needed to feed them and collect their eggs. Chicken ranchers began to apply the assembly-line techniques that Lyman Byce had used to build incubators, to distributing feed and collecting eggs. They installed conveyor belts, and machines for washing, grading, and packing the eggs. Cages with wire floors became a necessity to break the cycle of reinfection from coccidia, protozoa in an afflicted hen's droppings that contaminated the soil. Breeders began hybridizing chickens, striving for greater yields. All the hens produced a prodigious amount of manure. Neighbors were irate, just like the people who live near burning sugarcane fields.

Other economic realities came to bear. Poultry farmers have never been bolstered by government subsidies, but have had to grapple with the vagaries of production costs and supply and demand. The span across the Golden Gate, completed in 1937, brought Petaluma closer to San Francisco; improved highways decreased the time further. Better roadways, coupled with smoother transport, made the once-mighty steamboats carrying eggs from Petaluma to the city quaint and obsolete. The figurative narrowing of the gap between country and city made the farmland more valuable. Land prices went up. A bigger-is-better mentality was driving the competition in southern California and Oregon. Several thousand hens at one facility were not uncommon, more than the average Petaluma rancher could support, and in any event, zoning laws limited ranch expansion. And eggs, once the quintessential American breakfast, were usurped by dry cereals, whose manufacturers mounted a convincing advertising campaign highlighting their convenience for a hurried family where both parents worked and the children left early for school. It wasn't a hard decision for a small chicken rancher to sell his land and get out of a struggling business.

Today, the only Petaluma hatchery is the one I visited north of town, which hatches birds for meat, not to lay eggs. One family chicken farm remains. A brick building still stands on the main street with a relief of a chick emerging from a shell above the door. It was once home of the Poehlmann Hatchery; now it's a group of retail shops. Historical memorabilia, stored at the Petaluma museum, hold a record of the past.

Steve Mahrt's chicken ranch is small compared with most laying-hen homes today. Although I passed some old-fashioned chicken houses along the way—some listing precariously, others needing new roofs—I knew the Thayer egg plant, a division of J. S. West, was a different operation as soon as I pulled into the gravel driveway from a small road in a northern San Joaquin Valley town. Buildings looming higher than the tallest barn, with fans several feet in diameter protruding from their sides, made me readjust my concept of hen housing. These are twenty-first-century chicken coops. And the size of the trailers at the loading dock told me that more than a handful of eggs regularly left this processing plant.

Indeed, about a million and a half hens are busy laying eggs at Thayer at any given time. Between 150,000 and 200,000 new ones arrive every nine weeks. The hen houses are fully digitized; computers regulate the temperature, the lighting (sixteen hours a day), the amount of corn and soy feed and water dispensed; they count the number of eggs laid. Enclosed conveyor belts transport eggs to the adjacent packing plant; no one touches them. Seven hundred thousand dozen leave every week.

I found an empty parking place in the phalanx of vehicles across from a low building. Flowering plants and shrubs set off the door to a suite of offices. I entered, and a receptionist greeted me. Tom Silva, the manager and a vice president of the company, appeared immediately and led me to his office. Only his casual clothing reflected the farming nature of the business. I sat in a chair opposite his desk while we discussed modern-day chicken farming.

As at Petaluma Farms, only laying hens are here. Breeding farms in the Midwest send eggs to hatcheries in southern California and Washington, which then send baby female chicks to a different J. S. West location, where they're inoculated on a set schedule, just like human infants, to protect them against common chicken ailments. When the pullets start to lay eggs (at about eighteen weeks), they're transferred to the hen houses that dominate the view from the window. They lay for eighty-three weeks, with a molt sometime in the cycle when they stop laying for about six weeks. Eventually their production decreases; they may lay only seven eggs in a clutch instead of ten. Their egg-laying careers finished, these spent hens "go away," just like the old milking cows, and end up in canned chicken products, such as soup and broth.

Before we left for a tour of the processing plant, I asked Tom about an antique gadget on the windowsill, consisting of a gauge affixed to a metal pole, which was supported by a tripod. Raymond Haugh invented these devices in 1937 to calculate egg quality. An egg was broken underneath, then the middle pole lowered to measure the height of the white. This reading was correlated with the weight to give a Haugh Unit. The higher the number, the better the egg.

Now visual examination determines egg grades, which are affected by the age of the egg. When broken onto a surface, AA eggs cover a small area, the white is firm and thick where it surrounds the yolk, and the yolk stands tall. Grade A eggs spread over a larger area when cracked, and the white surrounding the yolk is not as thick. Grade B eggs spread even more and have watery whites and enlarged, flattened yolks. All eggs sold in retail stores must be Grade B or better, and most eggs are Grade AA or A.

As eggs make their way from hen to carton, the insides are examined by shining light through the uncracked shells to determine the grade. People, or electronic eyes, look at the size of the air cell (larger generally equals older), the outline of the yolk, and how close the yolk comes to the shell as the eggs twirl through the machine (close to the shell correlates with a thinner white). Because the light source originally came from candles, this process is still called candling.

We walked across the hall and stepped into a large room clanking with machinery. Conveyor belts bring eggs from the coops and tip them, end up, to go into the washers, which spray them with soap, rub them with brushes, then rinse them twice. Ironically, this removes a natural protective coating, not so important if they are sold fresh, but possibly exposing them to contamination if they are held too long. Thayer packs eggs for a number of customers; some request a film of mineral oil applied to the eggs, which seals the pores.

A conveyor belt moves the eggs to a chamber with lights underneath. Tom pulled aside a curtain so I could get a better look. I poked my head inside, but Tom told me to move to the left; I was in the eye of the cameras that scan the eggs for dirt. If any remains, they are rewashed. A test of the shells' integrity comes next. They run a gauntlet of tapping rods; if they crack, they're removed.

Next each egg is computer-weighed. After one more pass through a light machine, where a computer checks the inside for blood spots or other internal problems, they go to the packing lines. Although there are six designated egg sizes—jumbo, extra-large, large, medium, small, and peewee, calculated by the weight of a dozen eggs in the shell—most of the eggs here are either large or extra-large. "That's what the customers want," said Tom. At age thirty or thirty-two weeks, a hen will lay eggs this size, and specific breeds of chickens will lay the larger eggs at a younger age.

The number of packing options surprised me. Different customers have different needs: In addition to the familiar cartons on market shelves, cartons hold flats of eggs designated for restaurants, bakeries, and other food-service establishments; other cartons are stacked and shrink-wrapped for bulk outlets; and many have customized labeling. After packing, the eggs are whisked into a huge refrigerated room, but not for long. One hundred and twenty thousand eggs leave every day in refrigerated trucks kept at forty degrees Fahrenheit until they reach their destination, where they are transferred to walk-in refrigerators or temperature-controlled display cases. The goal is to keep the eggs at forty degrees Fahrenheit from hen to kitchen. About two years ago, this new government regulation went into effect, the same time that a thirty-day pull date on cartons was introduced.

As we retraced our steps, we passed the office of the resident USDA inspector. On-site inspection isn't mandatory, although complying with USDA and state standards is. Thayer has this service because some of the customers request it. "What does the inspector do?" I asked. "She checks the plant for cleanliness every day, before processing begins. We hand-clean all this equipment every night—hosing won't do, because of all the computers. Then she takes samples, one every ten thousand eggs or so, looking for correct weights and any flaws. If anything is wrong—incorrect weights, for example—the entire lot is rerun," Tom answered.

Back in his office, I asked one last question, even though I already suspected the answer. "Any chance to see the chickens?" "No, visitors aren't allowed in the coops," was Tom's response. Then, maybe in response to the crestfallen look on my face, he turned on his computer and walked me through a virtual tour of the chicken houses—not to view hens, but to see the tracking mechanism that monitors every aspect of bird and egg care.

The compartmentalized approach to chickens and eggs is at its apex. Little is left to fate. Breeders, usually in the middle of the country, produce chickens whose eggs will hatch into prolific egg-laying hens. The eggs travel to another location to be hatched into chicks. The females go to ranches where they grow until egg production begins. Then they are moved once more to do their work of laying eggs.

The eggs these hens produce may not be touched by human hands until you remove one from the carton in your kitchen.

However, there is one thing that humans haven't harnessed. The chicks that come out of the eggs are still close to an even split of males and females. No one has figured out how to hatch only, or predominantly, females.

There's another noteworthy thing about mass-produced eggs. In April 2000, the *San Francisco Chronicle* conducted a blind tasting of hard-boiled eggs by a panel of food professionals. The winner, with descriptives such as "classic," "beautiful yellow color," and "large yolk," outscored the second choice by twenty-six points. It was a Thayer Farm egg.

A week after my tour of the processing plant, I ate one of Gertrude's eggs, or maybe it belonged to one of her chicken-house comrades, I'm not sure. It had a brown shell because Gertrude and the other chickens my country neighbors keep are Rhode Island Reds. I put it in a pan, covered it with cold water, brought it to a simmer, then turned off the heat and set a timer for ten minutes. When it went off, I emptied the water from the pan and ran cold water in it until it overflowed.

The egg was a little hard to peel, indicating that it was newly laid. I sliced it into six pieces. Because of its size, I had suspected a double yolk, but my prediction was wrong. Although a dollop of my husband's aïoli would have been a good topping, I resisted the temptation and merely sprinkled it with sea salt and freshly ground pepper. The white was almost jiggly, just-cooked shiny slices that gave no resistance to my fork. The yolk, also just cooked enough to hold its shape, was deep yellow with a hint of orange.

The taste was surprisingly mild, no off flavors, a true egg essence. I hadn't cooked any other eggs to compare it with, commercial or fertilized. Gertrude and her sister hens have no love life, but their environment—an ample pen with a roosting house—seems ideal, a word I could use to describe the egg I ate.

⊚

And what of those eggs that are cracked but still intact? Or so dirty that the egg-washing machines can't get them sparkling? Although not good enough to be sold as shell eggs, they are still salvageable. The Thayer Farm in the San Joaquin Valley sends these "restricted" eggs to a processing plant they own in Oakland, California. The eggs are washed and candled. Then special machines crack them and they go to pasteurizers, either whole or separated into whites and yolks, that hold them at 140 degrees Fahrenheit for three and a half minutes to kill any pathogens. But the processing doesn't stop there. A customer can order whole eggs, frozen whole eggs with 10 percent salt added, whites with whipping aids, refrigerated or frozen, yolks with 10 percent added sugar, refrigerated or frozen. The packing sizes range from tanker trucks through 450-pound drums to nine-pound pails. Obviously, these are not for home use. Their customers are big businesses—bakeries and ice-cream makers. Thayer adds sugar, salt, and whipping aids because customers want them. (Eggs that are cracked and oozing, however, are sent to be processed into pet food.)

Robert Thayer, Sr., started this business almost eighty years ago, in the same spot. Eventually, his son took over the company, then sold it, about six years ago, to J. S. West, which owns both this plant and the farms in the San Joaquin Valley. The nondescript building is surrounded by small houses, some in various stages of disrepair, not far from the rapid-transit tracks in East Oakland. The morning I visited, a stray pit bull wandered the street, looking hungry. I waited until he got to the end of the block before leaving my car.

When this company started, the eggs were cracked by hand, a painstaking process that continued for another twenty years. (In those early days, they obviously didn't ship fifteen million pounds of egg products a year.) By the 1940s, others in the egg-cracking business began tinkering with machines that would do the work. The early machines cracked fourteen cases (360 eggs per case) an hour; present-day machines will crack 450 cases in the same time. The inventors of the machines didn't stop there. They dreamed up other equipment that large-scale food industries would embrace: machines that hard-boil eggs and peel them; another, called a "long egg machine," that introduces egg whites into a heated tube, then injects yolk in the middle, cooks the entire mass, cools it, and slices it, making perfect disks of cooked eggs. The same company that made Thayer's egg cracker also invented a reverse-osmosis machine that will take the liquid out of whites, concentrating the solids, which makes it easier to dry them.

I saw the egg cracker in action at the Thayer plant. It is a clever, if noisy machine. Graspers hold each egg as it moves down a line. At a certain point, a lever hits the grasper, forcing the two sides together to crack the egg. The grasper holds the yolk, while the white falls below. With the help of this wondrous device, the company processes 450,000 eggs a day, and this is considered a mom-and-pop operation in the giant world of egg cracking.

Jill Benson, a vice president of the company, occupies a small office above the egg-washing room. A colorfully painted wooden Humpty-Dumpty perches on a bookcase just inside the door. I asked her about in-shell pasteurization, a notion that came to the fore a few years ago, when President Clinton declared a war on *Salmonella enteritidis,* a strain of the bacteria that can exist inside eggs, by proposing that all eggs be pasteurized. The company investigated the method, a complicated one that involves sending whole eggs through a series of water baths of varying temperatures, but abandoned the idea as too costly, and as unacceptable to consumers because it often clouds the whites. The idea of mass pasteurization quietly died.

The bacteria that prompted the idea of in-shell pasteurization are present inside a small number of eggs, perhaps one in twenty thousand. They have also been found in chicken, pork, and even cheese. Other strains of salmonella, and there are many, are found in the intestinal tracts of animals, birds, reptiles, and insects. All these strains become a problem when they get transferred to food, which can happen by mishandling or by failure to clean a chopping board between uses. Children, pregnant women, the elderly, and people with compromised immune systems are more susceptible to being affected, because they may become ill after ingesting fewer bacteria than other people and they are more prone to complications. Although as many as two million people in the United States are sickened by salmonella each year, in only a small percentage are eggs implicated. Since 1995, the number of cases has been on the decline. The egg industry has been doing its share in this effort. It has applied control and sanitation measures at every stage of production and has offered guidelines for the consumer.

Refrigeration is the first step. Even if a freshly laid egg contains *Salmonella enteritidis*, it will be in small numbers; proper refrigeration will keep the bacteria from multiplying. Consumers should buy only unbroken eggs from a refrigerated case and store them in their carton in the middle of the refrigerator, not in the door. Eggs in any form should not be left at room temperature for more than two hours.

Cleanliness is the next defense. Everyone should wash hands before beginning food preparation, and wash utensils and cutting boards that have been used for raw foods before preparing other foods.

Proper cooking will kill any bacteria that might be present in the eggs. Specifically, salmonella is killed by cooking to 140 degrees Fahrenheit for three and a half minutes, or to an end temperature of 160 degrees Fahrenheit. This translates to a white that is firm and opaque and a yolk that has begun to thicken. Cooked egg dishes should be eaten immediately, or cooled to refrigerator temperature.

Dessert preparation brings special considerations. Because of their alkalinity, egg whites are less favorable to bacterial growth, but it is still possible that they could be contaminated. Many recipes in cookbooks twenty years ago called for raw eggs—whipped whites to give structure to cold soufflés, and yolks for richness in mousses. Now these preparations are not considered safe. Other problematic recipes are ice creams with lightly cooked custards, and undercooked meringues. But, dessert lovers, don't despair. There is a way to have a safe dessert and eat it too. A few alterations in cooking techniques make it possible.

Some dishes would be irrevocably changed if made with properly cooked eggs. Caesar salad is a prime example. In an effort to protect the restaurant-going public, the California legislature passed a law in January 1998 stipulating the end-cooking temperature for meat and eggs. A Caesar salad devotee could still bite into those crisp spears of romaine coated with a dressing of anchovy, olive oil, and raw (or barely poached) egg, as long as the waiter dressed the salad at the table. The practice represented full disclosure; the customer could see and thus approve of the egg. But many restaurants, including one noted for the salad, weren't equipped to comply. They didn't have room to dress salads at tableside. Customers objected to the government's taking such a parental role. They lamented the loss of their salad and made such an outcry that Carol Migden, an assemblywoman from San Francisco, sponsored a bill that allowed the use of raw eggs, provided the customer approved. The bill became law in July 1998. In celebration, the California Egg Commission, Moose's restaurant, and the mayor's office staged the tossing of a Caesar salad in Washington Square, across from the restaurant, that made the Guinness Book of Records—all 4,395 pounds of it. "The regulation was originally conceived to cover *E. coli* and salmonella, and it's seldom the case that a raw egg carries these bacteria," said Migden.

◎

People have attributed so much to the egg that the weight of the endowment seems enough to crack its deceptively fragile-looking shell.

The egg's life force has connected it to creation stories of mythical proportions that cross many cultures and times. And eggs are intertwined with other life-giving symbols: gods, birds, water. Early people seized upon the hatching of a chick from an egg to help them explain natural phenomena that were mysterious and awe-inspiring. They developed a notion of the egg as the origin of the world and the creator of all life. A vast ocean existed before the world began, and in many myths an egg bobbing on the water figures as the source of the world and life itself. The Assyrians believed that a fish pushed an egg from the Euphrates, from which a goddess hatched. A Chinese myth tells of an egg that emerged from the water to become dry land. Flood stories involve precious eggs. In some, heroes and tribal leaders hatch from eggs left on dry land by receding flood waters. In ancient Egypt, a god molded the earth egg from the mud of the Nile, a river whose banks provided fertile ground to grow crops.

Other myths involve a primordial egg hatching the sun god, the sun taking on the yolk's color. The setting of the sun into the same waters that supported the world egg connected the two. The egg and the sun were also connected as sources of life. It was sometimes thought that animals, including humans, were brought to life by the heat of the sun, just as crops thrived in its rays. Fowl were woven into the stories too. In one, a goose lays the sun egg; in another, a duck lays golden eggs, including one that is the sun egg.

In Mexico, the sun egg hatched from a mountain that split asunder—a fitting beginning, since mountains were venerated for their mass. In Indian lore, eggs rolled down the sides of a mountain to form rivers, a mythological answer to a natural phenomenon.

Serpents and dragons—sometimes good omens, sometimes evil—formed from earth that was once water, then laid eggs that hatched other dragons. These creatures guarded gold and silver eggs hidden in the earth, which were thought to grow within the yolk of the earth. In another myth, a snake fertilizes an egg laid by a young girl and starts the human race.

Other tales held birds responsible for the existence of humans. To people living on small islands surrounded by water, birds were revered because they were not bound to the land. This special status led to the belief that the first human was hatched from a bird's egg.

Taking the creation myths one step further, the egg came to be thought of as the seat of the immortal soul, which was thought to be separate from the body. Such a precious entity required careful guarding, and what better place than the egg? Since eggs hatch birds, they too became symbols of the soul, carrying the soul from the body at the time of death. The soul could also turn into a dove, thus bringing it closer to God; the Holy Ghost was assumed to take that form.

Eggs were also connected to sacrifices that would bring good fortune. Archaeological evidence suggests that early people in varying geographies believed that a blood sacrifice was essential if a new building's foundation was to be strong. At first, this was human sacrifice; people were buried in the foundation or in the walls. After years of the macabre practice, animals took the place of humans. Gradually, eggs, symbolic of life, replaced the animals, although for a while both were used. Excavators have found eggs, ranging in age from four hundred to two thousand years of age, buried in temple walls, houses, and town halls throughout Europe. There is at least one instance of both chickens and eggs being entombed.

Bridges, as important structures, also required sacrifices in the form of eggs mixed into the mortar that held them together. The rivers they spanned demanded offerings to prevent flooding and drownings, so people buried eggs in the banks. Since it was believed that the water spirits moved to the trees during the summer, plates of eggs were placed near the trunks. Some trees are still thought to possess special powers. In Jamaica, people gather around a sacred tree when someone is ill and hurl eggs at it so it will free the spirit of the afflicted person. Egg-breaking can also be used to predict the outcome of illness. In the East Indies, soothsayers throw an egg at a special egg-breaking board, and the placement of the small fragments of shell predict the patient's chances of recovery. The *New York Times* profiled an Indonesian medicine man who uses an egg placed on the stomach of an ill person to help diagnose the ailment.

The shapes that broken eggs assumed were used to predict the future throughout Europe, England, and Mexico. Eggs were augurs of comets and eclipses; pictures of these unusual occurrences supposedly appeared on them.

Unusual eggs, small or without shells, were viewed with suspicion as unnatural things to be feared. Supposedly they were laid by cocks, who put them under snakes or toads until monsters hatched. This belief was common throughout medieval Europe. Even the scientifically minded Ulisse Aldrovandi claimed to have seen many of the eggs.

When belief in witches was the norm, eggs figured into the picture. Witches not only flew on broomsticks, but sailed in eggshells. Thus it was essential that eggshells be smashed, rendering them useless to the witches—who were also thought to cast spells on cattle by burying eggs in their pastures.

The days on which eggs were set under hens to hatch were selected with great care. Friday was considered a bad day in Christian countries, because it was the day of the Crucifixion. The phases of the moon and the tides were taken into account as well. Setting eggs at ebb tide brought hens. Inland, farmers carried the eggs to the chicken in a blouse if hens were wanted, in a man's hat for roosters. (Unbeknownst to those setting the eggs, the sex of the gestating chicks had already been determined.) Uneven-numbered days were preferred, for even numbers were thought to hatch only cockerels.

The egg reaches its highest symbolic form in fertility myths. In parts of Africa, the egg's significance as a life force led to prohibitions on eating them, a practice thought to cause sterility, the price to be paid for destroying life. Conversely, other cultures esteemed eggs as a cure for sterility and impotence: Barren Jewish women ate double-yolked eggs; impotent men were advised to eat egg yolks every day.

Eggs were sometimes fed to laboring women to ease childbirth, and during a difficult birth, eggs were laid on a woman's garment in hopes that she would bear the baby as easily as a hen lays an egg. Eggs play a part in welcoming the newborn too. They were given as gifts and often added to the water for the child's first bath. A Chinese custom for a birth celebration includes giving a bowl of noodles, signifying long life, to each person in attendance. Each bowl also contains an egg, dyed red, to signify peace and happiness.

In Greece, Jewish women affixed an egg to the bride's veil to bring her good luck and many children. In other cultures, a bride carried an egg in the bodice of her dress, or stitched into another part of her clothing. The newlyweds often shared an egg to ensure long life and fertility.

Success in sowing crops, and in their subsequent growth and harvest, was vital to small rural communities, and farmers enlisted the power of eggs to ensure it. People transported chicken eggs to the fields, perhaps thinking that their life force would give power to the plant seeds. Some tribes of Asia put eggs in the basket that held the seeds to be planted, and placed these baskets beneath the central posts of their huts, where they believed their ancestral spirits to have lived. The spirits entered the egg and were then transferred to the field during the planting of the seeds.

Primitive people often attributed disease to evil spirits. Just as eggs could transfer good spirits to fields, they could be the medium to remove evil spirits from the sick. Exorcists employed eggs to accept evil spirits driven from the possessed. Eggs were fed to snakes to render them harmless. And ostrich eggs hang in churches of varying religions throughout the Middle East, Africa, and parts of Spain, sometimes stuck to the outside of minarets, symbolic of God's watchful care.

Just as eggs were prominent in fertility and birth rituals, they also played a part in funeral rites. Eggs, or egg shapes made from wood or stone, were often buried in tombs. The practice goes back to 2400 B.C., although even in modern Russia mourners offer eggs to a corpse. They may be sacrificial, or symbolic of resurrection, for it is the human condition to long for immortality.

Many mythologies connect the egg to resurrection; the Hindu spirit Prajapati forms an egg, then appears from within it; the phoenix was thought to live for hundreds of years, die, be consumed by fire, then rise from the egg that it had laid. By the first century A.D., the phoenix had become symbolic of Christ and his resurrection. And so eggs became associated with rebirth, resurrection, and the celebration of Easter. Some Catholic liturgists maintained that it was every Christian's duty to eat an egg at Easter.

The early Christians celebrated traditional Jewish festivals, and until the third century celebrated Easter at the same time as Passover. There is even a connection in the languages—"Pasch," the basis for many words to describe Easter, originates in the Hebrew "Pesach," which means "Passover." Eggs are prominent in Jewish traditions, and it may be that Easter eggs had their origins in Passover. The Passover seder includes a roasted egg to which various meanings are attached— the burnt offering carried to the temple at major festivals, and symbols of hope during persecution, of new life after the Egyptian captivity, and of the spring cycles of rebirth and regrowth.

Colored eggs have been used for Passover celebrations, dyed with onion skins, coffee grounds, or hay. The practice may have been borrowed from the Christians, although there is another festival, Lag b'Omer, that is celebrated with a picnic including eggs dyed the colors of the rainbow.

In Europe, red is the favorite color to dye eggs. The color itself is thought to be a good omen and avert evil. Legends bear this out, including the hen that laid a red egg at the birth of Severus Alexander, prompting a seer to forecast his eventual role as emperor. Another Roman, Marcus Aurelius, had his birth announced by a hen laying an egg spotted with red, also forecasting his eventual role as emperor. When this prediction became reality, the Romans exchanged colored eggs.

As time passed, simple dyeing of Easter eggs gave way to more elaborate forms, becoming a highly developed art, in Central and Eastern Europe especially. People in Poland were decorating eggs in the eleventh century, and in Germany and England in the thirteenth. Decorators dyed eggs, then made designs by scratching them to remove the color, or, more elaborately, dyed the eggs after applying wax in intricate designs, rewaxing and redyeing with as many as six or seven colors. Various motifs were employed, many with religious significance. Some small villages had a resident egg-decorator, usually an elderly woman who had practiced the craft her whole life. One Ukrainian woman was said to know more than one hundred designs. Another woman, in Moravia, had decorated over thirty thousand eggs.

Some decorators used wooden eggs, or porcelain. The form was taken to its most elaborate—and expensive—heights by Carl Fabergé, the court jeweler for the tsar's family, who fashioned an egg from gold, white enamel, and rubies as a gift from Tsar Alexander III to his wife. The tsar was so delighted that he commissioned Fabergé to make one each succeeding Easter, leaving the design to the jeweler's creative genius. Most opened to reveal miniature scenes. Those that still exist are either in museums or owned by royalty or the very rich.

And so the simple egg, with all its meanings, has inspired ordinary people, mystics, clerics, kings, leaders, and artists. It has become entwined with the human condition at its most essential and most ethereal.

❦

Do we dare to eat an egg? Object of awed reverence and receptacle of perceived supernatural might, an egg is more than food. But if we put it on a pedestal, we would forever deny ourselves its culinary possibilities. And esteemed as it is for its powers to predict the future, aid fertility, and provide almost perfect nourishment, it can also inspire astounding baking feats. I'm sure, if the egg itself could answer, it would encourage us to proceed, exploiting its wizardlike capabilities. It wants to show them off.

For the baker, eggs are a cornerstone of the craft. From the simple custards of the Romans to towering cakes for important celebrations, eggs are vital to many desserts. They have chameleon characteristics that shift their role from one dessert to another. When they're beaten, they can coax lightness into a cake by trapping tiny air bubbles that expand in the heat of the oven. A génoise cake is the quintessential example: A baker gently heats whole eggs and sugar until the sugar dissolves, then, with the help of an electric mixer, beats this liquid until it pales, thickens, triples in volume, and falls like soft clouds from the beaters. A quick folding in of flour and melted butter complete the preparation. The cake will rise in the oven. The egg's proteins will cook and give the airy cake its structure.

The same ingredients, in different proportions, will make a dessert soufflé, but it's still the power of the eggs, this time in the whites alone, that pushes the quivering top above the dish.

If they are mixed with milk, sugar, and cream, eggs take on a different form when baked. They become jiggly cups of goodness that fill the mouth with their unctuousness and slide down the throat. An eggshell-thin layer of burnt sugar on the top can provide a shocking but delightful counterpoint.

Egg yolks cooked with milk—carefully, so they don't scramble—are an essential part of good ice cream. A slow, gentle heating binds the eggs and milk and thickens them. When cooled and mixed with cream and flavoring, the result is ice cream of extraordinary smoothness.

Change the ingredients (yolks, sugar, wine) and the cooking method (beating over simmering water) and the result is a billowing, warm custard to be eaten immediately—zabaglione.

Egg whites alone have almost magical properties. Their thick albumen, composed of several proteins, is irrevocably changed by the simple act of beating. Agitation breaks the protein into long strands. Very fresh eggs whip into the most stable foam, but eggs a few days older will attain the most volume, important for making soufflés. Room-temperature eggs will whip to greater heights than eggs straight from the refrigerator. The rhythmic slapping of balloon whisks beating egg whites in copper bowls is more than a romantic holdover. Atoms from the copper bind with one of the white's proteins, which promotes cross-linking between the protein molecules, resulting in a foam that is creamier and not so easy to overwhip. But today's baker is more likely to use an electric mixer than a balloon whisk.

Egg whites beaten with sugar, shaped into triangles or disks, and baked in a slow oven expand slightly before the proteins coagulate and fix the shape. Then the baker can top the triangles with ice cream or fruit and make "sandwiches" from the disks. The whites and the sugar are almost like an oven-baked candy.

Eggs don't mind playing a minor role in desserts either. A beaten egg, gently brushed on a sweet yeast bread just before it goes into the oven, helps it brown and shine.

Although many desserts use whole eggs, today's baker often separates the yolk from the white, using one or the other, or adding them to the preparation separately. And so, just as eggs are compartmentalized in their production, their components are often segregated in the kitchen.

Chocolate Meringue "Sandwiches"

Chocolate lovers, rejoice—this is your dessert. Cocoa powder flavors flat disks of meringues, and rich bittersweet chocolate is the base for the filling that holds them together.

The components can be made ahead. Store the meringues, airtight, for up to 2 weeks, and the filling, refrigerated, for up to 5 days.

Let the assembled desserts sit at room temperature for 30 minutes before serving, so the filling softens.

8 SERVINGS

For the meringues:
1 cup (3½ ounces) powdered sugar
4 tablespoons Dutch-processed cocoa
3 large egg whites, at room temperature
½ cup (3½ ounces) granulated sugar

For the filling:
¾ cup (6 ounces) heavy whipping cream
8 ounces high-quality bittersweet chocolate, finely chopped

Make the meringues:

Preheat the oven to 250°F.

Draw 20 circles, 2 inches in diameter, 1 inch apart, on a piece of parchment paper. Put the paper in the baking pan, marked side down.

Sift the powdered sugar with the cocoa.

Put the egg whites in the bowl of a heavy-duty mixer. Beat the whites with the whisk attachment, starting on medium speed. When they start to froth, add about a third of the granulated sugar and beat until they become opaque and increase in volume. Add another third of the sugar and beat until they start to become firm, then turn up the mixer speed, add the rest of the sugar, and beat until they are stiff but still glossy. The whites will hang in soft, droopy peaks from the whisk when it is lifted from the bowl.

Remove the bowl from the mixer. Sift a third of the powdered sugar and cocoa over the bowl (this will be the second time it is sifted) and fold this into the whites. Use a rubber spatula to fold, going to the bottom of the bowl in the center and coming up along the side. Rotate the bowl slightly after every fold. Fold in the remaining powdered sugar in two stages, sifting it into the bowl each time.

Fit a pastry bag with a plain ⅜-inch tip, and fill it with the meringue. Starting in the center of each circle, pipe a coil, filling the circles.

Bake the meringues on the middle shelf of the oven until they are firm and can be detached from the paper, about 1 hour.

Cool the baking pan on a rack. When the meringues are completely cool, store them in an airtight container at room temperature.

Make the filling:

Bring the whipping cream to a boil in a medium saucepan. Remove it from the heat. Add the chopped chocolate, and let it sit for 5 minutes. Whisk the chocolate into the cream until it is smooth. Transfer the chocolate cream to a bowl, cover it, and refrigerate.

Assemble the desserts:

The filling should be the consistency of thick mayonnaise. If it is freshly made, cool it until it thickens; if made ahead, leave it at room temperature until it softens.

Pile a generous tablespoon of filling in the middle of 8 meringues. Gently place another meringue on top of each, being careful not to push down too hard, so that each sandwich maintains some height. Put the meringues in the freezer for 20 minutes.

Crush the remaining meringues between pieces of wax or parchment paper. Remove the filled meringues from the freezer. Using a small offset spatula or a kitchen knife, smooth the remaining filling onto the sides of the sandwiches. Roll each finished sandwich in the crushed meringues.

Refrigerate the desserts until 30 minutes before serving.

Variation:

To make these for a dessert buffet, pipe the meringues into 1-inch instead of 2-inch disks.

MERINGUE TRIANGLES WITH ALMONDS

Egg whites, sugar, and almonds, formed into triangles and baked in the oven, provide a base for your favorite ice cream or the ripest seasonal fruit. A smaller meringue triangle on top completes the picture. Unblanched almonds lend color and a stronger flavor.

Keep these on hand, stored in an airtight container, for a practically instant dessert.

16 TRIANGLES (8 LARGE AND 8 SMALL), 8 SERVINGS

⅔ cup (3½ ounces) whole unblanched almonds
1 cup (3½ ounces) powdered sugar, plus more for sifting
    over the triangles
3 large egg whites, at room temperature
3 tablespoons granulated sugar

Preheat the oven to 350°F.

Draw 8 equilateral triangles, with sides measuring 4 inches, 1 inch apart, on a piece of parchment paper that will fit in a baking pan. On the same paper, draw 8 more triangles with sides measuring 2 inches. Put the paper in the pan, marked side down.

Use a food processor to grind the almonds and 1 cup powdered sugar until they are a powder.

Put the egg whites in the bowl of a heavy-duty mixer. Beat the whites with the whisk attachment, starting on medium speed. When they start to froth, add 1 tablespoon of granulated sugar and beat until they become opaque and increase in volume. Add another tablespoon of sugar and beat until they start to become firm, then turn up the mixer speed, add the remaining tablespoon of sugar, and beat until they are stiff but still glossy. The whites will hang in soft, droopy peaks from the whisk when it is lifted from the bowl.

Remove the bowl from the mixer. Sprinkle about a third of the almonds and powdered sugar over the bowl, and fold this into the whites. Use a rubber spatula to fold, going to the bottom of the bowl in the center and coming up along the side. Rotate the bowl slightly after every fold. Fold in the remaining almond-and-powdered-sugar mixture in two stages.

Fit a pastry bag with a plain ⅜-inch tip, and fill it with the meringue. Starting around the outside edges, fill each triangle with the meringue. Sift a fine layer of powdered sugar over the triangles.

Put the baking sheet on the middle shelf of the oven, and turn the oven temperature down to 300°F.

Bake until the triangles are browned and crisp, and can be detached from the paper, about 50 minutes.

Place the baking pan on a rack until the triangles are completely cool. Carefully remove them from the paper, and store in an airtight container at room temperature.

To serve, place the large triangles on serving plates, top with a scoop of ice cream or sorbet, fresh fruit, or fresh fruit folded into whipped cream. Put a small triangle on top of each serving.

PROVENÇAL EASTER BREAD

Many countries make an egg-rich bread, decorated with colored eggs, for Easter, and France is no exception. This dough includes the typical Provençal flavors of orange-flower water and olive oil. Both France and Middle Eastern countries export the water to the United States. Although not essential, a French olive oil makes this recipe more authentic.

A word of caution about the whole eggs nestled in the dough— prick the larger end of the eggs with a straight pin before baking, to prevent explosions in the oven. Use a very fine paintbrush and food coloring to decorate the eggs with swirls, stripes, and other designs as well as solid colors. Do this after baking; prebaking decorations may stain the dough.

Consider the painted eggs to be decoration only. They will be overcooked, and may sit too long at room temperature, both before and after baking, to be safe.

1 LARGE RING, 10 SERVINGS

> *⅔ cup (5¼ ounces) warm (body-temperature) tap water, plus 2*
>   *tablespoons for glaze*
> *1¾ teaspoons active dry yeast*
> *8 large eggs: 3 at room temperature, 4 for decoration, and*
>   *1 yolk for glaze*
> *1 tablespoon orange-flower water*
> *3½ cups (1 pound 1¾ ounces) unbleached all-purpose flour*
> *⅓ cup (2½ ounces) granulated sugar*
> *1¾ teaspoons fine sea salt*
> *3 tablespoons extra-virgin olive oil, preferably French*

Put the ⅔ cup warm water in the bowl of a heavy-duty mixer, and sprinkle the yeast over it. Let it stand until it becomes creamy, about 5 minutes. Add 3 eggs at room temperature and orange-flower water to the bowl. Add the flour, sugar, and sea salt to the bowl.

Using a dough hook on low speed, mix the dough until the wet and dry ingredients combine, about 2 minutes. Turn the speed to medium, and knead for about 3 minutes. The dough will form a ball on the hook, but will be soft and not spring cleanly from the bottom of the bowl. Add more flour judiciously if the dough is too wet. Add the olive oil, 1 tablespoon at a time, letting the dough absorb the oil before adding the next addition. When all the oil is mixed in, knead for another minute. The dough will be soft and slightly sticky.

Remove the bowl from the mixer, cover it with plastic wrap, and let the dough rise at room temperature until it doubles in bulk, about 3 hours.

Turn the dough onto a lightly floured work surface. Shape it into a ball. Let it rest a few minutes, then make a hole through the center. Put a hand in the hole and lift the dough from the table. Insert your other hand in the hole from the opposite end and, using a hand-over-hand motion, enlarge the hole. It will take a few tries to make the hole large enough. Let this "doughnut" rest on the work surface between manipulations so it will relax. When the hole is about 5 inches in diameter, and the surrounding ring of dough is about 3 inches wide, put the doughnut on a parchment-lined baking pan.

Using a straight pin, prick tiny holes in the large ends of 4 eggs. Make 4 indentations in the ring of dough at equidistant points, going close to the bottom but not through the dough. Nestle the eggs in the dough, large end down.

Slip the pan into a plastic bag, shake it a few times to introduce air, and close the end. Let the dough rise at room temperature until double in bulk, 1 to 1½ hours.

Preheat the oven to 350°F.

When the dough has risen, remove the pan from the plastic bag. Separate the remaining egg, and beat the yolk with 2 tablespoons of water to make a glaze. Brush the dough with the egg-yolk glaze, being careful not to brush the eggs.

Bake the dough on the middle shelf of the oven. The bread is done when it is browned and sounds hollow when thumped on the bottom, about 30 minutes.

Put the pan on a rack until the bread cools, then decorate the eggs as described above.

COCONUT SOUFFLÉ

The secret ingredient in this recipe is the coconut milk, which isn't a dairy product at all, but the liquid from the tropical fruit. Buy it in Asian markets or in the specialty section in grocery stores.

The egg-yolk base can be made ahead, then refrigerated until needed. Gently reheat it over low heat before continuing. Thirty minutes before serving, whip the egg whites and fold them into the base. The air beaten into the egg whites gives this dessert its loft and texture. It will start to fall when it comes out of the oven, and certainly when it is being served, so take it to the table in all its glory and spoon it onto serving plates in front of your guests.

4 SERVINGS

Soft butter and granulated sugar for the soufflé dish
3 large eggs, at room temperature
1 large egg white, at room temperature
¾ cup (6 ounces) coconut milk (stir before measuring)
4 tablespoons granulated sugar, divided into 2 portions
1½ tablespoons unbleached all-purpose flour
2 tablespoons (1 ounce) unsalted butter
⅓ cup (1 ounce) flaked, sweetened coconut
1 tablespoon dark rum

Preheat the oven to 375°F.

Generously butter an 8-cup soufflé dish. Dust it with granulated sugar, and discard the excess.

Separate the 3 eggs, dropping the whites into the bowl of a heavy-duty mixer and the yolks into a small bowl. Add the additional egg white to the others in the mixer bowl.

Whisk a little of the coconut milk with 1 tablespoon of the sugar and the flour. Bring the rest of the coconut milk to a simmer in a medium saucepan. Whisk it into the sugar-flour paste. Return to the pan, and bring to a boil, whisking. Boil for a minute, to cook the flour. Remove from the heat, and whisk in the butter. Let it cool for a minute, then whisk in the egg yolks, one at a time. Stir in the coconut and rum.

Beat the whites with the whisk attachment on the mixer, starting on medium speed. When they start to froth, add 1 tablespoon of sugar and beat until they become opaque and increase in volume. Add another tablespoon of sugar and beat until they start to become firm, then turn up the mixer speed, add the remaining tablespoon of sugar, and beat until they are stiff but still glossy. The whites will hang in soft, droopy peaks from the whisk when it is lifted from the bowl.

Fold about a fourth of the beaten whites into the egg-yolk base, then turn the base into the mixing bowl and fold in the rest of the whites by hand. It's better to leave a few clumps of white showing than to overfold.

Pour the mixture into the soufflé dish, and bake it on the middle shelf of the oven until the soufflé rises and the top browns, about 25 minutes. Serve the soufflé at once at the table.

Snow Eggs (Oeufs à la Neige)

The egg shows off its range of abilities in this recipe. Two completely different tastes and textures from each of its components: Sweet meringue puffs from the whites, which are almost like eating air, float on a custard base made from the yolks.

4 SERVINGS

> 2 cups (16 ounces) whole milk
> ½-inch strip orange zest
> ½ vanilla bean, preferably Madagascar Bourbon
> 3 large eggs, at room temperature
> ½ cup (3½ ounces) granulated sugar, divided into 2 portions
> 4 teaspoons sliced almonds, toasted

Put the milk, orange zest, and vanilla bean in a medium saucepan. (Don't scrape the seeds from the vanilla bean yet.)

Separate the eggs, dropping the whites into the bowl of a heavy-duty mixer and the yolks into a medium bowl.

Bring the milk to a simmer. While the milk is heating, make a meringue with the egg whites, adding ¼ cup of sugar in 3 stages. Beat the whites with the whisk attachment, starting on medium speed. When they start to froth, add the first dose of sugar and beat until they become opaque and increase in volume. Add the second dose of sugar and beat until they start to become firm, then turn up the mixer speed, add the remaining sugar, and beat until they are stiff but still glossy. The whites will hang in soft, droopy peaks from the whisk when it is lifted from the bowl.

Dip 2 soupspoons in a glass of cold water. Scoop a generous amount of meringue into 1 spoon and, with the other, compact it and round the top into an egg shape. Slide the meringue into the simmering milk. Make 3 more "eggs," dipping the spoons into the water before forming each. You will have to cook them in 2 batches, 4 in each. Poach them for about 2 minutes, until they start to puff. Turn the meringues over with a slotted spoon, and poach 2 more minutes. They will be soft but will hold their shape when you remove them from the saucepan. Remove them with a slotted spoon, and place them on a plate lined with a tea towel. As they cool, they will deflate.

Remove the vanilla bean, split it horizontally, and scrape the seeds into the milk. Return the bean to the saucepan. Bring the milk to a boil.

Whisk the remaining ¼ cup sugar into the yolks in a steady stream. Slowly pour the hot milk into the yolks in a steady stream, continuing to whisk. Return this custard to the pan, and cook it over low heat, stirring constantly with a wooden spoon, until the custard thickens and coats the spoon. It will register 160°F on an instant-read thermometer. Don't let it boil.

Pour the custard through a sieve into a bowl. Put this bowl into a larger one filled with ice. Refrigerate it until it is cold.

Transfer the meringues to a plate and refrigerate them.

To serve, pour the custard into 4 bowls and top each with 2 meringues. Sprinkle the almonds on top.

Baked Alaska

A layer of cake, a mound of ice cream, and a topping of meringue sounds delicious enough, but to add a little tension, the dessert is traditionally placed in a hot oven just long enough to brown the meringue but not to melt the ice cream. To eliminate the nerve-racking part, use a propane torch (purchased at a hardware or kitchenware store) to brown the meringue. Two more nontraditional twists: Slices of apple replace the cake, and the portions are individual.

The ice-cream churning and the apple cooking can be done ahead. In a pinch, use purchased ice cream.

8 SERVINGS

The ice cream:
1½ cups (12 ounces) whole milk
½ teaspoon ground cinnamon
¾ cup (5½ ounces) granulated sugar
4 large egg yolks
1½ cups (12 ounces) heavy whipping cream

The apples:
8 slices firm apple, ½ inch thick, peeled and cored
2 tablespoons unsalted butter
2 tablespoons granulated sugar

The meringue:
4 large egg whites, at room temperature
2 tablespoons water
1¼ cups (8¾ ounces) granulated sugar

Make the ice cream:

Bring the milk to a boil in a medium saucepan. While it heats, mix the cinnamon into the sugar. Put the yolks in a medium bowl, and whisk in the cinnamon sugar in a steady stream.

When the milk is hot, slowly pour it into the yolks in a steady stream, whisking constantly. Return this custard to the pan, and cook it over low heat, stirring constantly with a wooden spoon, until the custard thickens and coats the spoon. It will register 160°F on an instant-read thermometer. Don't let it boil.

Pour the custard through a sieve into a bowl. Stir in the cream. Put this bowl into a larger one filled with ice water. When the custard is cool, remove it from the ice water and cover the bowl with plastic wrap. Refrigerate the custard for 5 hours or overnight.

Churn the custard in an ice-cream maker according to the manufacturer's instructions. Line a pan that will fit into your freezer with parchment paper. When the ice cream is ready, scoop it into 8 balls. Put the balls on the pan, and freeze them until they are hard.

Cook the apples:

Heat a skillet that will hold all the apple slices. Melt the butter in the pan. Sprinkle half of the sugar over the apples, then place them, sugar side down, in the pan. When they are cooked halfway through, sprinkle them with the rest of the sugar and turn them. Cook them until they are soft but not falling apart.

Finish the dessert:

Make the meringue: Put the egg whites, water, and sugar in the bowl of a heavy-duty mixer, then put this over a pan of barely simmering water. Whisk by hand until an instant-read thermometer reads 160°F, 4 to 5 minutes.

Immediately put the bowl on the mixer fitted with a whisk attachment. Beat on high speed until the mixture thickens, about 2 minutes. Turn the mixer speed to low, and continue to beat until the meringue is room temperature, a few more minutes.

Put the cooked apple slices on serving plates. Top each with a ball of frozen ice cream.

Fit a pastry bag with a medium star tip and fill it with the meringue. Thinly cover the ice-cream balls and the sides of the apple slices with a swirl of meringue. Brown the meringue with a propane torch. Serve the dessert immediately.

LICORICE ICE CREAM

The root of *Glycyrrhiza glabra* has been recognized for its ability to soothe sore throats and suppress coughs since Egyptian times, when the ground-up roots were mixed into pastilles. It also has a naturally sweet taste, which fosters its use in candy, although the black licorice ropes of penny-candy fame are not colored by the roots alone.

This ice cream, enriched by an egg-yolk base, has a light-buff hue. The taste intensifies with each swallow, haunting and soothing.

Buy licorice tea bags in a health-food store to make this dessert. Read the box to make sure that licorice root is the main ingredient.

1 QUART

1½ cups (12 ounces) whole milk
2 licorice-root tea bags
⅔ cup (4½ ounces) granulated sugar
4 large egg yolks
1½ cups (12 ounces) heavy whipping cream

Bring the milk and the tea bags to a boil in a medium saucepan with a heavy bottom. Let the liquid steep for 15 minutes. Remove the tea bags, pressing down on them to extract as much flavor as possible. Bring the infused milk back to a boil.

While the milk reheats, whisk the sugar with the egg yolks. Slowly pour the hot milk into the yolks in a steady stream, continuing to whisk. Return this custard to the pan, and cook it over low heat, stirring constantly with a wooden spoon, until the custard thickens and coats the spoon. It will register 160°F on an instant-read thermometer. Don't let it boil.

Pour the custard through a sieve into a bowl. Stir in the cream. Put this bowl into a larger one filled with ice. When the custard is cool, remove it from the ice and cover the bowl with plastic wrap. Refrigerate the custard for 5 hours, or overnight.

Churn the custard in an ice-cream maker according to the manufacturer's instructions.

SAFFRON ORANGE CRÈME BRÛLÉE

The contrasts in texture are what make this dessert so remarkable. The diner's spoon cracks through a thin layer of caramelized sugar, then slips into an unctuous custard. In the mouth the contrast remains, providing a sensory treat.

Union Pacific restaurant in New York makes *crème brûlée* in shallow dishes instead of the taller ramekins, which increases the crunch-to-custard ratio. Borrow their technique for a bit of caramelized sugar with every bite.

A propane torch, purchased at a hardware or kitchenware store, is the best tool for caramelizing the tops of the custards.

Drying out the saffron before mixing with the other ingredients accentuates its flavor.

For a particularly smooth, rich custard, use duck eggs if you can find them.

8 CUSTARDS

> *¼ teaspoon saffron threads*
> *2 cups (16 ounces) whole milk*
> *2 cups (16 ounces) heavy whipping cream*
> *½ cup (3½ ounces) granulated sugar, plus more for topping*
> *8 large egg yolks*
> *2 whole large eggs*
> *Zest of 1 orange, grated*

Preheat the oven to 300°F.

Arrange 8 shallow bowls, with 6-inch diameters at the top, in 2 roasting pans.

Bring a large pot of water to boil.

Put the saffron threads in a medium saucepan over low heat. Turn them with your fingers until they feel dry and brittle. Add the milk, cream, and sugar to the saucepan. Bring the liquid to a boil, stirring once or twice to dissolve the sugar.

While the liquid is heating, whisk the egg yolks and whole eggs together in a medium bowl. Slowly pour the hot liquid into the eggs in a steady stream, continuing to whisk.

Pour the mixture through a strainer into a large bowl. Add the orange zest.

Ladle 6 ounces into each bowl. Pour boiling water into each pan until the bottom thirds of the bowls are submerged. Cover the pans with foil.

Carefully set the pans on 2 oven shelves. (If your oven will only hold one pan, bake them one at a time, adding water to the second one just before it goes into the oven.)

Bake until the custards are set but still jiggly in the center, about 25 minutes.

Remove the bowls from the hot water, and refrigerate them until they are thoroughly chilled.

Just before serving, sprinkle sugar on the top of each custard. Using a sweeping motion, caramelize the tops with a propane torch.

Serve the custards immediately.

Variation: Duck Egg *Crème Brûlée*

Follow the instructions, but substitute duck eggs for the chicken eggs in these proportions:

6 duck egg yolks
2 whole duck eggs

ZABAGLIONE

Egg yolks don't get much better than this. Beaten into a warm froth, sweetened with sugar, and flavored with Sauternes or other late-harvest wine, this dessert can be made in minutes.

If you have some perfect berries, drop a few into each glass before spooning in the custard.

4 TO 6 SERVINGS

8 large egg yolks
½ cup (4 ounces) Sauternes, sweet Bordeaux, late-harvest
    Riesling, or late-harvest Gewürztraminer
¼ cup (1¾ ounces) granulated sugar

Bring a few inches of water to a simmer in a large pot. For cooking the custard, choose a bowl that conducts heat well, such as stainless steel. The bowl should fit over the pot so that the bottom does not touch the water.

Beat the egg yolks and wine in the bowl with a whisk. Add the sugar in a steady stream, continuing to whisk.

Put the bowl over the pot of barely simmering water. Whisk constantly until the eggs thicken, foam, and increase dramatically in volume, about 5 minutes.

Serve the zabaglione immediately in large wineglasses, with a smaller glass of the remaining wine on the side.

BUTTER

SOPHIE WAS OVERDUE. Her gestation period is normally forty weeks, but most offspring don't arrive exactly on time; an additional two weeks isn't unusual. She was huge and restless, and the brief spell of unseasonably hot weather ten miles inland from the Mendocino coast of California didn't help. Although this was her third pregnancy, it would be her first delivery in these new, more isolated surroundings. The midwife was worried about being so far from help, in case of a medical emergency.

The pregnancy dragged on for nine more days. Then, with a little help from the midwife, Sophie gave birth: It was a boy. People interested in milking cows would rather have girls, of course. But the day I visited, Judy Garrett proudly showed me the little guy. We walked from the back door of her Victorian house to the small barn, dogs sniffing at my ankles and chickens running out of the way. We entered to the smell of sweet hay. The newcomer sat with his legs curled under him in a corner, panting slightly in the heat. Judy spoke to him in a gentle voice while stroking his back. I thought he looked large for a three-week-old; he had almost tripled in size since birth. She hadn't decided whether to sell him soon or raise him for a few months. When the priority is milk, the male offspring go away. It wouldn't be the last time I heard this sentiment.

Next we walked to the enclosure that Sophie shares with a horse and another cow, this one a Dexter Kerry, black with horns. The animals came to greet us as we walked through the gate. "Sophie likes to be petted," Judy said as she ran her hands over the cow's back and scratched her head. The black cow's horns made me wary; I didn't touch her. Judy prefers the milk from Sophie, a Jersey; the Dexter's milk doesn't have the same sweet taste, in her opinion.

An interest in butter had brought me to the Garretts' home. Butter starts with cows, and I wanted to see the animals and learn more about the influences that come into play between the cow and a block of butter on a plate, or a piece of pastry with the taste and unctuousness that only butter can add.

Judy Garrett grew up near her grandmothers, who both milked cows. "I've always wanted a cow," she told me, and twenty-five years ago she got her wish when she saw a dairy cow for sale and bought it on impulse. She enlisted a neighbor to truck it to her house, and when it arrived, upset and with a full udder, Judy asked the neighbor how to milk. "Nobody can tell you, you have to do it yourself," was his reply as he pulled away. Judy tried without success. The cow kicked; Judy cried; not a drop of milk appeared. Then she took a nap, and when she awoke, she took her pail to the barn, sat on a stool next to the cow, and successfully milked her.

Sophie produces six to seven gallons of milk a day. For the moment, the calf gets four and Judy two. "What do you do with all the milk?" I asked. She used to sell it, but has stopped because of public-health concerns about bacteria in milk. So her family drinks it, and she bakes with it, churns it into butter, and perfects her skill of making cheese, yogurt, and kefir.

I was particularly interested in the butter-making process. After the fresh milk sits in the refrigerator for twenty-four hours, Judy skims the cream from the top. Jersey milk is known for its high butterfat content—there are about one and a half pints of cream per gallon of milk. The cream loses about two-thirds of its volume when it's churned into butter. I thought I spied a butter churner, a glass jar with a paddle attached to the lid, on a top shelf in the kitchen, and asked if that was what she used. Looking slightly sheepish, she admitted that she uses a blender to whir the cream until it separates; the fat globules coalesce, squeezing out the liquid. (I remember experiencing this process involuntarily the first time I tried to whip cream with a hand whisk in a hot kitchen. Instead of billowy mounds of cream to spoon onto a pie, I had butter for breakfast.) Then she pours the butter on the counter and works it with wooden spoons, kneading it with water until the water is clear and free of buttermilk. Next she adds a small amount of salt. This is sweet, not cultured, butter. (Cultured-butter makers add a bacterial starter to the cream, giving the butter a slightly sharper taste.) Because Judy doesn't pasteurize the cream, none of the naturally occurring enzymes and bacteria that give the cream flavor are killed.

I sat at the kitchen table, which was draped with a blue-and-white-checked cloth, waiting to taste batches of butter, a dry piece of toast ready to serve as a vehicle for transporting samples to my mouth. The stove sat at my back, and across from it was a black cast-iron model fueled by wood that Judy uses in the winter for both cooking and heat. Judy rummaged in the refrigerator and freezer for samples. Her refrigerator was full, but not with the usual suspects. There were jars of milk and cream, cheeses of many shapes carefully wrapped in plastic, and butter, some of it in paper cups and other batches wrapped in plastic, all dated.

The first butter Judy offered was three weeks old. I spread some on a piece of toast and took a bite. Although the butter crumbled slightly when spread, it wasn't dry in my mouth but smooth, with a sweet, clean taste somehow deeper and more satisfying than that of run-of-the-mill butter. No off flavors marred its pristine state. Next came a butter that had been frozen for a few months, a treatment that didn't compromise its integrity; it had the same satisfying flavor and texture as the first batch. Then Judy put a third specimen in front of me. This butter was only a few days old, but it had not been refrigerated. It was more complex, with a tangy bite that reminded me of cultured butter.

Judy milks the cow twice a day. After installing Sophie in the barn, she gives both herself and the cow what she described as a surgical scrub, washing her hands and arms and the entire underside of the cow with disinfectant. She is vigilant that no foreign matter should get into the milk, and because of her care and Sophie's good health, she is confident that the unpasteurized milk is safe to drink. Judy is the only family member who milks the cow. A neighbor takes over if she is away, but when he milks, she pasteurizes the milk. "It's not that I don't trust him," she said, "but I don't actually see the milking process."

She regrets that there aren't more family cows whose owners could provide a network of information and exchange. It's harder to know what to do when you're forced to rely on books, "an intellectual approach to something so natural," she said. If there were more people who knew about cows, they could consult one another about symptoms and remedies.

Although most people would feel burdened by the chore of twice-a-day milking, Judy enjoys it. For her it's a peaceful, primitive activity, almost meditative. Maybe that's the reason for her calm demeanor. She sees the tending of cows as a way of passing on family tradition. "My five-year-old granddaughter helps me with the curds. Someday she'll have the same memories that I had with my grandmother."

If you're in the market for a family cow, a Jersey is a good choice. With an average weight of nine hundred pounds, they are not large cows, but they produce more milk per pound than any other. And the milk is 4.5 to 6.5 percent butterfat, higher than from any other breed. It can be used as is or made into cheese or butter. People who work with cows say that Jerseys have a good disposition. Judy Garrett calls Sophie "the sweetest cow I've ever had."

◎

The extinct ancestor of the Jersey breed was the aurochs (*Bos primigenius*), which ranged throughout Eurasia and North Africa. These animals probably did not possess the passive disposition of dairy cows today, which may be the reason that they were not domesticated until 6000 B.C., after dogs, sheep, goats, and pigs. They were larger than other domesticated animals, and may not have been easy to manage.

As people changed from hunting and gathering to a more settled life that revolved around growing plants and raising livestock, they selected animals that had the social instinct to live in herds; were disposed to thrive and to breed in captivity; bore young that had a good chance of survival and matured relatively quickly; and accepted a human authority. The shift from hunting to herding didn't happen quickly. Most likely, hunters tracked certain herds, learned how to contain them, bred them, then selected animals possessing favorable characteristics for further breeding. Of the hundreds of animals that roamed the earth, only a handful were adaptable to human domestication.

It is unlikely that the first captive cows allowed humans to milk them. The reflex that allows milk to surge from a cow's udder into the teats so it can be expelled is hormonally induced and will not happen unless the cow is relaxed. Perhaps these first cows were kept for sacrificial ceremonies, or for barter. Later, their keepers began to exploit their potential. They were beasts of burden; their manure was used as heating fuel and fertilizer. When they became too old to be useful, they were slaughtered, and their carcasses provided meat, weapons, and tools (from horns), fat for lighting, and glue (from hooves).

The earliest evidence of humans' keeping cows for milk dates from the fourth millennium B.C. in Egypt and Mesopotamia. A frieze from a Mesopotamian temple depicts a milking scene with the people standing behind the animals, the same position used to milk goats, which were domesticated before cows. Dairying may also have been practiced farther north around the same time.

The Romans used cattle primarily as draft animals. The early Roman writers described a variety of oxen from throughout the country; none were milking cows. Nor were cows milked in parts of Africa and

Asia, a situation that holds true today, suggesting that this food avoidance stems from an inability to absorb lactose.

The freshness of milk was compromised by warm climates; it quickly fermented, depending on the ambient bacteria, either into a small-curd substance resembling yogurt, or into a primitive soft cheese with larger curds. Warm milk carried in a pouch made from an animal's stomach would have benefited from the stomach lining's rennet to aid in the conversion.

Butter may have evolved in a cooler climate, where agitated milk didn't ferment but separated instead. The earliest butter churn may have been a milk-filled container jouncing along with a Neolithic woman on a journey. She was probably surprised by its contents when she reached her destination—balls of solids suspended in milky liquid. Later, this effect was cultivated deliberately by suspending animal skins full of milk or cream from tree branches and swinging them to churn the contents. (The nineteenth-century writer and food-lover Alexandre Dumas had his own version of this method. When traveling, he filled a bottle with the local milk—cow, camel, horse, or sheep—then strapped it to his horse's neck. By the end of his journey, it was butter.) Much later came other vessels, small glass jars with dashers, suitable for making a pound or two of butter, and larger revolving barrels made from crockery or wood, which kept the cream from getting too warm. It could take thirty to forty-five minutes for granules of butter to appear in one of these churns, depending on the fat content of the milk and the temperature. Later, as butter began to be mass-produced, electricity and gasoline would be harnessed to run mechanized batch churns that could make five to six hundred pounds of butter at a time. Such churns are still used by some small producers in both France and the United States.

Butter and cheese were means of preserving a highly perishable product, especially before the days when farmers figured out how to keep cows in continuous milk production. Salt prolonged the life of butter, as did heating it, then evaporating the liquid and removing the solids, a method that is still used today in India to make ghee.

In its earliest uses, butter was offered as a religious sacrifice and used as an ointment for skin and hair as well as for food. But by the Middle Ages, dairying was an important economy in Northern Europe and Scandinavia, where butter was the preferred fat in the kitchen. The people of Flanders even used it to dress salads, and their love of butter spread to the nearby Île de France. But some regions satisfied the taste for fat in other ways—walnut oil in the Auvergne, Toulouse, and Savoy regions of France, olive oil along the Mediterranean. Religion also played a part. The Catholic Church forbade the use of butter on fast days, just as it proscribed meat and eggs, although the degree of proscription varied from place to place. Sometimes it was allowed during Lent; at other times, relegated to meat days. As the church's influence declined, the use of butter rose throughout Europe, especially in the North, where it was the preferred, and most readily available, cooking fat.

The Channel Islands, off the coast of Normandy, became the home of two dairy breeds that took the name of the islands where they originated. Purebred for almost six centuries, Jersey cows are one of the oldest dairy breeds. Guernsey cows are another prized breed from the Islands. In 960, the duke of Normandy sent monks to Guernsey Island to cultivate the land. They took dairy cows from Isigny and Brittany with them and developed the Guernsey breed from their herds. Jersey and Guernsey cows were noted for the quality of their milk, with its high butterfat content. Guernseys were particularly adapted to using the carotene in their feed, which gave their milk and butter its characteristic golden color. The mild weather and lush pastures of the islands permitted year-round grazing, and the cows were often milked in the fields. They led an idyllic life.

In nearby England, dairying slowly took hold as a profitable business. By the sixteenth century, England exported butter as well as bales of cloth, although it wasn't until the second half of the seventeenth century that commercial dairy production greatly increased. Meat was the most coveted food at the time, so the poor were the butter eaters. Even so, some villagers became known for their high-quality butter and cheese. By 1830, a semi-skilled worker in England, with a wife and two children, typically bought one pound each of butter and sugar a week.

In France, fat-based sauces replaced the vinegar-and-spice-laden mixtures of the Middle Ages. Cooks used a liaison of almond milk or egg yolks whipped with cider vinegar, a vestige of the past, but also invented a butter liaison to make white sauce. *Beurre blanc* was born. Butter and cream tamed the strong seasonings of prior times. Eventually, butter completely replaced the strong bases in French sauces, and with the advent of haute cuisine, these new liaisons became a distinguishing feature of the new way of cooking.

Cows arrived in the New World, along with pigs, goats, and sheep, on the second of Columbus's voyages. The cattle and pigs adapted to their new home better than the other animals; both were used primarily for meat. Yet cheese, bread, and butter were valued so highly that one group of early colonists carried all three to their new home in 1630. We can only imagine the condition of the latter two provisions upon arrival.

Although lard was a favorite fat for cooking and baking, the early Americans also used butter, especially to enrich the dough of their beloved pies. Fruit pies became a popular breakfast dish, the fillings altering with the seasons. There are recipes for apple pies in Martha Washington's *Booke of Cookery*, a seventeenth-century book that contains the accumulated recipes of several generations of an English family. One recipe gives general directions on how to make a short pastry, another for a sort of rapid puff pastry that is shaped into individual tarts and filled with cooked apples. Butter is the fat in both recipes. And the 1796 *American Cookery*, the first cookbook written by an American author, contains recipes for cookies made with butter.

Jerseys were first brought to the States in the 1850s. In 1874, when a good milk cow cost forty dollars, the Shafter family bought Jerseys and other breeds for their thirty dairy ranches in western Marin County, California. The gold rush of 1849 had created a need for food, especially dairy products. In San Francisco, salted butter was being imported from the East Coast or Chile. But the old fishlike smell of the East Coast butter and the lardlike texture of the Chilean import couldn't have been appetizing, even to hungry miners. By 1862, the dairy farms of Marin County, staffed by waves of immigrants from Switzerland and the Azores, became the major suppliers of butter to San Francisco. The rich grass of the Point Reyes Peninsula, saturated with fog, was a prime factor in the success of the dairy industry. One local called it "cow heaven." Another quipped, "The grass growing in the fields on Monday is the butter on the city tables the following Sunday." The dairymen milked the cows outdoors unless it was raining. Each milker had a string of twenty cows he milked by hand, a practice that didn't go out of vogue until the 1920s, with the advent of milking machines. A narrow-gauge railroad built in 1875 sped the butter to waiting dinner tables.

The world of dairy cows at the beginning of the twenty-first century is dramatically different from that of their predecessors. The most noticeable difference is in the cows themselves—black-and-white spotted Holstein-Friesians now dominate the picture. These large animals produce more milk than any other, twice as much as a Jersey. Their lives are more regulated, and they work harder—no slacking allowed! And they are not alone: On a small dairy farm, they may share their living space with one thousand other cows, some a few weeks old, others reaching the end of their milk-producing life. Larger operations have many more cows.

Crystal Cream and Butter Company, founded in 1901, then

bought by Carl and Gerda Hansen in 1913, is still housed on D Street in Sacramento, and is still owned by the Hansen family. They have contracts with sixty-six nearby farms that supply them with milk. One September day, Max Scheiber, a field manager for the company, agreed to take me on a tour of one of the contract farms a little south of Sacramento. He climbed out of his pickup in front of the creamery, ducking slightly so his large white straw hat would clear the truck. The rest of his attire fit his job description—a blue shirt, tips of cowboy boots poking from the bottom of his jeans. We got into his truck and headed for the freeway. He told me that his father had immigrated from Switzerland and started a dairy farm just north of Sacramento. "I used to milk cows when I came home from school," he recalled. After a dispute with his father, he left home and went to work at Crystal, where he has been for thirty years.

We pulled off the freeway and drove down a dirt road. The land was flat and bare, with mounds of drying manure and hills of grain fermenting under tarpaulins held in place by old tires, interspersed with blocks of corn ready for harvest. The dairy farmers grow the corn, not for produce markets, but to feed the cows. The temperature was in the eighties, and forest fires to the north fouled the air. We pulled into a driveway, passed a modest house with roses framing one side, and got out of the truck.

"We'll start with the new ones," Max said as he headed for a metal-roofed barn. Wooden stalls lined a central corridor. The room smelled of animals. As I followed Max, I stepped into a puddle of what I hoped was water. Small black-and-white calves peered at us from the enclosures. They all had ear tags, some with numbers, others with birthdates; the youngest was three weeks old. Unlike Sophie's calf, these newborns are removed from their mothers. For the first five days, they are fed antibody-rich colostrum, the first milk from the mother cow, then powdered milk for several weeks, before being moved to larger, semi-open pens, when they are introduced to mixed grain. One of these kindergarteners poked her muzzle through the pen's opening and sniffed my shirt. "Let her suck your fingers," said Max. I held out two fingers, and after first backing away, she sniffed them, then took them in her mouth and pulled hard with a pulsing motion. Her saliva was slimy and her tongue rough. Max said that the milking machines are more gentle. After a month, the cows graduate again to an open pen. As the heifers (cows who have never calved) come close to reproductive age, they are often moved to a separate place, especially if the farm has its own bull. Unplanned pregnancies are frowned upon.

When a heifer is eighteen months old, she is artificially insemi-nated, and not by just any bull. Lineage records, with high marks go-ing to heavy milk-producing offspring, are kept on all bulls. After the heifer calves, nine months later, the dairy farmer finally has a cow that helps pay her way by producing milk. She is milked for 305 days, dur-ing which time she is artificially inseminated. For the last two months of pregnancy, she is not milked. When she calves, the cycle starts anew.

Next we visited the milking cows. When they're not being led to the milking shed at twelve-hour intervals, they spend their days in large, roofed enclosures with long feed troughs on one side. Number 407 poked her head through metal bars for lunch. Being creatures of habit, the cows return to the same feeding stations. I picked up some of the feed. It was a mixture of grains, alfalfa, and silage, grain that un-dergoes anaerobic fermentation. The aroma was powerful, with an unpleasant acidic fermented smell that almost made me gag. "How can an animal who eats such strong-smelling stuff produce sweet milk?" I asked myself. But they seem to like it. When a cow's milk production starts to wane, after six or seven years, she "goes away"—there was that phrase again. "Where do they go?" I asked. "They go for food, but these aren't the steaks that you see at the Black Angus restaurants," explained Max. Some months later, I discovered that some of these spent dairy cows are used to make a special stew for the Feast of the Holy Ghost, an important cultural and religious event celebrated by Portuguese-Americans throughout California.

Because these cows weren't going to be milked for two more hours, Max took me to another farm, where milking was in progress. The cows stood patiently at the end of a large building. They had walked through a washer that sprayed their undersides and were "drip-drying" as they waited. Circular fans whirred, keeping flies out of the building. The surfaces were hard and noisy—concrete floors and clanking gates to keep the cows in the milking stanchions. A radio blared Mexican music, more for the workers than for the cows. There were two rows of milking stations and a depression down the middle of the floor between them. Two workers, wearing knee-high boots and baseball caps, attached the milking machines, which have sensors that detect the cow's empty udder, then automatically break the vacuum. The apparatus drops from the cow and is caught by a chain attached to a nearby bar. The worker need not be present.

The cows seemed to know what to do. As one group left, more moved into place. Each cow has a computer chip embedded in her ear that activates the delivery of individually formulated portions into a feeding trough at the head of the milking station.

The milk surged through pipes into large refrigerated stainless-steel tanks, their temperature monitored to stay below fifty degrees. Once a day, a driver hauling a stainless-steel tank truck arrives. He reads and resets the temperature graphs, measures the amount of milk in each tank by reading a metal rod suspended in the milk, somewhat like checking the oil of a car, records his findings, then attaches hoses to the tank and transfers the milk to his waiting truck, which he drives to the creamery.

Max drove us back to Sacramento, dropped me at the plant, and hurried off to visit a farm that was having refrigeration problems. Gene Gerwer, the quality-control manager, picked up as my tour guide. After the milk arrives at the plant, a centrifugal separator removes the cream. This machine can be adjusted to regulate the fat content of the cream. Here, the cream that's made into butter is 40 percent fat. Next it's pasteurized at 185 degrees for twenty-three seconds, then held at fifty degrees for eight hours, before going into the continuous churn. This step helps its texture. The metal sides of the churn obscure the inside workings of the machine, where giant beaters work the cream until it separates. The buttermilk drops into a vat; then augers force the fat solids through screens and impellers. Water is injected to rinse away traces of buttermilk, and if the butter is to be salted, a salt slurry is added. Then the soft finished butter drops into a large vat that looks like a giant bathtub, from which it's pumped to the packaging line. The butter room was as noisy as any other food-processing operation I've witnessed. That day, the workers were packaging salted pounds. The machines hissed and clanked as pliable butter was enclosed in paper, then packed in boxes, which rolled along chutes to waiting pallets. Gene handed me a wrapped pound. It almost squirted out of the paper; I had expected a harder block.

In California, there were no laws regulating the dairy industry until some culprits tried to sell margarine under the pretense that it was butter. In 1878, the California legislature enacted a law to prevent this deception, but there was no effort to back it up until the State Dairy Bureau was established in 1895. An inspection program was in place by 1905, and inspectors were hired at a wage of four dollars a day. As the years went by, legislators enacted more laws, narrowing the standards for milk and its products, and provisions were made to inspect each of them. These rules assured the public that it was buying a safe, stable product. The Pure Milk Law of 1915 required pasteurization. In California, by 1959, technological advances permitted the testing of milk for pesticide residue and antibiotics. Two years later, a law fixed the price paid to dairy farmers to milk's fat and solids-not-fat content, and this measure is still in effect today. I saw charts in the milk-storage room of the dairy I visited listing these measures for milk collected during the previous month.

In the last few years of the nineteenth century, butter was exhibited at various agricultural fairs, where it was judged on a scorecard based on a hundred-point scale. Flavor could earn a potential forty-five points; body, twenty-five points; color, fifteen points; salt, ten points; and package, five points. But no butter received a perfect hundred points, because the flavor component was never given a full score. This was the beginning of butter grading, and it evolved into the standards used today. Eventually, ninety-three became the top score; butter with a flavor score of thirty-eight is considered to be perfect. In California, it's called "First Quality." The USDA nomenclature is Grade AA.

Inspectors from the Department of Food and Agriculture inspect butter at the creameries once a month. Federal regulations require that butter have a minimum fat content of 80 percent. It is downgraded by points for tasting cooked, acidic, bitter, flat, malty, musty, or like feed, whey, or old cream. If the cows eat foods with a very pronounced flavor, such as turnips or garlic, they will be perceptible in the taste of the milk. Turnips caused quite a problem between 1912 and 1932 in Humboldt County, eventually forcing creamery operators to sign an agreement not to receive milk from dairies where turnips were planted, grown, or fed. Judy Garrett keeps her cow out of her apple orchard, because wild garlic grows there and taints Sophie's milk.

Defects in color and texture cost points too. If the body is crumbly, gummy, leaky, grainy, or sticky, the score goes down. The color must not be wavy, mottled, or streaked. However, the addition of color, in the form of annatto seed dissolved in vegetable oil, is permitted. The color of the butterfat itself derives from carotene in the feed, but because there is some difference in breeds' ability to maximize this uptake, and some seasonal variation if the cows graze for part of the year, most processors add color to make the butter uniform year-round, lest the public become uneasy. If salt is present, it must not be sharp or gritty.

A very small number of dairy farmers and creameries adhere to organic principles in producing milk and butter. The Straus family of western Marin County have been raising dairy cattle since 1941 on the same fog-shrouded hills overlooking Tomales Bay where the prolific farms of the nineteenth century once stood. Albert, the son, who lives in a house down the hill from the milking barn, switched to organic animal husbandry in 1992. I sat on a hay bale in a barn while he talked about the business, with a little prompting from his gregarious mother.

To produce organic butter, the cows must eat feed or graze in pastures that have not been treated with commercial fertilizers or pesticides. This led to a search for acceptable feed—alfalfa from Nevada, flax meal from Washington, soybeans from Iowa. But there are more prickly issues than what to feed the cows. Organic dairy farming precludes antibiotics and hormones to fight disease or aid reproduction. In a conventional dairy, if a cow gets mastitis, an infection of the udder, it is treated with antibiotics. That option doesn't exist here, unless the cow's life is in danger. Instead, Albert uses remedies that he learned from a veterinarian who subscribes to the principles of homeopathy, in which small quantities of herbs are administered to mimic a disease, inducing a response from the immune system. Albert has devised a way to administer these remedies under the skin. "It's hard to give pills to cows," he said.

Less stressed cows tend to be healthier, so at Straus the cows have room to move and graze when the fields are dry. They have individual bedding stalls—once padded with shredded government documents from the Mare Island Naval Station before it closed, now with rice hulls—and have the benefit of the cool coastal weather (cows would rather be chilly than too warm).

One hormone has been causing a furor since it was introduced in 1993, pitting governments against each other, enraging environmentalists, and fomenting public outcry. It is recombinant bovine somato-tropin (rBST), also known as recombinant bovine growth hormone (rBGH). Monsanto, the company that developed it, calls its version Posilac. Cows make bovine somatotropin in their pituitary glands to regulate milk production and growth. Scientists make recombinant bovine somatotropin in a laboratory, using bioengineering techniques, then sell it to dairy farmers, who inject it into cows on a regular basis to boost their milk production by as much as 15 percent. By 1998, farmers had used a hundred million doses of Posilac. By 1999, about 30 percent of the dairy cows in this country were receiving rBST.

On the surface, this sounds like better farming through the marvels of biochemistry. But it's not that simple. Before the Food and Drug Administration approved the drug, many tests on cows and lab rats scrutinized it to see whether it did indeed increase milk production, whether it was safe for the cows, and whether residues of the drug, along with another growth substance that it stimulates the cows to produce (IGF-1), were present in the treated cows' milk. And whether the milk was safe for humans. In November 1993, the FDA approved Posilac.

Some people were not happy, for rBST use had been shown to increase the incidence of mastitis in treated cows (an FDA-required package insert says so) and thus to increase the use of antibiotics to combat the infection. The overuse of antibiotics may in turn contribute to increased antibiotic resistance in bacteria, rendering penicillin, once the drug of choice for mastitis, ineffective. So, even though milk is routinely tested for penicillin residues and discarded if they are found, traces of other antibiotics could go undetected. Moreover, rBST can cause decreased pregnancy rates and other reproductive complications, and its use may reduce the useful life span of the cows; they may have to "go away" after three years instead of six.

Although the FDA unequivocally states that milk from rBST-treated cows is safe for humans, a few scientists have questioned the methodology of some of the research and, citing other studies, have concluded that IGF-1 can survive digestion and shows up in greater concentration in the milk of treated cows, which may cause intestinal maladies in the consumer. Others call for more research into uncharted areas, such as a possible relationship between rBST and bovine spongiform encephalopathy, mad-cow disease.

Recently, the European Commission raised questions about the safety of rBST in U.S. imports; the FDA rebuffed the inquiry. In January 1999, Health Canada, an agency similar to our FDA, refused to accept Posilac, citing animal safety issues.

To complicate matters more, rBST isn't detectable in milk; the consumer doesn't know what she's getting. For people concerned about their food's origins, this isn't acceptable. Max Scheiber told me that Crystal had received many calls asking if the milk they sold contained rBST, and that the creamery asked its farmers not to use the drug. Some milk products now carry labeling stating that they are rBST-free.

❧

In France, use of rBST is not an issue; the European Union has not approved its use. Aside from the absence of the hormone, what makes French butter so prized by many chefs and connoisseurs? In fact, the quality of French butter is so prized that some specially produced butters of a given provenance that meet certain standards are given an *appellation d'origine contrôlée* (*AOC*), like wine. The cream used to make butter classified as *AOC* must come from cows raised in a designated area surrounding the creameries; it must have undergone a slow maturation of at least twelve hours; it cannot contain colorants or preservatives; and it must be approved by a tasting panel, who evaluate the aroma, texture, and taste. If the panel isn't satisfied with the quality of the butter, the creamery receives a warning; after three warnings, it loses its *AOC* status.

A winter trip to France provided an opportunity to visit this land of dairy enchantment. The two most celebrated *AOC* butter-producing areas are to the west of Paris, one in the fertile lowlands not far from the Atlantic Coast, the other along wind-swept plains near the English Channel, areas whose weather permits grazing most of the year. The proximity to the ocean and the tangle of rivers running through both regions make the soil extremely fertile. The grasses that the cows eat contain healthy trace minerals and are high in carotenes, which give the butter a good color. In addition, the quality of the pastures translates into a butter high in oleic acid, which lends it plasticity and unctuousness.

My husband and I left Paris on the true first day of the new millennium and headed for the town of Niort, near the creameries of the Charentes-Poitou. The town lies forty miles from the Atlantic Ocean, where salt harvesters collect precious *fleur de sel*, and the renowned Cognac region is not far to the south. The Sèvre Niortaise River flanks one edge of the town. This is the same town where nuns once had a flourishing industry candying angelica. The autoroute was not as crowded as we expected; the traffic seemed to be flowing toward Paris, not away. Niort was a sleepy town when we arrived close to 6 p.m. Most stores and restaurants were closed for the holiday. A formidable dungeon from the Middle Ages stood facing the river just down the street from our hotel. Next to it was the market place, a large nineteenth-century structure with an elaborate iron-and-glass façade.

The next morning, we picked up our guide, who would take us to a small creamery in a nearby village. Madame Guérin is a small, bubbly woman with blond hair and well-cared-for porcelain skin who retired about five years ago, when she sold her cheese shop in town. She gave directions while talking nonstop. I had a hard time understanding her and was grateful that my husband, Sidney, was with me, since his French is better than mine. We drove on two-lane country roads with roundabouts for intersections. The route was lined with fallow fields of dark earth, some sporting stubble of some crop—corn, perhaps? The farther we got into the country, the less sure Madame was of the route, "*À droit ici—non, à la prochaine.*" But eventually she pointed to a low white building near a T in the road, and we pulled into the parking lot.

Monsieur Lieby, the director of the creamery, casually dressed and seated behind a desk in a small office, greeted us. There was no receptionist. He stood and explained the operation for more than an hour, excusing himself to answer the phone when it rang. La Fontaine des Veuves, a cooperative creamery, was established in 1904, and there is a legend connected to its name. During the Hundred Years' War, which spanned the fourteenth and fifteenth centuries, six men accused of instigating a revolt were driven from their village by the English mayor. They were found dead not far away. When the constable of Guesclin heard about the deaths, he arrived with his army and took the town from the English. Triumphant, he continued to a nearby château, also occupied by the English. A sad sight greeted him: The widows of the six dead men had also been slain. Their bodies lay next to a small spring, which became known as La Fontaine des Veuves (the Widows' Spring). Centuries later, when the creamery was erected nearby, it took the same name.

Today, twenty-three dairy farmers belong to the cooperative. With a production of 3.8 million liters of milk a year, it is the smallest in the region of Charentes-Poitou. Only six people work at the creamery, making butter, crème fraîche, and goat cheese. But this modest enterprise has been discovered by the likes of Alain Ducasse and Joël Robuchon, who buy butter here.

After a discourse on the history and facts of the company, Monsieur Lieby slid open a door a few feet from his desk, and we stepped into the production room. We carefully walked across a wet tile floor (creameries all seem to have wet floors, from the frequent hosing of equipment). Three people, dressed in white tops and trousers with knee-high white boots, were at work.

Trucks deliver milk into large tanks just inside the building. The milk is heated, then run through a separator, which removes the cream; the fat-free milk is transported away in tanker trucks for use elsewhere. Eighty percent of the cream is pasteurized; the rest is made into butter without this treatment. The butter maker adds a dose of lactic ferment to the cream and lets it sit until it develops the slightly sharp edge that is the hallmark of cultured butter. When it's ready, the cream is pumped into the steel churns, or *barattes*, which rotate for three hours, working their magic to transform cream into solid butter. This is the traditional way to make butter. The only innovation is stainless steel; before it was available, the churns were made from wood. (Wood-churn production persists at Échiré, another noted creamery in the region.)

Another tradition is kept alive here: Some of the butter is shaped by hand in wooden molds. We saw a woman deftly slap a chunk of cool but pliable butter into a mold, scrape off the excess, then unhinge the apparatus, revealing a half-pound of butter with a scalloped edge and a flower imprint on the top. This batch of butter was from raw cream without salt added, which according to our guide has a taste "*plus fine*"—more refined, a term he also used to describe butter made in a vat churn instead of a continuous churn. The taste is also affected by what the cows eat. During the spring and summer months, when they are in the pasture, the butter has a richer taste and a deeper color. In the winter, when grain supplements their feed, the taste is more bland, the color whiter, and the texture more crumbly. Good butter also depends on the process, he explained. Temperatures, amount of ferment, ripening time, speed, and length of time in the churn are all parameters that the butter maker must know and respect.

The creamery also makes salted butter, added either during the churning process or, if *grains de sel* (the large crystals from the nearby sea) are used, at the end. The latter practice is a recent one, introducing a grittiness that once would have been considered a fault. Sea salt was harvested off the coast of Charente and southern Brittany for centuries, until less expensive commercial salt became widely available after World War II, but recently French and American chefs have rediscovered this unadulterated gift of the sea and are embracing it with a passion. The butter makers took note. Now a piece of butter embedded with the precious salt can be melted on hot asparagus or tossed with roasted potatoes, providing a burst of texture and a clean, salty taste.

The butter here, like that made elsewhere in France, has a minimum fat content of 82 percent unless it is salted, in which case fat content can be slightly lower. The trend among both artisanal and larger producers in the United States to push the butterfat content higher—to 84 percent, even 86 percent—has not been taken up by the French. To them, taste remains of prime importance. The maximum water content allowed is 16 percent. And the members of the Fontaine des Veuves cooperative cannot give hormones or antibiotics to their cows, nor may feed contain genetically engineered substances. The director looked puzzled when I asked about rBST, as if it was the first time he had heard the term.

As we left the production room, we passed foil wrapped cubes of butter of different sizes, and squat wooden paper-lined baskets holding butter. Our host slipped several samples into a plastic sack and handed it to us. Then we returned to the car and retraced our route to Niort. Sidney remembered the way, so Madame could enjoy the drive.

@

The next day, we visited another cooperative creamery, in Celles-sur-Belle, closer to Niort. The marshes that hold water between Niort and the sea were swelling visibly from the rain. A cold rain greeted us as we stepped out of the car. Judging from the size and number of the buildings, I surmised that this was a larger operation than La Fontaine des Veuves.

A rather stern-looking woman seated behind a counter directed us upstairs to the office of Monsieur Cantet, the director. We sat opposite his desk while he told us about the creamery.

Sèvre & Belle is in the Charentes-Poitou *AOC* region. People started raising cows in the region after phylloxera destroyed the grapevines in the middle of the nineteenth century. The Arabs had introduced goats a thousand years before. For a long time, they were considered a poor man's cow and neglected, but as land use switched from grape growing to dairy farming, people used the goats' rich milk to make cheese. Sèvre & Belle was founded in 1893, and is one of the few remaining creameries that make a small quantity of butter from goat's milk; it was this curiosity that had enticed me to arrange a visit. I had never tasted goat butter, but if it tasted anything like goat cheese, I knew I had to try it.

Monsieur Cantet provided details of the churning process that filled out what we'd gleaned the day before. After the cultured cream is pumped into the *barattes*, it is churned at high speed for one hour. By that time, fat globules have started to form. The butter maker drains the liquid buttermilk from the churn, and the butter is washed twice in clear water to be certain that all the buttermilk is removed. Then the butter is churned until it is a solid mass.

Monsieur Cantet handed us gauzy jackets and hairnets. The wind whipped rain around us as we walked from one building to the next. We entered a room twice the size of the one at La Fontaine. Several of the now-familiar vat churns were rotating. Just opposite them, workers fed butter into packing machines. Another apparatus at the end of the room caught my eye. It was a continuous churn, smaller than the one I had seen in California. The inside chamber was exposed, unlike the one at home, so I got a better picture of how it works. Cream enters from a tube at one end. Inside, it is whirled at high speed, emerging from the other end as finished butter in a few minutes instead of two hours. The creamery sells this butter to bakeries and pastry shops at a lower price. It is not designated *AOC*.

Exiting from the building, we walked through a small room. When Monsieur Cantet opened the door, a rush of goat aroma engulfed me. We entered a room with equipment like that in the room we had just left, only scaled down. Our guide asked me not to take photos and hurried us through without comment. Later, when I commented that I hadn't thought it was possible to make butter from goat's milk because it came out of the animal in a homogenized state, Monsieur Cantet answered, "It can be separated, but it is difficult," and mumbled something about using slower centrifugal speed. Our host was cordial, but he wasn't going to reveal any trade secrets.

As we walked down a narrow corridor, Monsieur Cantet suddenly stopped and opened a door. A rush of welcome warm air hit my face. The room contained salt dryers, which extract moisture from the wet *grains de sel* before they go into the butter.

In a reception room in another building, which had been the former director's residence, stood a table set with packages of all the creamery's products. Plates held slices of bread spread thickly with butters and cheeses. First we sampled the butter from cow's milk. It was unctuous and almost nutty. Then Monsieur Cantet offered another plate. It was the goat butter. I had been dreaming about this moment for months. An expectation of the taste had formulated in my mind—the fresh earthiness of young goat cheese, but not as dry, fuller on the tongue. I picked up a piece of baguette covered with a thick layer of the butter and sank my teeth into it. My hopes of a new taste discovery were dashed. It had very little flavor, and the fat content seemed to explode all at once in my mouth. Even worse, it lacked even a hint of goatiness. What a disappointment!

Monsieur Cantet disappeared momentarily into the next room and returned with a bottle of Pineau de Charentes, the local fortified apéritif wine. He poured each of us a glass as we moved on to the cheeses, then offered more when that was gone. Given the hour (10:30 a.m.), we declined. In a show of French hospitality, he sent us on our way with a bag bulging with cheeses, butter, and a bottle of Pineau.

☙

Our next stop was in Normandy, noted for its butter and cream so thick that a spoon stands up in it. It is also noted for its caramels, made from the superior milk and cream of the region of Isigny. André Galliot began the first caramel-making operation there in 1932, and others soon followed. The formula wasn't complicated, although a perfect outcome—a soft, chewy consistency—required precise cooking. The ingredients weren't numerous—sugar, glucose, dextrose, and milk. It was the milk that made the difference. With a fat content of 26 percent, it was closer to cream. A slow cooking to 248 degrees allowed the distinct flavor, which came from the browning of milk proteins and milk sugars, to develop. Caramels are still made in the region and are prized beyond the borders of France.

We drove all day in the rain, then spent the night in Bayeux, home of the intricate tapestry that tells the story of the Battle of Hastings in 1066.

The next day, we set out along the coast to Isigny, the sky still almost dark even though it was 9:30 a.m. The cooperative of Isigny–Sainte-Mère is just outside the town. The town is small, but the cooperative is huge, encompassing dairy farms stretching north into the Cotentin Peninsula, past the World War II battle site of Sainte-Mère Église, and east toward the Pays d'Auge, more than a thousand farms in all.

Stainless-steel tanks the size of grain silos stood guard over the adjacent buildings, as if the chain-link fence surrounding the entire complex were inadequate. Across the road was a three-story modern office building. As we approached, automatic doors swung open, revealing a woman behind a large desk answering phone calls. "*Bonjour, Isigny–Sainte-Mère, ne quittez pas,*" she rattled, then repeated the same message to another caller. She seemed to be the telecommunications master for the whole building, and probably for the buildings across the street as well. When the phones quieted for a second, she looked at us. Sidney introduced us and gave her the name of the person we were to meet. She flipped another switch and announced our arrival into her headset.

Monsieur Courtois greeted us and suggested that we first watch a video about the company. It gave us basic facts, but the real stars in the film were not the machinery, or the Camemberts ripening in rows, but the cows. They got more airtime than anything else in the short film. They were all Normande cows. (Some of the farmers have Holstein-Friesians, but they aren't as photogenic.) The Normande breed was introduced to northern France by Viking conquerors in the ninth and tenth centuries. Initially, they were dual-purpose animals, milked and used for meat. Many were killed during the fighting of World War II, but their numbers have been replenished. Normande cows are large white animals with blotches of brown and black randomly distributed through their coats. They look like lots of other cows, but with one big difference—they all have big circles of dark brown around their eyes, like smudged mascara. The circles make their eyes look bigger, more soulful. They reminded me of panda bears.

The soundtrack peppered us with facts: Isigny–Sainte-Mère has the only *AOC* cream in all of France. The salt content of the butter is 2 percent. Camembert is dried for two weeks in 90-percent humidity, then it's wrapped and aged for three to four weeks. A Holstein-Friesian cow gives forty liters of milk a day. The cows are fed natural vegetable matter. The master butter maker tastes the butter every day. The factory has been there since 1930. In 1980, two cooperatives merged. In 1991, they built a factory in Japan to make Camembert. They collect two hundred million liters of milk a year. There are 525 employees. They make four million tons of butter a year.

Our tour of the factory traced the same steps as at the other creameries, only on a much larger scale. The size and sophistication of the equipment was staggering. As we walked through a room where boilers generate steam for the factory, I noticed a very large tank with fish swimming lazily in the water, an odd sight juxtaposed with the machinery. It had a curious feature. Water dripped into it from a pipe near the top, and water also dripped out the bottom into a drain. I was puzzled by the tank in such an unlikely setting. Monsieur Courtois explained that the fish were a test for the water. If it contains injurious substances, the fish will react to them first, like canaries in a coal mine.

Even in this highly automated plant, however, one function still needed a hands-on approach. At the end of one room, women took rounds of aged Camembert from wooden boxes, patted them between their hands to determine the degree of ripeness, then replaced them. Different customers want them at different stages of ripeness, so every cheese is tested—and human hands make the final call.

We left bearing more gifts and added them to our stash in the trunk of the car. It was the only time during the trip that I was grateful for the cold weather.

☙

My visits to the French creameries had not completely explained the mystique of French butter. Holstein-Friesian cows are as plentiful at home as abroad. Most of the animals in France spend some time in pasture, but so do some dairy cows in the United States. Cream is separated from milk in the same way. The minimum 82-percent French butterfat content exceeds the United States' 80-percent minimum, although some American butters are even richer. The best French butter is made from cream that has been allowed to mature, although some of the butter in the States is made from matured cream too. The most prized French butter is made in individual churns over a period of hours, not by the speedy continuous churning method. Some of the French butter is made from milk that has not been pasteurized.

And if the butter is salted, sea salt, either fine-grained or coarse, is used. In this country, only a very few small producers use vat churns, and even fewer use raw cream and sea salt.

I wanted to taste and compare the butters when we returned to Paris, and because some food-loving friends were in Paris at the same time, I hoped they could join us. But we ran out of time. So I carefully wrapped my golden nuggets in plastic bags, packed them in a small suitcase surrounded with clothes, and checked them (it would be cooler in the belly of the plane, I surmised) for the long trek back to California.

At home, I called friends and colleagues whose taste buds I trust and invited them to a butter tasting. I included some American butters that were noteworthy for their high fat content, their churning method, or their flavor. I cut pieces of butter and arranged them on plates, hurrying to finish so I could hide the wrappers before the tasters arrived. I meant this to be a blind tasting. The door bell buzzed just as I slid the last piece of butter onto a plate.

There were ten samples, five without salt and five with. Baguette slices were available, but most of us tasted the butters alone at first. The group started out serious and intent, tasting and scribbling notes. When each of us had made the round of our plates, we talked about the butters; then I "opened the envelope" and handed around sheets that matched names to the squares on the plates. Exclamations of surprise and affirmation went around the table. Our reactions dutifully recorded (I copied everyone's notes to analyze the next day), we brought out some protein to go with the butter. Plates of cured meats and smoked fish, more bread, vegetable salads with palate-cleansing vinaigrette, and bottles of wine passed hand to hand. We ended the evening a few hours later swirling glasses of Calvados and Vieux Prune, souvenirs of the trip.

No one butter was the clear winner. However, the French butters, all made in vat churns, and especially those made from unpasteurized cream, received the most favorable comments—*rich, ripe, nutty, cheesy, tastes of cream, long finish, floral, full-bodied, lactose finish, full of flavor.* Most of the American butters, even those made by the same methods and with higher butterfat than required by USDA standards, didn't have the same deep, satisfying flavor. Maybe the notion of *terroir* holds true for butter, just as it does for wine. And maybe the careful treatment of the cream, from maturation through churning, produces a different result. Or maybe practice makes perfect. As a country, we're still new at butter making. (In the interest of fairness, I should mention that one taster gave high marks to the American butters, and a butter tasting held by the *San Francisco Chronicle* food staff named a butter from Oregon with a butterfat content just above 82 percent as the favorite in a blind tasting that included imported butter.)

Unfortunately, some of the butters from my tasting, certainly those made from unpasteurized cream, aren't available here. And those that are imported are often shipped with cheese from the same region, whose stronger taste may infiltrate the more delicate butter.

෧

After seeing so much butter making, I decided to try my hand at the craft. Simple butter churns still exist, from glass jars fitted with wooden paddles to larger wooden tubs. Even shaking cream in a jar will eventually produce butter. When I approached the task in my kitchen, however, I decided to take a tip from Judy Garrett and let electricity do the work.

Cream is an emulsion of fat particles in liquid; the butter maker wants to separate the fat particles from the liquid so that they coalesce. Agitating the cream encourages the process and a proper temperature optimizes it. Since my home experiment was small in the world of butter making, I looked to the practices of the small manufacturers I had visited in France for guidance. At La Fontaine des Veuves, the churning temperature is fifty-five to sixty-four degrees, and at Sèvre & Belle they churn fast for one hour, wash, then churn slowly for two hours. I decided to let the cream come to sixty degrees, then mix it in a heavy-duty mixer.

The first cream was from a large California supplier. I let two cups warm to sixty degrees, then put it in the mixer bowl. Thinking that the paddle was more like an old-fashioned churn, I started with it. After mixing for a minute or two, I decided that the whisk would be better, so I switched. The cream got thicker and stiffer. Having whipped so much cream in my time, I almost instinctively turned off the mixer as it started to overwhip. It started to look chunky instead of smooth and fluffy; then, suddenly, the cream separated into its two components. Now chunks of butter were swimming in an opaque liquid. I dumped the contents into a sieve, saving the whey. Then I put the butter back in the bowl, added cold tap water, and sloshed it around. I poured it into the sieve again, then turned the butter out on a wooden work counter. I mashed and pushed it with a dough scraper; a fair amount of water came out, which I mopped up with paper towels. Some water still seemed to remain, so I put the butter back in the mixing bowl, thinking that beating it with the paddle might separate the liquid more, but my logic was backward. Instead of separating the liquid, the beating incorporated it. The yield was one cup of whey and one cup of butter—perhaps an inflated proportion of butter, because of the beating at the end. But the formula from La Fontaine des Veuves specifies that twenty liters of milk equals two liters of cream, which produces one kilo of butter, so the yield from my first try seems to be proportionate.

The next attempt was with cream from a small northern-California dairy. When I tried to pour it from the bottle, it wouldn't come out. Uh-oh, might be sour, I thought, but when I tasted a dab, it was sound. A quick mix with a table knife persuaded it to pour. Again, I let two cups come to sixty degrees. Using the whip seemed to be the best strategy, but I wanted to replicate the method, so I did the same thing, paddle first, then whisk. This butter was more yellow (different feed for the cows?), and I didn't get as much—only three-quarters of a cup, and one cup of whey—probably because I was more careful to work out all the liquid.

Both wheys tasted sweet, not like commercial buttermilk at all. And both butters tasted sweet, lacking the tang present in cultured butters. Their staying power was impressive. My husband found one hidden in the back of the refrigerator almost two months after it was made, and it still tasted fresh.

There is real butter, and there is fake butter, and they are not the same. Just as the French demonstrated their inventive prowess by producing sugar from beets during the English blockade in the early 1800s, they created another staple during the Franco-Prussian War. This time it was a replacement for butter, when the real thing was scarce. Spurred on by a challenge from Napoleon III in 1869, Hippolyte Mège-Mouriès came up with a cheaper substitute. Relying on shaky biological knowledge of how a cow produced something that became butter, he mixed the oil from beef fat (oleo) with skimmed milk and water, throwing in a strip of cow udder for good measure. His invention was surprisingly like the *véritable* item. He called it margarine, after the Greek word for "pearl," a name that reflected its glossy appearance. People liked the price, and some may have liked the taste. The new product became popular.

Within five years, margarine was introduced into the United States, and by 1881 it was being made in New York City. By the beginning of the 1890s, vegetable oils replaced some of the animal fat, making the taste more palatable.

About the same time that Monsieur Mège-Mouriès was working in France, Procter and Gamble, then a manufacturer of soap and candles, expanded their products to include refined lard, still a favorite American cooking and baking fat. In 1911, the company introduced Crisco, the first solid all-vegetable oil that didn't need refrigeration. It was made from cottonseed oil, which was converted from a liquid to a solid state by a process of hydrogenation worked out by German and French chemists in 1905. With the aid of a nickel catalyst, the carbon atoms in the liquid oil take on hydrogen atoms, which change some of the unsaturated fatty acids to saturated ones. Here was a product that shared the characteristics of margarines and animal fats—it could be spread on toast like butter, mixed into pie dough, even baked into cookies. It was particularly appealing to the Jewish community, because it didn't contain animal or dairy products. Procter and Gamble even published a Jewish cookbook that highlighted Crisco.

Margarine manufacturers eventually began using vegetable oils exclusively, and each decade had its favorite: coconut oil during the teens, cottonseed in the thirties, soy in the fifties. They tried to make their products look and taste like butter, adding coloring and flavoring, but butter sales outnumbered margarine until 1957. Some diehards insisted on baking with butter even after Procter and Gamble introduced butter-flavored Crisco in an effort to win over the recalcitrant.

When worries about saturated fat and its harmful health effects became primary topics of research and conversation, many Americans switched to margarine, because its saturated-fat content was much lower than butter's. To make it even lower, "lite" margarines appeared—not solids, but spreads that were lightened by beating in air or adding water. Woe to the baker who tried to use them, though. Their diminished fat content changed the chemistry, resulting in disappointing outcomes. (Whipped butter can also have disastrous baking results, for the same reason.)

Gradually, questions arose about the safety of hydrogenated oils. Maybe the miraculous process that changed them from liquid to solid came at a price. Hydrogenation changes the very nature of the fats by altering their form. The result is trans-fatty acids, an artificial version of fats that appear naturally in animal and dairy products. Scientists ran studies to measure the effect of different forms of fat on blood lipid levels. By 1990, the results implicated the manufactured fats as sharing saturated animal fats' ill-effect on blood cholesterol levels. The American Heart Association changed its guidelines to include trans-fatty acids in the saturated-fat category, and to suggest limiting their intake to 10 percent of ingested calories.

Margarine makers are fighting back. Now a number of spreads are made without trans-fatty acids, using emulsifiers to thicken them instead of hydrogenation. (Many commercial manufacturers of cookies, cakes, and crackers still use hydrogenated oils, however.) McNeil Consumer Healthcare, the makers of Benecol, are adding to their spread a plant stanol ester derived from pine fiber, which interrupts the absorption of cholesterol from the small intestine, thereby lowering blood lipid levels. Of course, one must use their product instead of, not in addition to, other spreads with saturated fats. As for the taste, the restaurant critic William Grimes, writing in the *New York Times* in December 1999, said it "exhibits absolutely no taste characteristics other than salt."

Procter and Gamble has come up with the most innovative approach yet—not a functional food that by virtue of one addition or another is healthier, but a completely synthetic one. Olestra is not a fat at all, but an unwieldy synthesis of sucrose and fatty acids. It has the "mouth feel" of fat, and it tastes like fat, but it is not absorbed by the body at all, not one drop. Alexandre Dumas, who prefaced his *Dictionary of Cuisine* with the phrase "man does not live on what he eats, but on what he digests," surely would have been appalled by this new substance.

Theoretically, a person could eat this fat to satiety, even beyond, without ill-effect. However, the human intestines are befuddled by the onslaught of Olestra's monstrous molecules. Unable to absorb them, they hurry them through, sometimes faster than the ingestor might like.

So far, Olestra is being used only in a few clearly labeled packaged foods—potato chips, for example. Fortunately, no Olestra "butter" is available, so we don't have to contemplate its use in baking.

Do we really need fat? A small amount is needed to transport the fat-soluble vitamins A, D, E, and K, and to provide linoleic acid, an essential fatty acid that we can't make. But Western diets bulge with fat; we eat too much of it—even more reason to choose judiciously which fats to consume, and save our butter consumption for desserts whose *raison d'être* demands it.

The quintessential pastry whose *raison d'être* demands butter is puff pastry. Its many names in different languages make its origins somewhat less straightforward. Both the Italian *pasta sfoglia* and the French *pâte feuilletée* mean "leafed pastry." The Greeks and Arabs made leafed pastry early on, using paper-thin sheets of phyllo dough. It may have been the pastry chefs in the courts of the dukes of Tuscany in the fifteenth century who realized that sandwiched layers of butter and dough, folded and rolled many times, would puff up in the heat of an oven. If so, we can thank them profusely for this ingenious discovery.

We can also thank those who wrote down the recipe. *The Good Huswifes Jewell, Part I*, written by Dawson in 1586, gives instructions for making a dough dotted with butter, folded, and rolled five or six times. Although the dough contains eggs, the process is the same as for making puff pastry. La Varenne gives instructions for puff pastry in *Pâtissier François*, published in 1651. Both *Martha Washington's Booke of Cookery* (seventeenth-century) and Richard Briggs's *The New Art of Cookery* (eighteenth-century) include puff pastry. The proportions are the same as those used today: equal parts of butter and flour by weight, with salt and water.

How best to approach the construction of a dough that allows a baker to conjure an undistinguished wad into a tower of buttery crispness? Books and cookware catalogues are full of hints and gadgets to bolster the confidence of hesitant bakers. Rolling pins, for example, come in tight-grained wood or marble. The marble is heavy and cool, generally several degrees cooler than the ambient temperature, which in theory keeps the butter in the dough from melting, especially at the hands of a slow-working novice or in a warm kitchen. Cool work surfaces made of granite or marble offer the same protection. Long ago, when I was a fledgling with doughs, my husband gave me a marble square for Christmas. We lugged it to Europe for a three-year sojourn in Brussels, during which I went to Paris to study at the La Varenne cooking school. One of the staff touted a restaurant where a young chef made innovative, startlingly good food, and I spent an evening watching him cook. He used puff pastry for both savory dishes and desserts. His kitchen was minuscule and hot from a wood-burning stove, so he rolled the puff pastry in the courtyard on an old table, and it was perfect. When I learned to make this delicate dough, I used my marble slab and a wooden rolling pin. Much later, when I had a bakery, I rolled all manner of doughs on a wooden or stainless-steel table; the marble-topped table was reserved for making chocolates. Practice and familiarity make a difference; fancy equipment isn't always needed.

But good butter is—an inferior product will mar the pastry's beauty. A high water content makes the butter fuse with the dough instead of maintaining the integrity of its layers. And the rancidity of age or other off flavors will ruin the pastry's delicate taste.

The multilayered dough itself is a stepping-stone to other creations. One with a impressive history is a *galette des Rois*. Throughout many European countries, there are special pastries used to celebrate the Epiphany, January 6, when the three kings visited the infant Jesus. All have a prize baked into them, ranging from something as simple as a dried bean to an elaborate porcelain figurine. The makeup of the cakes vary: in Friuli, a yeasted cornmeal bread fragrant with fennel and anise seeds; in Spain, a ring perfumed with rum and orange-flower water and flavored with preserved fruit; in England, a cake studded with raisins and other dried fruit; in Germany, a brioche sprinkled with almonds; in Portugal, also a cake from brioche dough. Even New Orleans has a "king's cake." In France, the composition of the cake runs the gamut. In the north, it is a dessert of puff pastry filled with an almond cream. *Pâtissiers* in the Sologne and Limousin, regions noted for their cherries, add them to the filling. In the south, the structure of the cake changes from puff pastry to a yeast-risen brioche. One bakery business in France, with twenty-nine locations throughout the country, bakes thirty-five to forty-five thousand of these special cakes around the time of the Epiphany. But no matter the venue, all contain a trinket—a *fève*—baked into the dough.

The notion of a baked good containing a prize has a long history that predates Christianity. Beans had great symbolic power—sacred, possessing supernatural powers for the Egyptians; representing continuity for the Romans. During the Roman Saturnalia, slaves were permitted to eat with their masters. Gambling was allowed too, and dice were thrown to choose a "king." The Christians eventually combined these pagan rituals into Epiphany celebrations. The person who receives the piece of pastry containing the "bean" becomes king or queen for the day. The wish that the winner is afforded stems from the bean's believed power to predict the future.

There is another explanation for this custom. During the Middle Ages, the monks of Besançon designated their leader each year on the eve of the Epiphany by hiding a piece of silver in a loaf of bread. The general populace took up the custom, replacing the silver with a bean, symbol of life and fertility. Eventually, the bread was replaced by cake, just as the bean evolved into images of the infant Jesus, which in turn were replaced by more elaborate representations.

The first porcelain figures were made in 1870. Now the large French *pâtisseries* commission special *fèves* for their *galettes*, some based more on popular culture (*The Lion King*, for example) than on religion. Perhaps the custom is reverting to its pagan roots.

Not content just to be the backbone for the *galette des Rois*, a pastry that is steeped in ancient history, puff pastry also offers its buttery crunch to a famous upside-down cake, the *tarte Tatin*. As is the case with other famous French foods, this pastry has a legend describing its birth. The Tatin sisters, Stéphanie and Caroline, ran the Hôtel Tatin in Lamotte-Beuvron, a small town south of Orléans. One evening in 1898, customers filled the dining room. In her haste to replenish the supply of desserts, Stéphanie put a pan of apples into the oven, failing to notice that there was no crust underneath. To correct her mistake, she hastily put the crust on top, then turned it out, apple side up, onto a plate after it had finished baking. *Voilà, la tarte Tatin*.

Apples, and sometimes pears, were the first fruits, but in more recent times, innovative (some might say disrespectful) bakers have used others. (Quinces and apricots are favorites of mine.) Whatever the whim of the baker, the fruit must be caramelized and the pastry crisp for this dessert to reach its zenith.

❦

Butter has been with us for millennia, but it is derived from something we can't make. This fundamental truth reflects the complex relationship that we have with dairy cows in the context of their domestication. We interfere in their reproductive process by removing their offspring, but continue to avail ourselves of their milk. We have created in them a dependency on humans by thrusting ourselves into their life cycles. Their demands are few—adequate water and feed, a decent place to live. Continuous milk production becomes their life purpose, and they willingly take on the role. We depend on them too, for without them milk and butter would disappear. The desserts that depend on butter for their special taste and texture would fail. Shortbreads and other butter-infused doughs would sag if other fats were used; they would become impostors. They demand the stand-up-and-notice-me taste that only butter can give. Thank you, cows.

Puff Pastry

Many people approach the task of making puff pastry with great trepidation. How can I allay their fears? When I watched a young French chef make this pastry in the courtyard outside his cramped kitchen in 90°F heat, the butter didn't melt, and in the oven, the pastry rose beyond expectation. In a cool kitchen, anyone can succeed.

Puff pastry rises in the oven because of its unique construction—thin sheets of dough separated by thin sheets of butter. This is accomplished by rolling the dough into a rectangle, then folding it onto itself, not once, but six times. (Each rolling and folding is called a turn.) With each turn, the layers become thinner and more numerous, resulting in 729 layers of butter sandwiched between 730 layers of dough when the pastry is ready for its final shaping. In the oven, air trapped between the layers, and steam formed from the moisture in the dough, push the layers apart and make the dough rise dramatically.

Although the dough needs some rest periods, the actual time spent manipulating it is only about 30 minutes from start to finish. Then it will rest in the refrigerator or freezer until its creator wants a dessert that only its multitudinous layers can provide.

Use a butter whose taste you like, provided it contains at least 82 percent butterfat.

ABOUT 2½ POUNDS OF DOUGH—ENOUGH FOR 1 *GALETTE DES ROIS* OR 2 *TARTES TATIN*, PLUS LEFTOVER DOUGH FOR *PALMIERS*

> *3¼ cups (1 pound) unbleached all-purpose flour*
> *1½ teaspoons fine sea salt*
> *1 pound unsalted butter, refrigerator temperature, divided into*
>   *4 ounces and 12 ounces*
> *1 tablespoon lemon juice*
> *1 cup (8 ounces) cold water*

Mix the flour and salt together in a medium bowl. Cut ¼ pound of the butter into ½-inch pieces. Put them in the bowl, and, using your fingertips or a pastry cutter, rub the butter and flour together. The butter will break into smaller pieces, each coated with flour. Continue until the mixture looks like a coarse meal.

Put the lemon juice in the water. Pour the water into the bowl, a little at a time, mixing with your other hand. Turn the resulting dough onto a lightly floured work surface, and knead it a few times, until all the dough is gathered into a ball. It will still look rough. Flatten it into a disk about ½ inch thick, enclose it in plastic wrap, and refrigerate it for 30 to 60 minutes.

Remove the dough from the refrigerator and put it on a lightly floured work surface. Roll it into a 13-inch disk, leaving a center area about 6 inches in diameter thicker and thinning the periphery, so that it has a shape like a hat lying on a table.

Take the remaining ¾ pound of butter from the refrigerator and, on a lightly floured work surface, beat it with a rolling pin into a disk about the same diameter and thickness as the fat center of the dough. Put the butter in the middle of the dough, and fold the edges over it. Now you have a piece of butter completely enclosed in dough.

Turn it over so that the folded side is on the work surface. Pound the package (not too hard) a few times with a rolling pin to flatten it somewhat. Roll the dough into a rectangle 20 by 11 inches, with one of the narrower sides facing you. Dust off any excess flour. Fold the bottom part of the dough up about a third of the way, then fold the top down, like a letter. Turn the dough so that the outer fold is on your left, like a book. Roll and fold the dough one more time. Make 2 finger indentations in the top of the dough to remind you that you have made 2 turns. Wrap the dough in plastic, and refrigerate 30 to 60 minutes.

Remove the dough from the refrigerator and repeat the process, rolling and folding the dough 2 more times. Make 4 finger indentations in the top of the dough, wrap it in plastic, and refrigerate 30 to 60 minutes.

If at any time the dough resists your efforts to roll it, let it rest a few minutes and try again. And if butter breaks through the dough, lightly flour that portion and continue.

Remove the dough, and roll it and fold it 2 more times. Now the dough has 6 turns (and 729 layers) and, after a rest of 60 minutes, is ready to be rolled and shaped to make the pastry of your choice. Either refrigerate it up to 3 days, or wrap it in 2 layers of plastic wrap and freeze it up to 1 month.

If the dough has been refrigerated more than 1 or 2 hours, gently beat it with a rolling pin before rolling it into its final shape. If it is frozen, defrost in the refrigerator for about 3 hours.

Apricot Tarte Tatin

When the Tatin sisters immortalized this pastry they used apples, but other fruits work just as well. The contrast between the flaky pastry that shatters when a fork passes through and the sweet softness of the fruit adds up to near perfection.

One 9-inch tart, 8 servings

> 1 pound puff pastry, made with butter (page 209)
> 1½ pounds ripe apricots, Blenheims if you can get them
> 2 tablespoons (1 ounce) unsalted butter
> ½ cup (3½ ounces) granulated sugar

Put the puff pastry on a lightly floured work surface. Roll it into a disk a little more than 10 inches in diameter and ⅛ inch thick. Put in on a parchment-lined baking pan, and refrigerate it for 30 minutes.

Preheat the oven to 400°F.

Remove the puff pastry from the refrigerator, and place it on a lightly floured work surface. Cut a 10-inch disk from the pastry. Be decisive, going through the pastry with a sharp knife or a pizza cutter in one motion so the edges don't crimp. Put the disk on the parchment-lined baking pan, and refrigerate it while you prepare the fruit. Reserve the excess for *palmiers*.

Cut the apricots into halves and remove the pits.

Make a trial arrangement of the fruit in a 9-inch cake pan that is 3 inches tall. Put the apricots in the pan, cut side down, arranging them snugly. Remove the fruit from the pan, and lay it out in the same pattern on a work surface.

Melt the butter in the cake pan over low heat. Add the sugar. Stir until the sugar melts and turns a medium-caramel color. Remove from the heat, and arrange the apricots in the bottom. They will sizzle as they hit the hot caramel. Be careful not to touch the sides of the pan.

Remove the puff-pastry disk from the refrigerator. Drape it over the apricots. It will be too big, but will shrink as it bakes.

Put the tart in the middle of the oven, and bake until the top is brown and puffed and the syrup is bubbling around the edges, about 50 minutes. The tart can be deceiving; you may think it's done before it is. The pastry must bake the entire way through, or it will be soggy. If in doubt, carefully lift up an edge to see if the bottom of the pastry looks baked. If it needs more time, turn the oven to 350°F and bake it another 5 to 10 minutes.

Remove the tart from the oven, and let it cool until the syrup stops bubbling, about 10 minutes. Shake the pan. If the apricots are sticking, heat it on top of the stove to free them. Place a serving plate upside down on top, then, wearing oven mitts, put one hand on the plate and the other on the bottom of the cake pan, and turn the pan onto the plate. The tart should fall onto the plate. If any apricots are stuck to the pan, re-move them and put them on the pastry. Serve the tart warm or at room temperature the same day that it's baked.

Galette des Rois

The particular construction of this pastry varies throughout Europe—the dough can be yeast-risen or puff pastry, the filling almond cream or candied fruit, and the flavorings rum or orange-flower water. This version is made in the north of France.

The person who gets the piece containing the bean is queen or king for the day. Some pastry shops in France supply a gold paper crown for the winner to wear.

ONE 9-INCH DESSERT, 10 TO 12 SERVINGS

> 2 pounds puff pastry, made with butter (page 209)
> ⅓ cup (1¾ ounces) whole blanched almonds
> 4 tablespoons (2 ounces) unsalted butter, at room temperature
> ½ cup (1¾ ounces) powdered sugar
> 1 tablespoon unbleached all-purpose flour
> 2 large eggs, at room temperature (one is used for glaze)
> 1½ teaspoons brandy
> 1 dried bean

Preheat the oven to 375°F.

Divide the pastry in two. Roll each piece into a disk a little more than 10½ inches in diameter and ⅛ inch thick. Stack them on a parchment-lined baking pan with another piece of paper between them. Refrigerate the pan while you make the filling.

Toast the almonds on a baking pan in the oven until they are lightly browned, about 5 minutes. Let them cool, then process them until they are fine but not a powder.

Put the butter in the bowl of a heavy-duty mixer. Beat it with the paddle attachment until it is soft. Add the almonds, sugar, and flour, and beat until everything is well combined. In a separate bowl, beat one of the eggs with a fork and add the brandy.

With the mixer running on medium speed, dribble the egg into the mixer bowl.

Remove the puff pastry from the refrigerator, and place it on a lightly floured work surface. Using a sharp knife or pizza cutter, trim the disks to about 10½ inches in diameter. Be decisive, going through the pastry in one motion so the edges don't crimp, which would hamper the pastry's rise. Reserve the excess for *palmiers*.

Return one disk to the parchment-lined baking sheet. Smooth the filling on top, leaving a ¾-inch border around the edges. Put a dried bean on the filling. Brush water on the exposed border, being careful not to get the water on the edges. Drape the other disk over the first. Firmly press around the outside border to adhere the 2 pieces, being careful not to crimp the edges. Using a fork, beat the other egg with 1 tablespoon of water. Brush the top with this egg glaze, again being careful not to dampen the edges. Refrigerate the pastry for 30 minutes.

Preheat the oven to 400°F.

Remove the pastry from the refrigerator, and brush it a second time with the egg wash.

Put it on the middle shelf of the oven, and bake it for 40 minutes. Turn down the oven to 350°F, and bake until the top is well browned and the sides look dry, about 15 more minutes.

Cool it to room temperature on a rack before serving.

PALMIERS

A pastry that is a caricature of a palm tree—what could be more fanciful? These butter-rich pastries come in many sizes, from as big as a large hand to a one-bite version. Make these from puff-pastry scraps, such as the edges left from cutting disks for *tarte Tatin* or *galette des Rois*. They vary in size with the amount of puff pastry on hand.

Line a baking pan with parchment paper.

Lightly flour a work surface, and generously sprinkle it with granulated sugar. Line up the scraps from a puff-pastry dessert, dampening the edges and overlapping them slightly. Press the strips together to make a rough rectangle, with one of the short ends facing you. Use a rolling pin to make the thickness even. Sprinkle the dough with granulated sugar. Fold the edges to the middle, like a book. Now "close the book." Turn the pastry 90 degrees, and cut into ½-inch pieces. Lay them, cut side up, on a parchment-lined baking pan, spaced 3 inches apart. Sprinkle them with more granulated sugar. Refrigerate them for 20 minutes.

Preheat the oven to 425°F.

Bake the *palmiers* on the middle shelf of the oven for 10 minutes. Turn the cookies over, and sprinkle them with more sugar. Return them to the oven, and bake until they are brown and the sugar begins to caramelize, 8 to 10 more minutes. Cool the baking pan on a rack.

For pastries with a little more crunch, use raw sugar crystals instead of granulated sugar.

Sandy Mullin, who tested this recipe, suggested a touch of ground cinnamon mixed with the sugar for a slightly different twist.

CARDAMOM COINS

Butter is the dominant flavor, but the gingerlike punch of the cardamom adds another dimension. Serve a few of these cookies on the plate with the Pineapple with Rum Sauce (page 64), or eat them alone, at any hour of the day.

ABOUT 2 DOZEN COOKIES

> *1 cup (5 ounces) unbleached all-purpose flour*
> *1 teaspoon ground cardamom*
> *Pinch of fine sea salt*
> *8 tablespoons (4 ounces) unsalted butter, at room temperature*
> *¼ cup (1¾ ounces) granulated sugar*
> *¼ teaspoon pure vanilla extract, preferably Madagascar Bourbon*

Sift the flour with the cardamom and salt.

Mix the butter and sugar in the bowl of a heavy-duty mixer with the paddle attachment until they are combined. Do not cream to a light, fluffy stage. Too much air beaten into the dough will make the logs hard to shape and encourage the cookies to spread, rather than hold their shape, when baked. With the mixer running, dribble in the vanilla. Add the flour, and mix until a soft dough is formed. Do not overmix it.

Turn the dough out onto a lightly floured work surface. Shape it into a log 1 inch in diameter. Roll it in plastic wrap, and refrigerate until firm, a few hours.

Preheat the oven to 375°F.

Slice the log into ¼-inch pieces. Place the rounds on a parchment-lined baking sheet. Bake until the edges are browned and the centers are a light golden brown, about 10 minutes. Cool the cookies on a rack. Store them in an airtight container.

CLASSIC SHORTBREAD

Traditional Scottish shortbread is made with 1 part sugar, 2 parts butter, and 3 parts flour. Rice flour or cornstarch can replace some of the flour. Its original form, an oatmeal bannock marked with a symbol of the sun, was served at pre-Christian celebrations.

Here is an example of simple ingredients in the right proportions adding up to perfection. The butter anchors the recipe. Shortbread is equally welcome at breakfast, with tea or coffee, or after dinner.

ONE 9-INCH ROUND, 8 TO 10 SERVINGS

⅓ cup (2½ ounces) granulated sugar
½ vanilla bean, preferably Madagascar Bourbon
1⅓ cups (6⅔ ounces) unbleached all-purpose flour
¼ cup (1¼ ounces) cornstarch
Pinch of fine sea salt
⅓ cup (1¼ ounces) dried cherries, roughly chopped
10 tablespoons (5 ounces) unsalted butter, refrigerator temperature, cut into ½-inch cubes

Preheat the oven to 350°F.

Put the sugar in a medium bowl. Split the vanilla bean lengthwise, and, using the tip of a paring knife, scrape the seeds into the sugar. Reserve the pod for another use. Rub the seeds into the sugar with your fingertips to distribute them evenly. Add the flour, cornstarch, salt, and cherries. Mix everything together with your hands. Add the butter pieces, and, using either your fingertips or a pastry cutter, mix them into the dry ingredients until the mixture looks like a coarse meal.

Turn the dough onto a work surface. Knead it until it holds together. Press it as evenly as possible into a fluted 9-inch tart pan that is 1 inch deep. Prick the dough all over with a fork, going to the bottom of the pan.

Bake the shortbread on the middle shelf of the oven until the top is lightly brown, about 25 minutes. Cool the pan on a rack, then carefully transfer the shortbread to a plate. Store it wrapped in plastic wrap.

GALETTE BRETONNE

Brittany, the northwestern province of France with dramatic tides and craggy shoreline, is noted for its lightly salted butter. This same butter finds its way into many of the region's desserts.

Rather than trying to replicate the butter of Brittany, use unsalted butter and add a pinch of salt to the flour.

This recipe is an adaptation of one from *Les Recettes de la Table Bretonne* by Francis Hinault and Joseph Koscher. I like the near-shortbread texture. Use your favorite dried fruit.

ONE 9-INCH CAKE, 8 TO 10 SERVINGS

> *Soft butter for the pan*
> *3 tablespoons (2 ounces) raisins*
> *3 or 4 pieces (2 ounces) dried fruit, finely chopped*
> *2 tablespoons dark rum*
> *Scant 2 cups (9 ounces) unbleached all-purpose flour*
> *Pinch of fine sea salt*
> *2 teaspoons baking powder*
> *10 tablespoons (5 ounces) unsalted butter, at room temperature*
> *½ cup (3½ ounces) granulated sugar*
> *4 large egg yolks, at room temperature (one is used for the glaze)*

Preheat the oven to 350°F.

Generously butter a 9-inch fluted tart pan with a removable bottom that is 1 inch deep.

Soak the raisins and the dried fruit in the rum while you prepare the other ingredients.

Sift the flour with the salt and baking powder.

Put the 10 tablespoons of butter in the bowl of a heavy-duty mixer. Beat it with the paddle attachment at medium speed until it is creamy. With the mixer on low, add the sugar in a steady stream. Beat the butter and sugar until the mixture is lighter in color and fluffy.

Beat in 3 of the egg yolks, one by one. Beat in the flour until it is just combined, then add the raisins, dried fruit, and rum.

Scoop the batter into the tart pan, and push it with your fingers to the sides, filling the pan. Smooth the top with a small spatula.

In a small bowl, beat the fourth egg yolk with a fork. Brush it on the top of the cake with a pastry brush.

Score the top of the cake in a decorative pattern, using the tip of a sharp knife.

Put the cake on the middle shelf of the oven, and bake until the top is well browned and a skewer inserted into the cake comes out clean, about 35 minutes.

Cool the cake, then transfer it to a serving plate.

Fig Flans

These flans are distinguished by the unusual additions of butter and flour, resulting in a sweet that's like a hybrid between custard and cake.

In Brittany, this flan—called *far Breton*—is usually made with prunes and baked in a cake pan. This recipe trades chopped dried figs for the prunes, and individual tart pans for the larger one. Use fluted tart pans with solid bottoms, and serve these flans warm from the oven.

6 FLANS

> *Soft butter for the pans*
> *1⅓ cups (10⅔ ounces) whole milk*
> *3 tablespoons (1½ ounces) unsalted butter*
> *2 large eggs, at room temperature*
> *½ cup (3½ ounces) granulated sugar*
> *½ cup plus 1 tablespoon (3 ounces) unbleached all-purpose flour, sifted*
> *1½ teaspoons pure vanilla extract, preferably Madagascar Bourbon*
> *6 (4 ounces) dried figs, finely chopped*

Preheat the oven to 375°F.

Generously butter 6 tart pans.

Bring the milk and butter to a boil. While the milk is heating, put the eggs in the bowl of a heavy-duty mixer. Beat them with the whisk attachment at medium speed until they become frothy. With the mixer running, add the sugar in a steady stream. Turn up the mixer speed, and beat until the mixture almost triples in volume and thickens.

On medium speed, beat in the flour.

On low speed, add the milk in a steady stream. Add the vanilla.

Pour some of the mixture into each of the tart pans. Distribute the figs evenly among the pans. Fill the pans to the top.

Bake the flans on the middle shelf of the oven until they are puffed and browned, about 25 minutes.

Let them cool for a few minutes, then unmold and serve them.

A Sweet Quartet

TODAY, DESSERT MEANS SOMETHING SWEET to end a meal. This is a relatively new concept; the word itself comes from the French *desservir*, to clear the table, a term coined in the middle of the sixteenth century. During the Middle Ages, sometimes after the table was cleared, a few nuts, raisins, and fruit may have been brought out, or, as a special treat, comfits, which were seeds or nuts covered with sugar.

But that's not when people began eating sweet things. Wild bees supplied the first burst of sweetness to the human diet, and early people braved their stings to collect it. Fruit was another source of sweetness, the variety depending on geography and climate. During the Middle Ages, when diet was heavily influenced by the humoral theories of Galen, raw fruit was looked upon with suspicion, but when it was cooked with sugar in preserves or tarts, and its medicinal glories stressed, it was deemed safe. The Chinese discovered the preserving power of ice about the eighth century B.C., and built ice houses that cooled by evaporation. Later, they hauled ice from winter rivers to caves, turning them into primitive but efficient refrigerators. By the sixteenth century, plums and loquats were packed in ice for transport. Indians and Italians also collected ice, but probably more for making sorbets than for preserving.

Licorice root, primarily used for medicine, was sweet too. Its botanical name, *Glycyrrhiza*, is derived from the Greek word for "sweet root."

But the discovery of sugarcane stands supreme in the history of desserts. As sugar became more plentiful in the centuries that followed, it was used in more sophisticated ways. By the sixteenth century, the well-to-do ate sweets in most courses of their meals.

At the end of the Middle Ages, cookbooks began to appear, and from them we can form a better picture of what some people ate and how they cooked it. In the Middle Ages, pastry cooks worked in their own kitchens without written recipes, so the sources are not as plentiful. Those dessert recipes that were published assumed that most kitchens lacked ovens; hence directions for pies cooked on top of the stove, coals heaped on their lids, and numerous recipes for pancakes and fritters. Bread was purchased from the local baker, who also cooked in his oven casseroles brought by the townspeople.

The rough foundations of French pastry appear in *Patissier François* of 1654, generally attributed to La Varenne, which is the first detailed account of the art of pastry making. Recipes include many that could be found in a contemporary French pastry book: puff pastry, pie crusts, tarts, cream puff pastry, egg and sugar foams for cakes, cookies and puddings, even a version of ladyfingers.

Although the pronounced change in French cuisine that theoretically arrived from Italy with Catherine de Médicis is more myth than reality, she did orchestrate elaborate festivals to bolster the image of the court during periods of internal strife. These masquerades included entertainment, and of course lavish banquets. Most of the food was cold; the emphasis was on sweets. Sugar sculptures adorned the tables, a hint of what was to come a few centuries later with the elaborate creations of Antonin Carême.

A hundred years later, when Princess Marguerite-Louise traveled to Italy to marry Cosimo, heir of the grand duke of Tuscany, the Italians rose to the occasion by producing a plethora of sweets. Tall *trifoni*, centerpieces designed by painters and sculptors and executed by sugar masters, lined banquet tables. Pastry makers cut marzipan into *fleur de lys*, and sweet delicacies poured in from all of Italy—fruit pastes, *dragées*, and comfits. The Florentines had perfected the art of constructing elaborate molds for freezing ice into the shape of goblets and other serving vessels, which were also included in the banquet.

Southern Europe didn't dominate the world of pastry as civilization moved out of the grip of the Middle Ages. Vienna had a thriving pastry culture with specific entities—in 1661, the gingerbread makers had their own guild; there were also guilds for sugar, chocolate, marzipan, cake, and candy makers. Although the first sugar bakers came in 1514, the arrival of Spanish and Burgundian nobles, with Burgundian pastry makers in tow some years later, influenced the growth of the field. Some specific treats stood out—sweetened whipped cream went on everything; special fried yeast cakes were everywhere during Fasching, the special time between Epiphany and the start of Lent. They were fried in an array of fats, but only at Vienna's temple of pastry were they cooked in butter.

Christoph Demel bought a pastry shop from the descendants of the Dehne family in 1857, eighty years after they had opened. If strudel is king here, the various tortes are queens and princesses. Some are egg- and butter-rich, many replace flour with almonds or other nuts to give them body, and the *Windtorte* is a fancy version of the French *vacherin*, an egg-white meringue filled with berries and of course whipped cream.

Verticality defined French table settings of the seventeenth and eighteenth centuries. Confectioners employed sugar to make elaborate architectural creations that dominated the center of the table. If there is one name linked to these fanciful arrangements, it is Antonin Carême, pastry chef extraordinare of haute cuisine. One of numerous children from a poor family, he learned his craft by working from a young age in Paris pastry shops. One of his employers allowed him time to visit the royal library, where he read cookbooks and pored over architectural prints. In 1803, he opened his own shop. In his book, *Le Pâtissier Royal*, he gives instructions, including drawings, for many *croquembouches*, a word that means "crunch in the mouth." The predecessors of these were the towering centerpieces, sometimes inedible, that had been used earlier in France, Italy, and England. Carême built his simpler versions in a plain round mold with tapering sides, using all manner of pastry and fruit. Orange sections, candied chestnuts, and pieces of iced cake were affixed to the inside of the mold with cooked sugar; then the mold was heated to release its prize. Choux pastries were the base of other towers. At that time, travelers to Turkey wrote glowing accounts of their visits, and anything Turkish became exotic, providing a theme for other *pièces montées.* Carême made a *sultane*, an elaborate sugar turban resting on a base of almond paste. Two of Carême's followers, Gouffe and Urbain-Dubois, pushed these pastry forms to excess, creating extravaganzas of glazed harlequin lozenges and pedestals supporting nougat cornucopias overflowing with candied fruit. These creations were often topped with elaborate sugar cages. By the end of the nineteenth century, Escoffier called for a return to taste over form.

Leading up to and throughout the primacy of haute cuisine, a *cuisine bourgeoise* maintained a low-profile existence. People made simple desserts at home, often using regional ingredients. A pair of books written in the mid-seventeenth century by Nicolas de Bonnefons, *Le Jardinier François* and *Les Delices de la Campagne*, were aimed at those who lived the bourgeois life. Many had modest gardens to grow fruit and vegetables. Bonnefons had a seed business and could furnish customers with the ones he recommended in his books. He listed fruit by season, a forerunner of the modern-day farmers'-market sensibility. The recipes leaned to a simpler approach—fewer spices, used to complement rather than to overpower the true flavors. Some had no spices at all. A recipe for a baked apple was seasoned only with butter and sugar.

In the New World, gardens and orchards were common, and early cookbooks listed recipes for custards and methods of preserving fruits. *American Cookery* incorporated recipes for the new foods corn and pumpkin and gave instructions for making johnnycake. Pies, which had their origin centuries before in Europe, were popular with the colonists and remain a favorite, in both restaurants and homes today. The quintessential American dessert may truly be an apple pie.

About the same time the new Americans were making johnny-cakes, the English were perfecting elaborate fruit jellies, made with syrup and set with gelatin. Some sported layers of different flavors and colors; others were composed in elaborate molds. Nevertheless, the creators of these confections surely would have flinched at the proliferation of molded desserts and salads, some with marshmallows and carrots, that would become the rage in America during the 1950s.

The modern restaurant, be it a roadside diner or a refined room of tables set with crystal and linen, always includes dessert offerings. The setting defines the choice, from mass-produced synthetic sweets to a list of carefully constructed concoctions of the choicest ingredients. Visitors at the earliest restaurants, which were really inns for travelers, were lucky to get bread and soup. There probably wasn't a dessert in sight. The birth of the restaurant as we know it was in France toward the end of the eighteenth century. The word originally referred to meat bouillon, the main offering at the first such establishment, owned by Boulanger, near the Louvre. He also served other dishes, much to the dismay of the caterers' guild, who tried unsuccessfully to drive him out of business. Seeing his victory against the guild, others opened similar businesses, which included separate tables covered with linen, and printed menus. The French Revolution dissolved the guilds and eliminated the jobs of many cooks for the aristocracy. Some of the unemployed struck out on their own and opened restaurants. People flocked to them to eat the haute cuisine that was once the domain of the privileged, gorging on truffles, pâtés, sorbets, and ice creams. Restaurants in Paris grew in number from one hundred just before the Revolution to three thousand during the Restoration. Cafés graduated to *salons de thé*, serving small savories along with pastries and confections. The vacationing European middle classes, who did not own villas, opened up another opportunity. Luxury hotels, spearheaded by César Ritz and Auguste Escoffier, opened all over Europe. The rivalry between the kitchen cooks and pantry cooks, common in large households during the seventeenth century, probably continued in these new venues. Carême commented on the condescending air of the *cuisiniers* by asserting that if one was to be a complete cook it was necessary to first be a distinguished *pâtissier*.

The rivalry continued in a more subtle form throughout the next century. Pastry chefs often had to work around the cooks, avoiding garlic-laden cutting boards, or in cramped corners of the kitchen. But conditions have improved dramatically, especially in the last decade. Now pastry chefs have status. Desserts are no longer an afterthought on the bottom of the menu. A separate listing of sweet creations is ceremoniously presented to the diner after the plates and bread crumbs are removed. And the fabricator's name is printed on the bottom of the page. The long-held medieval notion that sweets should be interspersed throughout the meal has been eclipsed; they now claim their own place. The diner settles in for the final course, anticipating its wonder just as she did the beginning of the meal.

Trends in pastry shift, just like trends in cuisine. The architectural displays worthy of Carême on both dinner and dessert plates may be the rage for a few years, then give way to simpler food—meat loaf and lemon-meringue pie, perhaps gussied up if the restaurant's prices are high. Sometimes the two philosophies coexist—a formal French restaurant presenting elaborate dessert plates, and an American restaurant heading its dessert menu with apple crisp. Cooks of both kitchen and pantry look for new ways to express their notions of cuisine, but the challenge to pastry chefs may be greater because of their limited repertoire of ingredients. They are kicking up their heels in their newfound celebrity. Desserts have no boundaries. In expensive restaurants, a piece of cake is no longer simply put on a plate and served. A mound of ice cream may slump beside it, and edible sugar decorations may jut from both. Dots of sauce may circle the edge of the plate. For this to work, the textures and flavors must harmonize like a perfect chord.

The front-of-the-stage pastry chefs look to the unexpected to enliven their offerings. Some employ spices and herbs to jolt the taste buds. Others borrow from unlikely sources—ice-cream sandwiches, lollipops, marshmallows. One chef in the land of corn makes sweet-and-salty popcorn wedges, then pairs them with chocolate mousse. Sometimes unleashed imaginations spiral into failure—tobacco in desserts?

Owners of pastry shops follow their own vision, with a nod to trends. Italian *pasticcerie*, French *pâtisseries*, and American bakeries coexist happily in the same cities, some adhering to standard formulas of their craft, others venturing into the less familiar. Sometimes an old standby gets dressed up and brought to center stage—pound cake, for example. This cake appreciated by English, French, and Americans has many faces. The original recipe, equal parts by weight of flour, eggs, butter, and sugar, has been altered over time—some of the eggs replaced by other liquids, and baking powder or soda used to boost the leavening power. Such a simple cake can be flavored countless ways—with coffee, tea, or even chai; dried fruits of every description; chocolate; anise, coriander, or poppy seeds; ginger; citrus. The shape can be a simple loaf or a more formal decorative ring. It is welcome at breakfast, teatime, or after dinner. This basic cake presents endless opportunities for capturing the flavor of the moment.

Those who make desserts at home are a stalwart group. Once the excitement of dessert creation is instilled in a person, it is hard to abandon. Some people will stretch their capabilities, striving to conquer challenging recipes and increase their repertoire. Others stay with a comfortable selection that brings success. But all those working in home kitchens join their fellow creators in restaurants and bakeries striving to bring delicious endings to meals. More often than not, the main players in these dessert inventions are sugar, almonds, eggs, and butter.

The four elements interweave in good desserts the same way instruments blend together in a quartet performance. Sometimes, one instrument takes the lead, another echoing the same line or providing a contrast to it. Each instrument has its anchoring point to the whole. As the musicians play, the instruments create a sound that is four-dimensional. If it were translated from an auditory to a visual form, it would occupy a physical space. A spectacular dessert does occupy real space, but its essence is hidden in its physical being. Flavors coexist, waiting to be released when the diner begins to eat. Both desserts and music disappear—when only crumbs remain on the plate, and when the musicians stop playing. But both can be stored in memory, to be relished once again, anticipated a second time.

What are the forms that dessert components can take? Sugar can be high or low—a loud, dominant theme or a stable undertone. It can be raspy or mellow. It can be playful or austere.

Almonds are versatile. They can have bassoon qualities, when they replace flour in the very structure of a dessert; or they can be like a piccolo, a sprinkling on the top; or a burst of surprise, like the sounding of a horn.

Eggs provide subtle structure, like violas, or lightness, like violins. The more numerous they are, the stronger their part. Sometimes they are just a wisp, a faint note, as when they glaze a dough.

Butter most often provides the bass tone. It sounds low, resonant notes; it anchors like a cello or a viola da gamba. Although it sometimes has solo moments, just like the deep-throated string instruments, it is best suited to playing the continuo part.

The pastry maker chooses and mixes the ingredients, composing. Then she plays all four parts, reading the recipe like a score.

A Dessert Buffet

Not many people will refuse an invitation to a dessert buffet. And for the host, it's an opportunity to visit with friends without the last-minute focus and delicate timing necessary to prepare a full-course dinner. Instead, you can mingle with your guests and have as much fun as they do, sipping champagne and tasting a panoply of sweet offerings.

Choose from a selection of recipes that can be made ahead and don't need refrigeration. Make at least four, or as many as eight. The number of guests will determine the quantity of each. There are many possibilities scattered throughout the preceding chapters. The sugar chapter's selections include Peppermint Lollipops (page 67), Popcorn Balls with Cashews (page 65), and Molasses Spice Cake (page 60). Chocolate Meringue "Sandwiches" (page 155), from the egg chapter, would satisfy the most intense chocolate craving. Almond recipes are numerous: Almond Butter Cookies (page 102), Almond Chocolate Drops (page 104), *Financiers* (page 105), and A Trio of After-Dinner Almonds (page 114). Possibilities from the butter chapter are Cardamom Coins (page 217), *Palmiers* (page 216), and Classic Shortbread (page 218). Licorice Ice Cream (page 168) is even a possibility, kept cold in a large bowl of ice. For a riveting finale to the evening, evoke the spirit of Antonin Carême and make a *croquembouche*.

CROQUEMBOUCHE

This dessert celebrates sugar, almonds, eggs, and butter as no other could. It is a free-standing pyramid of cream puffs filled with almond pastry cream. Lightly caramelized sugar holds the tower together. Jordan almonds scattered randomly between the puffs add visual appeal.

The *croquembouche* can be made in stages: the pastry cream up to 4 days ahead; the batter for the cream puffs made, piped into circles, and refrigerated the day before assembly. Bake the cream puffs early in the afternoon the day of the buffet. Fill the puffs and assemble the dessert in the late afternoon, then keep it in a cool place until you bring it triumphantly to the table.

25 SERVINGS

The pastry cream:
3 cups (24 ounces) whole milk, divided into 2½ cups and ½ cup
1 cup (7 ounces) granulated sugar, divided into halves
9 large egg yolks
6 tablespoons (1¾ ounces) cornstarch
1 to 1½ teaspoons pure almond extract

The cream puffs:
¾ cup (6 ounces) whole milk
¾ cup (6 ounces) water
1¼ teaspoons fine sea salt
2 teaspoons granulated sugar
12 tablespoons (6 ounces) unsalted butter, at room temperature, cut into rough chunks
1½ cups (7½ ounces) unbleached all-purpose flour
6 large eggs

The caramel:
1¾ cups (12¼ ounces) granulated sugar
⅓ cup (2½ ounces) water

15 to 20 sugar-coated (Jordan) almonds, or lightly toasted almonds

Make the pastry cream:

Put 2½ cups of milk and ½ cup granulated sugar in a large saucepan. Bring to a boil, stirring once or twice to dissolve the sugar.

While the milk is heating, beat the egg yolks and ½ cup granulated sugar in the bowl of a heavy-duty mixer with the whisk attachment.

In a separate small bowl, whisk ½ cup of milk with the cornstarch. When the yolks and sugar are pale and thick, whisk in the milk and cornstarch.

Pour the hot milk into the mixing bowl in a thin stream, continuing to whisk. Return this custard to the saucepan. Cook it over medium heat, whisking constantly, until the custard starts to thicken. (It will look as if it's curdling.) Turn down the heat, and continue to whisk until it comes to a boil and is thick and smooth.

Transfer the pastry cream to a bowl, cover with plastic wrap so that it is touching the top of the cream, and refrigerate at least 4 hours or up to 4 days.

Make the cream puffs:

Draw 30 circles, 1½ inches in diameter and 1 inch apart, on a sheet of parchment paper that will fit on a baking sheet. Draw 25 more circles on a second piece of parchment paper. Put the pieces of paper, marked side down, on baking sheets. (Check to be sure the marks show through.)

Put the milk, water, salt, sugar, and butter in a medium saucepan. Bring to a boil, stirring once or twice. When the liquid is boiling and the butter melted, add the flour all at once, and turn off the heat. Stir the mixture with a wooden spoon until it is a smooth paste. Return the pan to a low heat, and cook, stirring, until the paste starts to make cooking sizzles, a few minutes.

Scrape the paste into the bowl of a heavy-duty mixer. Beat it on medium speed with the paddle attachment. Add the eggs, one at a time, waiting until each is incorporated before adding the next.

Fit a pastry bag with a ½-inch plain tip, and fill it with the batter. Pipe a mound of batter onto each circle. Tamp down the points on the top of each one with a damp finger. Refrigerate the baking sheets overnight.

Bake the cream puffs:

Preheat the oven to 400°F.

Remove the baking sheets from the refrigerator and place them in the oven. Depending on your oven capacity, you may have to bake the sheets one at a time. If so, keep the second one refrigerated until you are ready to bake it.

Bake the puffs for 30 minutes. Turn down the oven to 350°F and bake 10 more minutes. The puffs should be browned and crisp. Cool the baking sheets on a rack.

Assemble the *croquembouche*:

Remove the pastry cream from the refrigerator and whisk in 1 teaspoon of the almond extract. If the flavor is too faint, whisk in an additional ½ teaspoon.

Make a small hole in the bottom of each puff with the tip of a paring knife or with a ¼-inch pastry tip.

Fit a pastry bag with a ¼-inch plain tip, and fill it with the pastry cream. Pipe cream into each puff through the hole in the bottom. Put the filled puffs on a baking sheet.

Make the caramel:

Choose a medium heavy-bottomed saucepan, an unlined copper sugar-pot if you have one. Fill a large bowl with cold water.

Mix the sugar and water in the pot. Cook the syrup over medium heat, stirring once or twice, until the sugar dissolves. Wash any sugar crystals from the sides of the pan with a brush dipped in cold water. Continue to cook, without stirring, until the syrup shows just a hint of golden color. This may take 10 to 15 minutes. Check the color by putting a drop on a white plate.

When the syrup is ready, plunge the bottom of the pan into the bowl of cold water to stop the cooking. The syrup will be very hot.

Dip the filled cream puffs in the syrup:

Spread a piece of parchment paper on a surface to receive the finished puffs.

Prop the saucepan holding the syrup on a work surface, protecting it with a pot holder, so that the syrup pools on one side of the bottom. Dip the top of each puff into the syrup, either by holding it at the very bottom or by using tongs. (Caution: The syrup is very hot. Have a bowl of ice water handy to immerse your fingers in immediately if they come in contact with the syrup.)

Put the dipped puffs, right side up, on the parchment paper; the caramel will harden quickly.

Finish the assembly:

Line the perimeter of a large round serving plate with strips of parchment paper to catch dripped syrup. Leave room in the unlined center of the plate to make a circle of 9 cream puffs.

Dip one side of a puff in the syrup, and place it on the serving plate with the caramelized top facing out. Dip the side of another puff in the syrup and attach it alongside the first, and continue until a circle of 9 puffs, tops facing out, is completed. If the syrup becomes too thick, reheat it over low heat to thin it.

Build a second circle of 9 puffs on top of the first. Continue building, securing the structure with caramel, decreasing the number of puffs in each succeeding circle to make a conical tower. Put one final puff, right side up, on the top. (You will probably end up with a couple of extra puffs, which can be used as replacements in case of breakage.)

Dip the pointed ends of the almonds into the syrup, and push them randomly into spaces between the puffs. Dip a fork into the syrup, and swirl it in circles around the finished pyramid so threads of sugar will envelop it. (When you are finished, you can clean the syrup pot by filling it with water and bringing it to a boil to melt the remaining syrup.)

Remove the strips of paper protecting the edges of the plate. Keep the *croquembouche* in a cool place until serving time.

To serve, cut puffs from the tower with a sharp paring knife. Serve 2 per person.

BIBLIOGRAPHY

Aldrovandi, Ulisse. *Aldrovandi on Chickens: The Ornithology of Ulisse Aldrovandi*, vol. 2, book 14. Translated by L. R. Lind. Norman: University of Oklahoma Press, 1963.

Allen, Gray. *The Almond People.* Sacramento: Blue Diamond Growers, 2000.

"Almond Board Calls for Americans to Take the Cholesterol Challenge." *The Cracker: The Official Voice of the International Tree Nut Council for the World Tree Nut Trade*, no. 3, September 2000.

Amendola, Joseph, and Donald Lundberg. *Understanding Baking.* New York: Van Nostrand Reinhold, 1992.

American Egg Board. *Eggcyclopedia.* Park Ridge, Ill.: American Egg Board, 1999.

Amor, Catherine. *Les Bonbons.* N.p.: Éditions du Chêne-Hachette Livre, 1998.

Barty-King, Hugh, and Anton Massel. *Rum, Yesterday and Today.* London: Heinemann, 1983.

Becker, Raymond B. *Dairy Cattle Breeds: Origin and Development.* Gainesville: University of Florida Press, 1973.

Blount, W. P. "History of Chick Sexing." In *Sexing All Fowl: Baby Chicks, Game Birds, Cage Birds.* Loyl Stromberg, editor. Pine River, Minn.: Stromberg Publishing, 1977.

Braker, Flo. "Making Desserts with Nutty Frangipane." *Fine Cooking*, March 1999, pp. 60–65.

Brennan, Georgeanne. "Marzipan Trail to Germany Built a Town Tradition." *San Francisco Chronicle*, March 31, 1999.

Brenner, Joël Glenn. *The Emperors of Chocolate: Inside the Secret World of Hershey and Mars.* New York: Random House, 1999.

Broekel, Ray. *The Great American Candy Bar Book.* Boston: Houghton Mifflin, 1982.

Brothwell, Don and Patricia. *Food in Antiquity.* New York: Frederick A. Praeger, 1969.

Caton, Mary Anne, editor. *Fooles and Fricassees: Food in Shakespeare's England*. Washington, D.C.: Folger Shakespeare Library, 1999.

Child, Julia, and Simone Beck. *Mastering the Art of French Cooking*, vol. 2. New York: Alfred A. Knopf, 1970.

Clutton-Brock, Juliet. *A Natural History of Domesticated Mammals*. Cambridge: Cambridge University Press, 1999.

Conrad, Glenn R., and Ray R. Lucas. *White Gold: A Brief History of the Louisiana Sugar Industry 1795–1995*. Lafayette: University of Southwestern Louisiana, 1995.

Cooke, D. A., and R. K. Scott, editors. *The Sugar Beet Crop*. London: Chapman and Hall, 1993.

Corriher, Shirley O. "The Amazing Culinary Powers of Eggs." *Fine Cooking*, April–May 1966, pp. 76–77.

Crane, Eva. *A Book of Honey*. New York: Charles Scribner's Sons, 1980.

Cunningham, Isabel Shipley. *Frank N. Meyer, Plant Hunter in Asia*. Ames: Iowa State University Press, 1984.

Darwin, Charles. *On the Origin of Species*. A Facsimile of the First Edition. Cambridge, Mass.: Harvard University Press, 1964.

David, Elizabeth. *Harvest of the Cold Months*. New York: Viking, 1994.

———. "Savour of Ice and of Roses." *Petits Propos Culinaires*, no. 8, June 1981, pp. 7–17.

Davidson, Alan. *The Oxford Companion to Food*. Oxford: Oxford University Press, 1999.

Davis, Robin. "One Egg Stands White and Yolk Above the Rest." *San Francisco Chronicle*, April 19, 2000.

Der Haroutunian, Arto. *Pâtisserie of the Eastern Mediterranean*. New York: McGraw-Hill, 1989.

Diamond, Jared. *Guns, Germs, and Steel*. New York: W. W. Norton, 1997.

Doyle, Brian. "The Joy of Sexing." *Atlantic Monthly*, March 2000, pp. 28–31.

Dumas, Alexandre. *Dictionary of Cuisine*. New York: Simon & Schuster, 1986.

Edwards, John. *The Roman Cooking of Apicius.* Point Roberts, Wash.: Hartley & Marks, 1984.

Everett, Thomas H. *The New York Botanical Garden Illustrated Encyclopedia of Horticulture.* New York: Garland Publishing, 1980.

Feibleman, Peter S., and Editors of Time-Life Books. *American Cooking: Creole and Acadian.* New York: Time-Life Books, 1971.

Ferrer, Sacha. "Histoires de Fèves et de Fabophiles." *Figaro,* January 6–7, 2001.

Field, Carol. *Celebrating Italy.* New York: William Morrow, 1990.

Fisher, Michele C., and Paul A. Lachance. *Nutrition and Health Aspects of Almonds.* Sacramento: Almond Board of California, 1999.

Flandrin, Jean-Louis, and Massimo Montanari, editors. *Food: A Culinary History.* New York: Columbia University Press, 1999.

Frisch, Karl von. *Bees: Their Vision, Chemical Senses, and Language.* Ithaca, N.Y.: Cornell University Press, 1950.

————. *The Dancing Bees.* London: Methuen, 1966.

Fussell, Betty. *The Story of Corn.* New York: North Point Press, Farrar, Straus and Giroux, 1992.

Gardner, Frank D. *Live Stock and Dairy Farming.* Philadelphia: John C. Winston Company, 1918.

Gérardin, Martine. "Galette des Rois: Un Savoureux Mystère." *Figaro,* January 6–7, 2001.

Grammatico, Maria, and Mary Taylor Simeti. *Bitter Almonds: Recollections and Recipes from a Sicilian Girlhood.* New York: William Morrow, 1994.

Greenspan, Dorie. "Butter with a Pedigree: Ah, the French." *New York Times,* January 17, 2001.

Grimes, William. "But How Do They Taste? A Food Critic Answers." *New York Times,* December 12, 1999.

————. "The Tart That Turned France Upside Down." *New York Times,* November 22, 2000.

Grohman, Joann Sills. *Keeping a Family Cow.* New York: Charles Scribner's Sons, 1981.

Guthrie, Edward Sewall. *The Book of Butter.* New York: MacMillan, 1923.

Healy, Bruce, and Paul Bugat. *The French Cookie Book.* New York: William Morrow, 1994.

————. *Mastering the Art of French Pastry.* Woodburg, N.Y.: Barron's, 1984.

Heiser, Charles B., Jr. *Seed to Civilization.* Cambridge, Mass.: Harvard University Press, 1990.

Hess, Karen, transcriber. *Martha Washington's Booke of Cookery.* New York: Columbia University Press, 1995.

Hesser, Amanda. "From the French Marshes: A Salty Treasure." *New York Times,* May 6, 1998.

Hinault, Francis, and Joseph Koscher. *Les Recettes de la Table Bretonne.* Paris: Éditions Casteilla, 1986.

Hubbell, Sue. *A Book of Bees.* New York: Random House, 1988.

Hunziker, Otto Frederick. *The Butter Industry.* La Grange, Ill.: Published by the Author, 1940.

Jenkins, G. H. *Introduction to Cane Sugar Technology.* Amsterdam: Elsevier Publishing Company, 1966.

Jeunet, André, and Ginette Hell-Girod. *Les Recettes de la Table Franc-Comtoise.* Besançon, France: Éditions Cêtre, 1993.

Jourdain, Robert. *Music, the Brain, and Ecstasy.* New York: William Morrow and Company, 1997.

Judkins, Henry. *The Principles of Dairying.* New York: John Wiley & Sons, 1924.

Kann, Kenneth L. *Comrades and Chicken Ranchers.* Ithaca, N.Y.: Cornell University Press, 1993.

Kester, Dale E. "The Biological and Cultural Evolution of the Almond." *I Congresso Ibérico de Ciéncias Horticolas,* proceedings, vol. 4, 1990.

Kester, Dale E., and Warren C. Micke. "The California Almond Industry." *Fruit Varieties Journal,* vol. 38, no. 3 (July 1984).

Kiple, Kenneth R., and Kriemhild Coneè Ornelas. *The Cambridge World History of Food*. Cambridge: Cambridge University Press, 2000.

Kirkpatrick, David D. "Snack Foods Become Stars of Books for Children." *New York Times*, September 22, 2000.

Kummer, Corby. "Better Butter." *Atlantic Monthly*, June 1998, pp. 98–102.

Langer, Patrick. *Calissons d'Aix: Nougats de Provence*. Barbentane, France: Éditions Équinoxe, 1999.

Leaver, J. D. *Milk Production: Science and Practice*. London: Longman, 1983.

Lenôtre, Gaston. *Desserts Traditionnels de France*. Paris: Flammarion, 1991.

———. *Ice Cream and Candies*. Woodbury, N.Y.: Barron's, 1979.

Levey, Martin, and Noury Al-Khaledy. *The Medical Formulary of Al-Samarqandi*. Philadelphia: University of Pennsylvania Press, 1967.

Livingston, David. *A Good Life: Dairy Farming in the Olema Valley*. San Francisco: National Park Service, Department of the Interior, 1995.

Longgood, William. *The Queen Must Die and Other Affairs of Bees and Men*. New York: W. W. Norton, 1985.

Lowenberg, Miriam. *Creative Candy Making*. New York: Weathervane Books, 1979.

Lowry, Thea. *Empty Shells: The Story of Petaluma, America's Chicken City*. Novato, Calif.: Manifold Press, 2000.

———. *Petaluma's Poultry Pioneers*. Novato, Calif.: Manifold Press, 1993.

Maeterlinck, Maurice. *The Life of the Bee*. New York: Dodd, Mead, 1901.

McGee, Harold. *On Food and Cooking*. New York: Charles Scribner's Sons, 1984.

Mintz, Sidney. *Sweetness and Power*. New York: Penguin, 1985.

———. *Tasting Food, Tasting Freedom*. Boston: Beacon Press, 1996.

Montagné, Prosper. *Nouveau Laroussse Gastronomique*. Paris: Librairie Larousse, 1967.

Morgan, Miriam. "Sugar, Sugar." *San Francisco Chronicle*, March 31, 1999.

Morse, Roger A., and Nicholas W. Calderone. "The Value of Honey Bees as Pollinators of U.S. Crops in 2000." *Bee Culture*, vol. 128, no. 3 (March 2000), pp. 2–15.

Mydans, Seth. "An Outpatient Exorcism (It Was Only a Crab)." *New York Times*, August 27, 2001.

Newall, Venetia. *An Egg at Easter: A Folklore Study.* London: Routledge & Kegan Paul, 1971.

North, Mack O. *Commercial Chicken Production Manual.* Westport, Conn.: AVI Publishing Company, 1978.

Ostrander, Gilman M. "The Making of the Triangular Trade Myth." *William and Mary Quarterly*, 3rd series, vol. 30 (1973), pp. 635–44.

Pliny the Elder. *Natural History.* Loeb Classical Library. Cambridge, Mass.: Harvard University Press, 1940.

Renner, H. D. *The Origin of Food Habits.* London: Faber and Faber, 1944.

Roberts, Paul. "The Sweet Hereafter." *Harper's*, November 1999.

Rolph, George. *Something About Sugar.* San Francisco: John L. Newbegin, 1917.

Root, Waverley. *Food.* New York: Simon & Schuster, 1980.

———. *The Food of France.* New York: Alfred A. Knopf, 1958.

Rosenburg, Michael. "New Discovery in Turkey: Nuts May Be the Original Staple Food." *The Cracker*, January 1996.

Russell, Kiley. "Beekeepers Bitter over Fire Ant Inspections." *San Francisco Chronicle*, February 14, 2001.

Salmon, Alice Wooledge. "Enduring Fantasies." *Petits Propos Culinaires*, no. 8, June 1981, pp. 49–59.

Scott, Cintra. "How Sweet It Is." *New York Times Magazine*, November 19, 2000.

Severson, Kim. "Butter's Back." *San Francisco Chronicle*, December 13, 2000.

Sheraton, Mimi. *Visions of Sugarplums.* New York: Random House, 1968.

Sheridan, Richard B. *Sugar and Slavery.* Baltimore: Johns Hopkins University Press, 1973.

Simmons, Marie. *The Good Egg.* New York: Houghton Mifflin, 2000.

Smith, Page, and Charles Daniel. *The Chicken Book.* Athens: University of Georgia Press, 2000.

Steen, Mrs. J. Wesley, editor. *The Story of Steen's Syrup and Its Famous Recipes.* Abbeville, La.: N.p., n.d.

Street, Len, and Andrew Singer. *Butter, Milk & Cheese from Your Back Yard.* New York: Sterling, 1976.

Tannahill, Reay. *Food in History.* New York: Three Rivers Press, 1988.

Torres, Félix. *Le Gout d'Un Terroir Isigny.* Strasbourg, France: Éditions Ronald Hirle, 1999.

Toussaint-Samat, Maguelonne. *Douceurs de Provence.* Avignon, France: Éditions A. Barthélemy, 1988.

Traynor, Joe. *Almond Pollination Handbook.* Bakersfield, Calif.: Kovak Books, 1993.

Untermeyer, Louis. *A Century of Candymaking.* Boston: Barta Press, 1947.

USDA. *Beekeeping in the United States.* Agriculture Handbook No. 335. Washington, D.C.: U.S. Government Printing Office, 1971.

Vickery, V. R. *The Honey Bee: A Guide for Beekeepers.* Westmount, Quebec: Particle Press, 1991.

Ward, Susie, Claire Clifton, and Jenny Stacey. *The Gourmet Atlas.* New York: Macmillan, 1997.

Wechsberg, Joseph, and Editors of Time-Life Books. *The Cooking of Vienna's Empire.* New York: Time-Life Books, 1968.

Weeks, Charles. *Egg Farming in California.* San Francisco: Schwabacher-Frey Stationery Co., 1920.

Westrich, Lolo. "The Californians." *Frontier Chicken,* July–August 1985.

Wheaton, Barbara Ketcham. *Savoring the Past.* Philadelphia: University of Pennsylvania Press, 1983.

Willats, P., J. S. Forsyth, M. K. DiModugno, S. Varma, and M. Colvin. "Effect of Long-Chain Polyunsaturated Fatty Acids in Infant Formula on Problem Solving at 10 Months of Age." *Lancet,* vol. 352 (August 29, 1998), pp. 688–91.

Williams, C. Trevor. *Chocolate and Confectionery.* London: Leonard Hill Books, 1964.

Wilson, C. Anne. *The Book of Marmalade.* Philadelphia: University of Pennsylvania Press, 1999.

Wolfe, Linda. *The Literary Gourmet: Menus from Masterpieces.* New York: Harmony Books, 1962.

Zeuner, Frederick E. *A History of Domesticated Animals.* London: Hutchinson, 1963.

Zohary, Daniel, and Maria Hopf. *Domestication of Plants in the Old World.* Oxford: Oxford University Press, 1988.

ACKNOWLEDGMENTS

Working on this book has reminded me that people involved in food are always generous, willing to share knowledge and tastes with those interested in their work.

I am grateful to all the people named in these narratives who shared their farms, orchards, herds, flocks, laboratories, and processing plants with me. Their generosity helped me find the basic truths in these stories.

In addition, there are others to whom I am grateful. In the sugar world, thanks to Steve Tan and Diane Thomas at C&H Sugar, to Ed Parolini at Spreckels, and to Sue Muniak at Charlotte's Confections. And to Phyllis Kaliher, who led me to New Orleans Rum. Even though he is mentioned in the sugar story, another thanks to Dr. Ben Legendre, my gracious host in Louisiana, who went out of his way to help me understand sugarcane processing.

David Haas, Jean-Claude Bauer, and Robert Reynolds were instrumental in helping me make contacts in France. Thanks also to Flo Braker, Gregory Johnson, Michèle Morainvillers, Michael Recchiuti, Elizabeth Falkner, Allison Hooper, and Jonathan White for helping me sort out the intricacies of butter.

Les Seely and Randy Oliver helped me understand bees, and Dr. Tom Gradizel, Dr. Dale Kester, and Dennis Meinberg explained almonds. Thanks also to Susan Brauner at Blue Diamond and Liz Prueitt.

In the egg world, Jim Reichardt, Bob Pierre, Kim Severson, Monroe Fuchs, Debbie Belt, Mark Gamaza, and Jim Olsen generously shared time and information. A special thanks to Sondra Costello for arranging a visit to Petaluma Farms.

Recipe testers Sandy Mullin, Marion Norberg, Susan Hersey, Les and Jennifer Seely, and Pat Robison helped clarify instructions.

Thanks to Gary Luke, who helped me envision this book, and to Becky Saletan for taking it on. Also thanks to Jeff Seroy, Sarita Varma, Suzanne Wickham-Beaird, and Karen Schober. And to Carole Bidnik for her enthusiasm, and to Martha Casselman for her never-ending encouragement.

And thank you, Sidney, for everything.